A CONTEMPORARY LOOK AT
THE FORMULA OF CONCORD

A Contemporary at the Formula

Look

# of Concord

Publishing House
St. Louis

The medal that appears on the cover was struck in 1930 to commemorate the 400th anniversary of the Augsburg Confession (1530). The medal carries profile bust portraits of Martin Luther, Philipp Melanchthon and the Elector John of Saxony, with their names and insignia.

Concordia Publishing House, St. Louis, Missouri
Copyright © 1978 Concordia Publishing House
Manufactured in the United States of America

Library of Congress Cataloging in Publication Data

Main entry under title:
A Contemporary look at the Formula of Concord.

1. Lutheran Church. Formula of Concord.
I. Rosin, Wilbert, 1923-
II. Preus, Robert D., 1924-
BX8069.4.C66   230′.4′1   78-5341
ISBN 0-570-03271-7

---

2 3 4 5 6 7 8 9 10 11 WP 89 88 87 86 85 84 83 82 81 80

CONTENTS

Abbreviations

AC	Augsburg Confession
Ap	Apology of the Augsburg Confession
BOW	*Bondage of the Will*
CR	*Corpus Reformatorum*
Ep	Epitome of the Formula of Concord
FC	Formula of Concord
KJV	King James Version
LC	Large Catechism
LW	*Luther's Works,* American edition
RSV	Revised Standard Version
SA	Smalcald Articles
SC	Small Catechism
SD	Solid Declaration of the Formula of Concord
WA	Weimar edition of Luther's works

6

NOTES ON THE AUTHORS

Dr. C. George Fry is professor of historical theology and director of mission education at Concordia Theological Seminary, Fort Wayne, Ind.

Dr. Lowell C. Green is professor of history and theology at Concordia College, River Forest, Ill.

Dr. Henry P. Hamann is professor of New Testament and vice-president of Luther Theological Seminary, Adelaide, South Australia

Dr. Harry Huth is associate professor of systematic theology at Concordia Theological Seminary, Fort Wayne, Ind.

Dr. Richard Klann is professor of systematic theology at Concordia Theological Seminary, St. Louis, Mo.

Dr. Eugene F. Klug is professor of systematic theology at Concordia Theological Seminary, Fort Wayne, Ind.

Dr. Robert Kolb is assistant professor of religion and history at Concordia College, St. Paul, Minn.

Prof. Kurt Marquart is associate professor of systematic

theology at Concordia Theological Seminary, Fort Wayne, Ind.

Dr. Robert D. Preus is president of Concordia Theological Seminary, Fort Wayne, Ind.

Dr. Wilbert H. Rosin is president of Concordia College, Milwaukee, Wis.

Dr. David P. Scaer is professor of systematic theology and editor of Concordia Theological Quarterly, Concordia Theological Seminary, Fort Wayne, Ind.

Prof. Bjarne W. Teigen is president emeritus of Bethany Lutheran College, Mankato, Minn.

FOREWORD

*T*hat more than 8,000 theologians could agree on a statement
of Christian doctrine after decades of discord and debate was
indeed a significant achievement. That the Formula of Concord
of 1577 has survived the test of 400 years is more significant. But
that intense study is being devoted to the Formula today and
that it is seriously being considered as useful for a genuine
ecumenical endeavor sets that 16th-century document apart as
one of the truly great achievements of all time.

The Formula is sufficient evidence of the enduring vitality
and vigor of Lutheranism after the death of the Great Reformer.
Martin Luther's Biblical emphasis on individual faith might well
have led to the disintegration of Lutheranism, had it not been
for the persistent and consistent reliance on the Holy Scriptures
as the sole authority for faith and life. Pere Daniel Olivier, well-
known ecumenical Catholic Reformation scholar, contends that
the Lutheran principle of justification by faith could not provide
stability and that it leads to individualism. He also asserts that it
was rather the force of Luther's personality that held
Protestantism together. The Formula is evidence that the
principle of *sola scriptura*, which leads to an understanding and
acceptance of *sola fide* as well as *sola gratia*, was the binding
factor. Scriptural authority—"Here I stand"—was the essential

principle. Morever, *sola fide,* justification by faith, meant far more than a subjective faith that depended on the individual. That doctrine could be understood only in the Biblical context of the fall of man and the redemption and all that it entails.

The Formula's *Entstehungsgeschichte,* outlined in the first part of this volume, shows that history can teach future generations. It also proves that faithful reliance on the Scriptures ultimately brings the blessing of religious concord. Some Lutheran groups have turned away from the authority of the Bible, contending that the Bible is not to be taken as it speaks to the reader but that it requires the interpretation of the 20th-century mind to determine what is to be believed.

Lutherans who seek peace and concord in the church today, not only among Lutherans but among all Christians, can learn from the 16th-century experience. The renewed interest in the Formula of Concord at this time is not an interest growing merely out of the 400th anniversary. It is based on the firm conviction that a faithful study of the Holy Scriptures will lead to harmony and understanding, though not necessarily to external unity of all church organizations.

Nor does the current interest in the Lutheran Confessions stem from a spirit of triumphalism. There is far too much need for repentance for that, as there was in the history of Lutheranism throughout its first 400 years as well as in the immediate past. On the other hand, sincere joy and appreciation of the Lord's guidance and blessing is in order. Gratitude for the endurance and effectiveness of the Formula should not contribute to divisiveness or to separation from the rest of Christendom. The Formula intended to unite, and it could well become the basis for unity with all Christians, since it is simply an exposition of Biblical truths.

Because a study of the Formula carries with it the possibility of uniting Christians, the purpose of the essays in the second part of this volume is to provide the reader with a clear statement of the doctrines treated in the Formula, enlarging on points that need clarification especially for the 20th century. The eminent theologians who have contributed to this volume deserve our sincere thanks. If these essays contribute to a better understanding of 16th-century Lutheranism, to a wholesome modern day ecumenical endeavor, to a better understanding within the church of Christ, and to a furtherance of our common Christian mission, their efforts will be well repaid.

Robert D. Preus
Wilbert H. Rosin

HISTORICAL BACKGROUND OF THE FORMULA OF CONCORD

Robert A. Kolb

𝒥n 1500 Europe was ripe for reform. Particularly in the church the call for reform in head and members was being voiced loudly and clearly, especially by the humanists, participants in the rising intellectual movement of the day. The call conformed to the traditional medieval concept of reform: a call for improvements in church life along moral and institutional lines. Onto this scene came Martin Luther. His concept of reform grew out of his own spiritual struggles and envisaged an essentially different kind of reformation, one that reacted against the current teaching of the church and concerned the proclamation of the gospel more than moral life and institutional structures. Luther's criticism of the church attracted many who had their own complaints, different from his basic concern, and who had little or no conception of Luther's personal reaction against medieval religion. Some of his earlier supporters realized quite early that their flirtation with Luther's reformation could not last since his concept of reform differed radically from their own. Others remained in the stream of reformation he had unloosed because they believed that their own concerns were largely identical with Luther's or were best served by remaining in his camp. But because Luther's followers came out of different backgrounds and because their cares and concerns were shaped by different issues and events, conflict within the 16th-century ecclesiastical movement for reform in Germany was inevitable. Not only between Zwingli and Luther, between Anabaptists and Evangelicals, but also within the Wittenberg Reformation discord arose among those who had committed themselves to the reformation of the church.

Controversy Within the Wittenberg Reformation During Luther's Life

Philip Melanchthon was already recognized as a brilliant humanist scholar in 1518, when he joined the Wittenberg faculty at the age of 21. He and Luther quickly became very close friends, and their friendship lasted until Luther's death in 1546. Not only was Melanchthon converted to Luther's understanding of the Gospel; he also exerted a significant influence on Luther's own theological development.[1] In contrast to Luther's scholastic education, the background from which Melanchthon proceeded was that of the humanistic training in classical studies he had received at the universities of Heidelberg and Tübingen. His humanistic training caused Melanchthon to approach certain doctrinal issues anthropologically; in contrast, Luther, reacting against certain anthropocentric emphases in his scholastic training in theology and against similar elements in the popular religion in which he had been raised, approached theological questions theocentrically. At least in part because of this difference in background and orientation, two of Luther's earliest disciples, Johann Agricola and Nikolaus von Amsdorf, found serious, though different, reasons for disagreement with Melanchthon while Luther was still alive. Both men had accepted Luther's developing theology before the posting of the Ninety-five Theses, i.e., well before Melanchthon came to Wittenberg. Both seized upon emphases in Luther's thought particularly his rejection of work-righteousness, in reaction to the theology of their own earlier instructor.

Agricola came to Wittenberg to study in 1515, and he and Luther soon became close friends. He shared Luther's reaction against the legalism of the medieval religious system, and this led him already in his early writings to denigrate the law and to exclude it from any role in the life of the believer.[2] Agricola brought his views into the public arena by attacking Melanchthon's stress on the preaching of the law in the articles of instruction (composed in 1527) for the reforming visitation of Saxon churches. Melanchthon was concerned that public morality be preserved, and he was shocked by the low standards of moral life he discovered in the typical Saxon parish in the course of the visitation. Agricola must have been irritated in 1526, when Melanchthon received an appointment as professor of theology in addition to his position on the Wittenberg arts faculty, for Agricola himself had coveted the new theological chair. Melanchthon's emphasis on the preaching of the law heightened this irritation, and in 1527 Agricola criticized Melanchthon publicly.

Agricola's reaction against late medieval work-righteousness took form in his teaching that the Gospel reveals God's wrath and produces contrition as it proceeds to effect forgiveness of sins. God fashioned the law for the Jews, and Christ ends its reign in the lives of believers. Implicit in this teaching was Agricola's understanding that sin is primarily unbelief, the breaking of the First Commandment. In his reaction against the medieval preoccupation with actual, commited sins, he almost ignored such sins. This led him to his belief that the preaching of the Law is not necessary in any way for bringing sinners to Christ since the Gospel alerts man to his sin and his need for salvation.

Luther patched up the rift between Agricola and

14

Melanchthon in 1527, and Agricola continued his service as rector and then pastor in Eisleben. At his own initiative he abruptly left his charge at Eisleben in 1537 and returned to Wittenberg. Luther welcomed him and his family and tried to excuse his hasty departure to Agricola's patron in Eisleben, Count Albrecht of Mansfeld. Luther arranged a post as lecturer for Agricola at the university, but tension developed quickly because Agricola attacked the use of the Law in the church and claimed that Luther had abandoned his original position and became again a preacher of the Law because he opposed Agricola's antinomianism. Luther felt betrayed by his friend, but at first he did not take seriously the difference in their views of the relationship between Law and Gospel. The dispute simmered for more than a year, and then it erupted in early 1539, when Luther challenged Agricola's position in open, formal disputation at the university. In a series of four such disputations Luther presented his understanding of the role of the Law in the life of the Christian.

Slow to become angry at Agricola, Luther forged several reconciliations with his cantankerous disciple, but finally he felt that he had been pushed too far by Agricola's sniping. He called for condemnation of Agricola's doctrine of the Law. Others at Wittenberg tried to moderate Luther's wrath, though they had formerly opposed Agricola more strongly than Luther. After a number of unsuccessful attempts to induce Agricola to accept Luther's position, the faculty, under Luther's leadership, moved to suspend Agricola's right to teach. Agricola responded with formal proceedings before the Elector, charging that Luther had lied about him. When the Elector forbade Agricola to leave Wittenberg while the whole case was pending, Agricola decided to flee. He became court preacher at Berlin for Elector Joachim II of Brandenburg. A formal reconciliation with the Wittenbergers was announced later, but Agricola continued to deny any role for the Law in the life of the Christian.

Unlike Agricola, Amsdorf never broke with Luther; the two remained firm friends until Luther's death. But Amsdorf became increasingly suspicious of Melanchthon after the city of Magdeburg called him from Wittenberg to be its ecclesiastical superintendent in 1524. At that distance Amsdorf and Melanchthon could no longer talk out their problems with Luther over a glass of beer in the evening. In his reaction against the semi-Pelagianism of his scholastic teachers, Amsdorf was naturally uneasy with certain expressions of the humanist Melanchthon, who was trying to do justice to the anthropological and psychological elements in the human experience of faith.

Amsdorf expressed to Luther his misgivings over Melanchthon's phrase "good works are necessary for eternal life." He filed a brief in favor of Conrad Cordatus, a doctoral candidate at Wittenberg, who attacked his professor, Caspar Cruciger, for teaching that contrition is a *conditio sine qua non* for justification. Cruciger defended himself by citing Melanchthon as the source for his view. Privately Amsdorf also criticized the second edition of Melanchton's *Loci communes,* published in 1535, for its implication that the human will plays a role in conversion and that in human affairs the will has freedom of choice and events are contingent. But Amsdorf avoided taking issue with Melanchthon in print, and so their differences did not attract public attention. In 1543 Melanchthon again aroused Amsdorf's distrust when he joined with Martin Bucer in composing a plan for the reformation of the archbishopric of Cologne at the request of the archibishop-elector, Hermann von Wied. In a critique prepared at the request of the Saxon Elector, John Frederick, Amsdorf noted that the plan was unnecessarily vague on the freedom of the will and the real presence of Christ's body and blood in the Lord's Supper. Again, Amsdorf chose not to take public issue with Melanchthon at this time.[3]

When Luther died in 1546, the tensions between those who shared Amsdorf's concerns and those who had learned to appreciate Melanchthon's perspectives were not readily apparent on the surface of the Wittenberg movement. They might not have surfaced in the dramatic form they did, had not political events within the empire moved quickly in the months after Luther died; these events created an entirely new situation for his followers.

16

The Smalcaldic War and the Interims

Within weeks of Luther's death Emperor Charles V felt free of all threats from inside and outside His German lands that had kept him from trying to eliminate schism and heresy in the Holy Roman Empire of the German Nation. He had outlawed Luther and banned his movement at the diet of Worms in 1521, but his government did not find itself in a position to commit troops to the enforcement of the edict for a quarter century.

Even the Hapsburgs, Charles and his brother King Ferdinand, did not launch war against the Evangelical churches as such. Instead, they publicly tried to separate their military campaign from the religious issue (though privately Charles stated that the eradication of the Lutheran heresy was a primary goal of his military action). In the summer of 1546, the emperor outlawed the two most prominent Evangelical princes, Elector John Frederick of Saxony and Landgrave Philip of Hesse, not on charges of heresy but for other irregular or illegal acts. Philip's bigamy and John Frederick's seizure of the bishopric of Naumburg-Zeitz helped compromise their position and gave the emperor a pretext for attack. Charles effectively cut the two princes off from the active and even the moral support of other Evangelical princes, although some Evangelical cities joined minor princes from the north in supporting their cause. Charles also used the religious issue to keep Catholic princes in line, so that they would not try to enhance their own power at the expense of the emperor's by siding with the outlawed Evangelical princes.

Among the Evangelical princes who took the Hapsburg side in the ensuing war in late 1546 and early 1547, the most active and most prominent was Moritz, duke of Saxony and Elector John Frederick's cousin. His parents had raised him as an Evangelical, and when his father, Duke Heinrich, succeeded Moritz's uncle, the arch-Roman Catholic, Duke George, the "Albertine" part of Saxony became Evangelical.[4] However, Moritz had served in Hapsburg armies and had become a close friend of both Charles and Ferdinand. Futhermore, he coveted the electoral title and lands that had fallen to his cousin's side of the family. He occupied John Frederick's lands when the Elector marched south with Philip of Hesse in the autumn of 1546. The Evangelical forces frittered away some advantage and then moved north again at the beginning of winter so that John Frederick could reclaim his lands from Moritz. He did so rather quickly and overran most of Albertine Saxony as well. But in the spring the Hapsburg brothers came to assist Moritz. Composed largely of Spanish troops brought from Charles' Iberian domains, the imperial army defeated John Frederick and Philip at Mühlberg on the Elbe, April 24, 1547. John Frederick, now a prisoner, was forced to sign the Wittenberg Capitulation on May 19. This treaty gave Moritz the electorate of Saxony and reduced the holdings of John Frederick's sons to the Thuringian, or western, portion of his former lands.[5]

Charles left Saxony a triumphant victor. With the exception of the city of Magdeburg and a few principalities or cities in the far north, his German lands lay at his feet, responsive to his will. He began to impose that will at the imperial diet which met at Augsburg in September. He appointed a group of theologians to prepare a statement of faith and practice that would define German religious life during the interim before the Council of Trent would issue definitive regulations for the Christian West. A committee of three was designated by this group to formulate the statement. Its members were Johann Agricola, Evangelical maverick and court preacher for Elector Joachim II of Brandenburg, and two Erasmian Roman Catholics, Michael Helding, suffragan bishop of Mainz, and Julius von Pflug, newly installed bishop of Naumburg-Zeitz. Two Spanish theologians from Charles' retinue and his brother Ferdinand's court preacher assisted them.[6]

Charles promulgated his *Declaration on Religion* on May 15, 1548. Popularly known as the "Augsburg Interim," it granted two minor concessions to Evangelicals who obtained special permission for them: communion in both kinds and the right of priests to marry. It also imposed Roman dogma, expressed in the manner of the Erasmian reform party, on Evangelical lands. The Interim linked justification to the gift of *charitas* and thus to the performance of good works. It restored

18

the power of papal bishops and the authority of the pope. It affirmed all seven medieval sacraments and their use in the church. It defended the medieval practice of the mass and insisted that the Evangelicals use its traditional form and trappings as well as the sacramentals connected with various aspects of religious life. The Interim threatened the end of Luther's movement and of the Evangelical churches.

Charles V used his Spanish troops to enforce the Interim where he could, chiefly in southern Germany. Württemberg and a number of southern Evangelical cities, including Constance, Strasbourg, Augsburg, and Nuremberg, were occupied by imperial forces, and their princes and officials were compelled to submit to imperial authority, though in some cases compromises were fashioned. Other Evangelical princes also agreed to use the Augsburg Interim as the basis of religious life in their lands in an attempt to avoid further difficulties with the emperor. Actually, various degrees of compliance with the Interim were obtained in various places. In the entire dukedom of Württemberg, only two Evangelical pastors consented to remain in their congregations and conduct their ministries according to the Augsburg Interim.[7] Hundreds of Evangelical preachers were driven into exile, but the priests who replaced them were often too few in number and too unpopular to bring about substantial change in the religious convictions of the people. The city of Constance was one of the few places in which the faith of the Augsburg Interim was permanently imposed, for the city was incorporated into Hapsburg territory. After the Peace of Augsburg allowed most lands to choose between the Augsburg Interim and the Augsburg Confession, the Evangelical lands returned to the Lutheran confession.

The opposition to the Augsburg Interim began almost immediately after its publication. Though only in Magdeburg could presses issue material critical of the emperor's plans, a number of sharp critiques of the Interim's theology and of its Evangelical coauthor, Agricola, appeared in mid-1548. They denounced the document and rejected any thought of compromise with the emperor and the Roman party.[8] More cautious criticisms also found their way into print. Among them was one by Melanchthon. But he was afraid of imperial retaliation, and he was embarrased when this private memorandum against compliance with the Interim, addressed to his new lord, Moritz, was published in Magdeburg.[9]

Melanchthon and his colleagues in Wittenberg did not have to share the fate of many Evangelical pastors: escape and exile. Instead, they were placed in a peculiarly ticklish situation. The Wittenberg theological faculty found itself in late spring 1547 subject to Moritz, whom they had accused of being a traitor to the Evangelical cause a few months earlier. Moritz, however, was in no position to bear a grudge against the Wittenberg theologians, since he needed their support if he was to woo and win the population of John Frederick's lands and retain that of his own lands. The new elector of Saxony was caught in a vise after the victory at Mühlberg. On the one hand, he felt pressure from his Hapsburg friends, who were not about to keep their oral promise, made before the war, that Moritz would not have to change his faith and that of his lands. On the other hand, he felt pressure from his estates and subjects, who were uncompromisingly Lutheran in spirit and doctrine. Charles had shocked Moritz by imposing the Augsburg Interim on Evangelical lands and then by insisting that even Moritz had to bring his lands into compliance with it. In order to secure room for maneuvering, Moritz tried on the one hand to convince the Saxons that the return of Spanish troops to Saxon soil was a genuine threat and that he was doing his best to stave off the Hapsburgs and their occupation forces as the electoral Saxon government began to search for some compromise solution. On the other hand, he did his best to convince Charles and Ferdinand that his own independent course was more than token compliance with the Augsburg Interim, for in 1548 he still believed that his hold on his electorate and his new lands was no stronger than his ability to keep the emperor's favor.

Moritz's secular counselors favored strong compliance with Hapsburg policy; his theologians rejected the Augsburg Interim. Melanchthon and his colleagues did suggest that certain compromises in indifferent matters might be possible, however, in order to keep Spanish troops from Saxon soil and thus keep

Evangelical preachers in Saxon pulpits. Through his secular counselors and the new Roman Catholic bishops in Saxony, Moritz applied pressure on the theologians to forge a compromise plan for Saxon religious life. This compromise, dubbed the Leipzig Interim by its opponents, was adopted by the Saxon estates assembled at Leipzig in late December 1548.

The Leipzig Interim satisfied no one in trying to placate the emperor while trying to preserve the heart of Lutheran doctrine. The basic principle of this Interim was concession on indifferent matters (adiaphora) and retention of the Evangelical understanding of justification. The document does stress divine grace and mercy as the causative factor of justification. Christ's atoning work brings forgiveness of sins, it states. But the phrase "through faith alone" is omitted, and the role of good works in the Christian life is emphasized. Faith, hope, and love are necessary for salvation, according to the Leipzig Interim.[10]

Its authors viewed the Leipzig Interim as a document of compromise chiefly in its concessions to what they considered adiaphora. The Leipzig Interim reintroduced confirmation, holding out hope it could be transformed from a spectacle into an examination of faith. The Interim also accepted private confession before communion and extreme unction "practiced according to apostolic usage." It restored much of the Latin rite of the Roman mass as well as the traditional ceremonial of the old worship service. Worship in electoral Saxony was designed to appear much as it had before Luther. Moritz's theologians also conceded the restoration of the canonical hours and services in memory of the dead. They planned for the reintroduction of many of the old festival celebrations, including Corpus Christi and the Marian holidays. According to this second Interim, meat would not be eaten on Fridays and Saturdays in Saxony, in obedience to the civil ordinances of the empire (namely the Augsburg Interim). The most difficult part of the new formula for the Saxon estates to accept was that which dealt with the right of the bishops to ordain. The Saxon bishops were all papal appointees after the Smalcaldic War, but Moritz's theologians were willing to acknowledge their right to ordain all pastors if the bishops did not persecute the Gospel and if they strove for good order in the church. Candidates for ordination had to be presented to the bishop by the patron of the congregation, a stipulation that insured control by Evangelical lords over the churches in their lands.

The Leipzig Interim was forged by men of good will and genuine concern for the preaching of the Gospel they had learned from Luther. They were not trying to betray their faith, as their opponents charged. But they were men in a different situation, of a different spirit, and perhaps with less grasp of the realities of parish life, than those who began immediately to criticize the Interim. For example, one of those who framed the Leipzig Interim, Prince Georg of Anhalt, had always favored conservative ecclesiastical practices. As Evangelical administrator of the bishopric of Merseburg 1544—50, he propagated Luther's concept of justification by grace through faith, but what to others were papalist trappings had always been to him proper Christian forms.[11] Johann Pfeffinger, pastor and professor in Leipzig, had served Moritz since his accession in 1542, as had others who participated in the composition of his Interim.[12] These men knew that Moritz had established and supported the Evangelical faith in his lands, and they were confident that his compromising only expressed his desire to retain as much of Luther's reformation as possible while avoiding an imperial invasion of his lands. Wittenbergers, like Johann Bugenhagen and Georg Major, shared Melanchthon's concern that their faith and their university not be further threatened, and so they went along with their preceptor in agreeing to the terms of the Leipzig Interim.

Melanchthon was in a particularly delicate situation. He had incurred the wrath of Charles V for a number of reasons, and Moritz's defense of his leading theologian against imperial pressures obligated Melanchthon to his prince. Pfeffinger and others who had been close to Moritz before the Smalcaldic War were Melanchthon's former students and friends, and they welcomed him into their prince's service. Furthermore, Melanchthon was genuinely concerned about the threat of Spanish troops and the religious suppression and persecution that their renewed presence in Saxony would bring. In addition,

22

he believed that the stars foretold an early death for Charles V; buying a little time through compromise would be worthwhile since a new emperor would soon mount the throne. Nor was the basic principle of the Leipzig Interim alien or offensive to Melanchthon: concessions in adiaphora for the sake of the church's peace ought not harm anyone's conscience. He therefore acceded to the desires of the new elector of Saxony. His personality and background, combined with his current situation, made it difficult for him to take any other course. His own makeup and his responsibilities in Wittenberg prevented him from considering seriously the options pursued by an exiled bishop like Nikolaus von Amsdorf, or a student on the run like Matthias Flacius Illyricus, or a pastor escaped from the south like Nikolaus Gallus. They and a number of others like them were lodged somewhat safely for the time, at least—in the outlawed city, the embattled fortress, Magdeburg.

The Interims Controversies

Magdeburg was theoretically subject in both secular and ecclesiastical realms to the archbishop of Magdeburg, but the desire of its citizens to be free from his control had coincided nicely with their conviction concerning religious reformation, which had been introduced by Amsdorf and others in the 1520s. In 1548 the city became a haven for those who opposed the Augsburg Interim, and under the leadership of Amsdorf and Flacius, a young, brilliant Italo-Croatian student at Wittenberg until 1549,[13] a concerted effort against the Leipzig Interim developed there. The group at Magdeburg and others who shared their general orientation were called "genuine Lutherans" or "Gnesio-Lutherans" by their opponents, and their movement remained strong until it was coopted by the Concordianist movement three decades later.

In England two parties arose in the church of the reformation, Anglicans and Puritans. Similarly, circumstances in Saxony led to the development of two groups within its young Lutheran church. One group favored, or at least could be content with, a reformation relatively more conservative from a late medieval perspective. The other group wanted to take

Luther's insights in their full radicality, at times expressing them in an even more radical fashion that Luther himself had. The conservatives have been named the Philippists because of their allegiance to their preceptor, Philipp Melanchthon; and the radicals were the Gnesio-Lutherans, a better term than the other epithet assigned them by the Philippists, "Flacianists." For not all Gnesio-Lutherans followed Flacius; the fissiparous tendencies of the group led them to fight with each other, including their most brilliant representative.

As noted above, the differing attitudes toward the reformation that became somewhat concrete in the rather loosely associated groups called Philippists and Gnesio-Lutherans did not arise only after or because of the crisis of the Smalcaldic War. These differing attitudes and concerns had existed earlier, but the events in the wake of the Smalcaldic War did trigger the battles over these concerns between the two perspectives. The nature and shape of the disputes within the Wittenberg reformation were influenced greatly by the poisonous atmosphere in Saxony after the war; in that atmosphere political considerations and personal recriminations played a large role in decisions concerning what was best for the Evangelical church of Saxony. From Magdeburg came charges that Moritz of Saxony was a newborn Antiochus Epiphanes and that his theologians had betrayed Luther's church to the Antichrist of Rome in the Leipzig Interim. Such criticism threatened to upset Moritz's precarious hold on his lands, both his new lands and his old lands, since his people were solidly Evangelical. So from his theologians in Wittenberg and Leipzig came countercharges that the men of Magdeburg were rebels and riffraff, outlaws and schismatics. Adiaphora, compromise with the Roman church on matters considered indifferent by the electoral Saxons, became the focal point for a bitter rivalry that grew up between friends, between two groups of the students of Luther and Melanchthon. The political necessities of those on each side provided the spark for a quarter century of intense, harsh exchanges of charges and countercharges.

The Gnesio-Lutheran attack on the Leipzig Interim poured forth in the course of 1549 and 1550 from the presses of

Magdeburg. Since Magdeburg was practically the only place in the empire where criticisms of either Interim could be published, Caspar Aquila called the city the "chancellery of God." Between 1548 and 1551 nearly 200 such tracts appeared from Magdeburg presses.[14]

The Magdeburgers objected to the presuppositions and judgments concerning adiaphora that had led the electoral Saxon theologians to forge the Leipzig Interim. Amsdorf, Flacius, and Gallus set down their basic principle: "In a case where confession of faith is demanded, where ceremonies or adiaphora are commanded as necessary, where offense may be given, adiaphora do not remain adiaphora or indifferent but become matters of moral precept, in which God must be obeyed."[15] Amsdorf, Flacius, and Gallus did not care how theologians might explain away their concessions to Rome. They were concerned about the effect of the concessions of the Leipzig Interim on the average Saxon parishioner. The Interimists were declaring that it was better to compromise appearances than to have Spanish troops and papal priests marching into Saxony. The Magdeburgers were really no more secure in the outlawed, and for a time besieged, city of Magdeburg, but they felt safer, or took the imperial threat less seriously, or choose to ignore that threat and to concentrate on the pastoral needs of the parishioner. They replied to the electoral Saxon theologians that the average parishioner saw as much as he heard in worship. If he saw the surplice and the candle, he would believe that the Wittenbergers who had reintroduced these medieval practices had returned to the message of the old days as well. He would not hear the gospel because the reminders of Rome seemed to indicate that Luther's successors had forgotten it. The exiled pastors at Magdeburg had lived their ministries among people for whom words were less important than symbols. As a professor, Melanchthon was at a disadvantage when it came to reading the popular mind. He and his colleagues had responded to other pressures and a somewhat different concern.

The Magdeburgers also criticized the Wittenbergers for permitting secular officials to interfere with what should have been strictly a matter for the church. This stance of independence and readiness to criticize secular officials for applying pressure to the church was, of course, easier for those in Magdeburg than for those in Moritz's employ. However, several Gnesio-Lutherans later earned exile for standing by this basic principle, which Flacius in particular enunciated in 1549 and 1550.

Controversy over the Interims became unnecessary after the Truce of Passau in 1552 and the confirmation of its arrangements in the Religious Peace of Augsburg in 1555. These documents established the right of the prince to determine which faith, that of Rome or Wittenberg, would be the faith preached in his lands. Thus, at Augsburg in 1555 the confession made there a quarter century earlier became a legal, though politically inferior, confession for the cities and princes of the Empire that chose to hold it. The Interims were dead. As a matter of fact, the Leipzig Interim had been enforced only in a few areas in which Moritiz's officials felt it would not arouse too much opposition.

However, the controversy had burned too hot for immediate extinction. The Gnesio-Lutherans insisted that the Philippists repent publicly for their composition and defense of the Leipzig Interim. Although Melanchthon admitted that he had taken the wrong stand in the crises of 1548,[16] he and his associates refused to submit to the kind of public penance Flacius and his friends insisted on. So the two parties continued to exchange verbal and printed blasts on the subject of the Interim throughout the 1550s. They also found other issues to dispute.

The Majoristic Controversy

One exchange in the course of the controversy over the Leipzig Interim led to another controversy, namely over the proposition "good works are necessary for salvation." In late 1551 Nikolaus von Amsdorf replied to accusations against the Magdeburgers made by two of his old friends, Johann Bugenhagen and Georg Major, both firmly within Moritz's theological camp at Wittenberg. Amsdorf made a special point of the omission of the *sola fide* in the Leipzig Interim, and he

26

criticized those who taught that good works are necessary for salvation. In his reply Major emphasized his own insistence on justification through faith alone but also stated:

> This I confess; I have previously taught and still teach and want to teach my whole life, that good works are necessary to salvation, and I say openly and with clear and plain words, that no one will be saved through evil works, and no one will be saved without good works, and I further say whoever teaches otherwise, even an angel from heaven, is accursed.[17]

Amsdorf and other Gnesio-Lutherans replied immediately with stinging critiques of Major's proposition and person. In his reply to Amsdorf, Major had tried to shift the focus of the dispute away from Amsdorf's comments to the person of Flacius, the foreigner, the "Wend," who was dabbling in theology without a divine call to teach or preach.

In 1552 and 1553 Major issued tracts defending his understanding of his proposition. He insisted that he had always taught that salvation is given only by God's grace through faith in Christ. But he also insisted that faith produces works, that faith is always joined to new obedience. Therefore, the works of the Christian man, he emphasized, are a necessary part of his salvation.[18]

Major was echoing Melanchthon's concern for Christian ethical standards and was well aware of the danger of antinomianism in the Evangelical camp. As a member of the Saxon consistory he was faced directly with problems of moral breakdown within a Christian land. Amsdorf, on the other hand, could never forget that papal supporters who had tried to eradicate the infant Evangelical movement in Magdeburg in the 1520s had used the concept of the necessity of good works for salvation as a weapon against the preaching of Luther's message. Amsdorf was further convinced that Evangelical lay people only a generation away from late medieval concepts of salvation could understand words like "good works are necessary for salvation" in only one way. Flacius shared his sensitivity to the problem of shifting definitions in the debate with Major and to the likelihood of misrepresenting the fruits of faith as the seed of faith when Major's proposition was used. For Flacius was certain that both "good works" and "salvation" were still defined by most Germans as they had been before Luther. Flacius continued to point out that no matter how thoroughly Major tried to explain his new nuances for the two terms, he could not avoid being misunderstood. Again, a difference of perspective can also help explain the dispute between Major and his opponents. Major was studying the human reaction to God's gift of salvation and stressed that this gift produces good works. The Gnesio-Lutherans were anxious to maintain that human works do not contribute to salvation.

Although the pressure of attack against Major was diverted temporarily to his friend, Justus Menius, who tried to defend Major's concern without defending his proposition, Flacius and his colleagues continued to treat the suggestion that good works are necessary for salvation as a serious threat to Luther's understanding of the gospel. Even Melanchthon disavowed the proposition in 1555. Major promised in 1558 and a number of times thereafter that he would never use the words again. But he did not disavow the proposition and continued to suggest that good works are necessary for the retention of salvation or that good works do receive their own reward in heaven, so the Gnesio-Lutherans remained suspicious and critical of his proposition and of his explanations of it.[19]

One phase of the Gnesio-Lutheran reaction to Major caused a separate minor controversy. Amsdorf had insisted on the necessity of good works in Christian living, as a result of faith, throughout his attack on the concept that they are necessary for salvation. However, in an effort to clarify his concern over Major's proposition, he formulated one of his own: "good works are harmful for salvation." He indicated in a tract on his proposition that good works are harmful when one trusts in them for salvation.[20] Most theologians on both sides of the Majoristic controversy knew what he meant and ignored him. But since he had made some very pointed attacks against the other side, a few Philippists could not help but charge him with antinomianism, in part also because of their concern that

28

Evangelical lay people could well get the idea that freedom from the law, as Luther proclaimed it, meant also freedom from works. No serious dispute grew up around Amsdorf's proposition.

Major found almost no supporters for his proposition, though in some locations brief controversy over his proposition arose between local clergymen. The matter might have sunk quickly from public view, had Major been able to extricate himself more convincingly from his unfortunate formulation. But without public repentance the Gnesio-Lutherans could also not be satisfied that the proposition had been properly removed from Lutheran theological circles, and so the issue lingered in the public exchanges between Gnesio-Lutherans and Philippists until the Formula of Concord ended the debate.

The Synergistic Controveries

Related controversies over the human role in salvation arose in Saxony while the Majoristic controversy was taking place. One was begun by Johann Pfeffinger, superintendent and professor in Leipzig, who had studied at Wittenberg in the 1520s and become a loyal friend of Melanchthon. He served Moritz as pastor, professor, and ecclesiastical advisor from the duke's accession in 1541. He helped compose and defend the Leipzig Interim. Therefore, when he suggested in public disputation in 1555 that man is able with his own natural powers to assent to the Word, to grasp the promise, and not resist the Holy Spirit, Gnesio-Lutherans found it impossible not to suspect that he was denying the sole efficacy of God's grace. Strangely enough, they waited three years before attacking his view.

As a student of Melanchthon, Pfeffinger had learned that the human will, along with the Word and the Holy Spirit, is the third factor in conversion.[21] (Melanchthon had not made it clear that the will becomes a factor in conversion only as a result of the action of the Holy Spirit through the Word upon it.) The humanists of the Philippist school were wrestling with the psychological aspects of the relationship between God and human beings in a way in which the Gnesio-Lutherans were not.

29

Pfeffinger was struggling with the problem of determinism and human reaction to God's grace when he wrote, "we attribute some cooperation to our will, [but] his sort of assent and grasping takes absolutely nothing at all away from the aid of the Holy Spirit." Yet he qualified and obscured his insistence on the primacy of the Holy Spirit by adding that the "Holy Spirit is received in this way by those who seek [Him], that is, by those who do not spurn or reject Him, but who seek His aid with groaning."[22]

Amsdorf criticized Pfeffinger for this position in 1558, at the same time that Flacius and Johann Stolz, court preacher for the dukes of Saxony, published their critiques of Pfeffinger's theses.[23] Pfeffinger replied, but he was never able to make it clear whether the human will could cooperate with God's grace before or only after the Holy Spirit moved that will. The controversy moved quite quickly beyond Pfeffinger at Leipzig into ducal Saxony itself, to its new university at Jena.

Because the sons of John Frederick had lost the university of Wittenberg to Moritz as a result of the Wittenberg Capitulation, they founded their university at Jena in 1548. It received its imperial charter a decade later. The new university was unavoidably a filial institution of Wittenberg since Saxon academics had all studied with Melanchthon and Luther in the second quarter of the 16th century. Jena's first professor of theology and philosophy, Viktorin Strigel, came to Jena on Melanchthon's recommendation. Only 24 when he arrived there in 1548, the brilliant Strigel became something of a Wunderkind in ducal Saxon public life. He felt his position severely threatened in 1557, when Flacius, four years his elder, was called to be his colleague on the theological faculty. He also must have resented what he regarded as Flacius' unfair treatment of their common mentor, Melanchthon, for Strigel, though he had faithfully served his Gnesio-Lutheran princes in Jena, was still sympathetic towards, and on good terms with, Melanchthon. Furthermore, the intellectual influence of his preceptor remained paramount in Strigel's thinking.

For three years the two maneuvered for position within the ducal Saxon church. Their antagonisms drove them into open conflict in 1557, when Duke John Frederick the Middler decided to further Lutheran unity by publishing a *Book of Confutation* to refute the errors of current concern in the Evangelical movement in Germany. The duke asked Strigel and two of his friends to work on this book, but they refused unless Amsdorf and Flacius would be completely excluded from any part in the project. The duke consented to this condition. The three proceeded to formulate a rough draft, which they offered to the duke in early 1558, repeating their expressed stipulation that Amsdorf and Flacius have no role in its composition.

Strigel and his friends hardly recognized their text when Flacius and his friends completed their revisions.[24] This affront to Strigel's party only heightened the tension and friction within the ducal Saxon church. Yet for the next two years the Flacian party was able to control the affairs of that church. Johann Wigand and Matthias Judex, friends of Flacius from Magdeburg, won appointments to the theological faculty at Jena. Strigel struggled against Flacian ascendancy, in part by making the *Book of Confutation* an issue. The duke required subscription to the *Book* from all members of the clergy and faculty in his land, and Strigel refused to subscribe for a number of doctrinal reasons. He hoped to defeat Flacius and regain his leading position in the ducal Saxon church by defending the stance he had learned from Melanchthon at Wittenberg 15 years earlier.

Strigel's resistance enraged John Frederick the Middler, and the duke had his professor arrested and imprisoned in the spring of 1559. After enforced meditation upon the *Book's* position in two ducal castles, Strigel still could not formulate his position, particularly on the role of the human will in conversion, to the satisfaction of the duke's clerical advisors. But pressure from the emperor and other Evangelical princes, together with John Frederick's own concern for pure doctrine and his weariness with the wrangle among his theologians, made the duke press for settlement. He rejected Strigel's suggestion for a synod of all Lutheran churches and opted for Flacius' proposal for a disputation between himself and Strigel. It was held at the ducal court in Weimar.

The disputants did not discuss all the issues put before them; the duke became impatient with the proceedings and placed the disputation in permanent recess after 13 sessions. Free will and its role in man's conversion was the central issue during the disputation, and in the context of the discussion of this issue a new controversy was born. Flacius wanted to describe man with Biblical terms; Strigel wanted to use the terminology of Aristotelian anthropology in discussing man's role and nature in conversion. Flacius blundered onto Strigel's field of battle, adopted his terms, and countered the claim that original sin was an accident in man with the assertion that man's very substance since the fall is original sin. Flacius was charged with Manichaeism. This may have contributed to John Frederick's growing disillusion with him.

Strigel defined man's will after the fall as a neutral, unbound active force; that was for him not so much a theological as a philospophical premise. Flacius believed the human will is bound and unable in any way to turn to God; he was thinking on a theological plane. Strigel argued that man remains God's creature and that his will retains its mode of acting *(modus agendi)* in spite of sin, which is only—in Aristotelian terms—an accidental property of man's subtance, which is good because it was created in the image of God. Flacius asserted that original sin is not merely accidental but has permeated and perverted the whole substance of man, who as a result of the fall is shaped essentially in the image of Satan, not in the image of God. Flacius did distinguish man's material substance from his formal substance. The formal substance of man is the image of God and the righteousness with which God created him, according to Flacius. From his theological perspective that is the most important part of man. The fact that his material substance remains much as it was before the fall is far less significant than is his loss of his original righteousness and his assumption of a spiritual image in rebellion against God, in Flacius' view. He believed that any other assessment of the human situation did not take seriously the total break between God and man which sin causes.[25] Flacius developed and maintained the basic position he had set forth at the Weimar

Disputation of 1560 throughout the rest of his life at great personal cost.

By 1560 his prince was becoming uncomfortable with more than Flacius' anthropology. Duke John Frederick the Middler could not tolerate the Flacian party's insistence that the government not interfere with the affairs of the church, and his counselors, who had always remained friends with the Strigel party, finally persuaded him that Flacius and his comrades should be purged. In the winter of 1561 (winter always being a good time to exile foes) the duke fired and deported Flacius and Wigand.

In 1567 Flacius presented his anthropology and his view of original sin as the substance of human beings in a special appendix to his *Key to the Sacred Scriptures.* Although the initial reaction to this presentation from his Gnesio-Lutheran friends was favorable, a number of them joined with Joachim Mörlin and Martin Chemnitz in criticizing Flacius' doctrine as Manichaean. Former supporters from Jena, Simon Musäus and Johann Wigand, joined Tilemann Heshus in reversing their stand on Flacian anthropology, and Flacius was forced to respond to the criticisms of those who, he believed, should naturally have shared that view of man. The debate over original sin continued until Flacius' death; one of the last rounds was his dispute in a series of tracts with Jacob Andreä, who ardently sought Flacius' support for his own plans for concord, but who found Flacius' expressions on original sin extravagant and misleading.[26] After Flacius' death a few of his disciples defended his position, but all the formulators of Lutheran concord condemned Flacian anthropology.

Controversies over Law and Gospel

Related to the disputes between Philippists and Gnesio-Lutherans of the 1550s and 1560s were several disputes over the relationship of law and gospel in Lutheran theology. Although the charge of "antinomianism" was thrown about quite easily during two of these disputes, none of the participants shared Agricola's view that the law had absolutely no role to play in the Christian life.

These disputes grew out of a concern similar to that of Agricola, but out of a reaction against work-righteousness and the use of the Law as at least a partial means of effecting one's own salvation. The first controversy did not find its way into public print until 1568. At the Altenburg Colloquy the Philippist representatives from electoral Saxony accused one Gnesio-Lutheran, Anton Otto, of crass antinomianism. But no extended public discussion resulted even from that false accusation. The dispute in which Otto had played a small role over a decade earlier arose out of the Eisenach Synod of 1556. That synod had been called to examine charges of Majorism against Justus Menius. Among its decisions was this: "Good works are necessary for salvation theoretically in the doctrine of the Law." That formulation was attacked by Amsdorf, by Otto, who was a pastor in Nordhausen, and particularly by Andreas Poach, pastor in Erfurt. Flacius and Wigand dealt with Amsdorf's objections; Joachim Mörlin of Braunschweig carried on the dispute with Poach in this controversy which pitted Gnesio-Lutheran against Gnesio-Lutheran. Amsdorf, Otto, and Poach were concerned that even this formulation would encourage reliance on one's own works for salvation. Flacius and Mörlin argued that the Law is the basis of judgment only if its demands are indeed the requirement for life as God originally created it for his human creatures.[27]

More public and more serious was the controversy between two of Agricola's colleagues in Brandenburg in the late 1550s and early 1560s. Andreas Musculus had studied at Wittenberg in the late 1530s and had become both a friend of Agricola and a disciple of Luther before accepting a call to Franfurt an der Oder as pastor and professor in 1540. In 1557 Melanchthon's disciple, Abdias (Gottschalk) Praetorius became professor of Hebrew at Frankfurt. He was welcomed to Brandenburg by another Philippist, Georg Buchholtzer, a preacher at Elector Joachim's court. Buchholtzer was already locked in a duel with Agricola in Berlin. Agricola and then Musculus took exception to Praetorius' use of the proposition "good works are necessary" and fought a five-year running battle in print, in preaching, and in the lecture hall. Students in Frankfurt generally favored

Praetorius, the clergy in Brandenburg was divided, and Joachim tried a number of times to reconcile his quarreling professors. Although he supported Musculus' position, he was never alientated from Praetorius and used him as a counselor and legate until Praetorius moved to Wittenberg in 1563.

Musculus taught that good works are produced freely through the Holy Spirit in the Christian life; Praetorius said that good works are a necessary part of the Christian life. Musculus knew what such a statement could mean to the lay people of Brandenburg less than a generation after the Evangelical faith had been established there. He was convinced that many parishioners would interpret talk about the necessity of good works as a soteriological statement and revert to, or be reinforced in, their old belief that doing good works saves. Praetorius, on the other hand, shared the concern of his Philippist colleagues over antinomianism. He knew that lay people could interpret Luther's message of freedom from the law as freedom from doing good works. Coupled with court intrigue and personality clashes as this controversy was, it is no wonder that its debate was particularly bitter. Both sides were trying to make a point that was important for the church in Brandenburg. Both sides misstated their own concerns and ministerpreted their opponents' concerns. Musculus won a reputation as an antinomian that even his subscription to article six of the Formula of Concord could not remove.[28]

The definition of "Gospel" was also debated, though not extensively, by a few representatives of the Gnesio-Lutheran and Philippist camps in the late 1550s and 1560s. Strigel and others who had studied under Melanchthon recognized a wider definition of the word, one that included the preaching of repentance. Strigel and Flacius disagreed over this definition during their feud in ducal Saxony at the end of the 1550s, and the dispute was taken up in print by the Wittenbergers Paul Crell and Christoph Pezel in 1570. Their position was criticized by Wigand, who agreed with Flacius that "Gospel" in its proper sense means simply the good news of the forgiveness of sins in Jesus Christ.[29]

The disputes between Philippists and Gnesio-Lutherans

actually took place in the context of, and because of, a complex of political and personal tensions which grew out of the Smalcaldic War. But their disputes only inflamed a division of opinion and expression that existed within the Wittenberg reformation at least a decade before Luther's death. Differences of perspective brought Gnesio-Lutherans and Philippists to different concerns as the Evangelical movement developed. Both sides were steeped in Biblical theology, and both sides were trained as Melanchthonian Aristotelians. But the Gnesio-Lutheran preference for Biblical terminology and the Philippist desire to use Aristotelian concepts, e.g., in the synergistic controversy, is symptomatic of the approach of the two schools to questions of doctrine. More often than not, the Gnesio-Lutherans wanted to safeguard divine grace and so defined issues from a strictly theological perspective, whereas the Philippists were striving to answer questions from an anthropological point of view.

The Philippists seemed more at home in human society, more a part of the total political unit in which they lived. Thus, they were ready to submit to their prince through compromise, while the Gnesio-Lutherans were more often willing to defy him for principle. The Gnesio-Lutherans demanded from their hearers a strict obedience to the will of God, but their ethical expressions are formulated out of a concern that Christians follow Christ. Philippists shared that concern, but they also felt responsible for the preservation of public morality. When all the political and personal factors are stripped away, serious concerns and strikingly different points of view remain as factors that separated the two parties within Saxon Lutheranism of the first 30 years after Luther's death. The political and personal gave form to their substantial disagreement.

The Osiandrian Controversy

Gnesio-Lutherans and Philippists alike were disturbed by the theology of Andreas Osiander at about the same time the seriousness of their own division was becoming apparent, and their brief dispute with him cast its shadow for a generation over the deliberations of German Lutheranism. Osiander had studied Old Testament with Johannes Reuchlin, great German Hebraist, at the University of Ingolstadt in 1520, and there he had absorbed the Platonic philosophical orientation of the Florentine Academy and his mentor's love for the cabala. As the clerical leader of the Reformation in the city of Nuremberg, he became one of the most prominent south German Lutherans and participated in the Marburg Colloquy, the Smalcald meeting of 1537, and the colloquies at Hagenau and Worms; he took part in the deliberations that led to the Augsburg Confession. His career in Nuremberg ended when the Augsburg Interim was introduced in the city. in 1548.[30]

A quarter century earlier Albert of Prussia (1490—1568), grand master of the Teutonic Knights, who ruled Prussia, had been converted to Lutheranism by Osiander's preaching. He had often invited Osiander to join him in Königsberg, the capital of the duchy created when he secularized the Knights' lands and made them Evangelical in 1525. So Osiander sought refuge at his court in early 1549. Several circumstances contributed to his instant unpopularity there. Albrecht made Osiander the pastor of the parish in the old quarter of Königsberg at a salary somewhat larger than his predecessor's. The duke insisted that the faculty of his new university accept Osiander as a lecturer in theology, though he had no academic degree that would qualify him for the position. By becoming a member of the faculty of the University of Königsberg, Osiander joined a group that had been squabbling incessantly and sometimes bitterly since the university's inception in 1542. The newcomer's initial disputation, on Law and Gospel, was greeted in typical fashion, with a sharp attack by an arts instructor, Matthias Lauterwald, who had studied at Wittenberg. Lauterwald's objection to Osiander's view of repentance did not strike at what would become the heart of the Osiandrian controversy, but in April 1549 it began the turmoil centered around the man.

Although Melanchthon approved Osiander's theses on Law and Gospel, relations between Osiander and the Philippists deteriorated in 1549 and 1550 with Osiander's attack on the Leipzig Interim and on a professor at Leipzig over the interpretation of the Old Testament concept of the heaven of heavens. Melanchthon attacked Osiander only after his views of justification were published in late 1550.

In December of that year Osiander's *Whether the Son of God Would Have Had to Become Man If Sin Had Not Entered the World* appeared, answering its title's question with a yes.[31] As the image—i.e., the visible, substantial form—of God, Christ would have become a man to assume headship of the church and to unite humanity fully with God. This diminution of the significance of the fall and of sin in salvation history aroused an immediate outcry among most other Lutherans. At the same time they were objecting to Osiander's view of justification, which had been published only weeks earlier in the form of a disputation.[32] In it Osiander condemned the concept of the imputation of Christ's righteousness to the sinner through faith. Instead Osiander taught that saving righteousness comes to the believer through the indwelling of Christ in him and that this righteousness is solely the essential righteousness of the divine Son of God, not the righteousness won by Christ through his suffering, death, and resurrection. Osiander wanted to comfort the sinner with the assurance that a real, ontic righteousness was present within him through faith. Osiander distinguished redemption, which took place 1,500 years earlier on the cross, from reconciliation or justification, which brings the believer into a marriage relationship with Christ now as the indwelling Christ and the believer become one flesh and one spirit. That relationship is created and maintained by faith, Osiander insisted, explaining that faith is created by the inner Word, Jesus Christ, which is borne by the outer Word, in its preached and written forms. Osiander repeatedly claimed and tried to prove that he and Luther had come to the same conclusions (though independently of each other, Osiander averred), but his exposure to the Florentine Platonism of Pico della Mirandola had given Osiander a far different basis or foundation on which to build his theology than Luther's Occamistic instructors had given him.

Not only the Philippists and Gnesio-Lutherans who had studied under Melanchthon but also Amsdorf, an older

Wittenberger, recognized this immediately. Although Osiander was probably correct in saying that his views had not changed since the 1520s, he had not presented them as fully before he came to Königsberg. Now all of the Wittenberg Reformation rose up against him. Within the Prussian church Osiander had few allies. Joachim Mörlin, exiled from Göttingen because of the Augsburg Interim, tried to reconcile with Osiander's position what he had learned from Luther and Melanchthon at Wittenberg, and this Gnesio-Lutheran played a mediating role in Königsberg for a short time after his arrival there in early 1551. But he soon joined the Prussian opponents of Osiander. Another professor, Francesco Stancaro, Italian exile and briefly Hebrew instructor in Königsberg, criticized Osiander's claim that Christ saves people only through his divine nature, by teaching that Christ saves only through his human nature. His position was also rejected by those who were opposing Osiander.[33]

Mörlin and his anti-Osiandrian party in Prussia were reinforced by a shower of critical memoranda and pamphlets from Evangelical quarters throughout northern Germany. Duke Albrecht solicited official judgments from most Evangelical princes and cities; he also received a great number of unofficial reactions. They all joined Melanchthon in insisting that people are saved through faith by the imputation of the merits of Christ's suffering and death, his obedience and blood. God the Holy Spirit does dwell in believers and sanctifies them, Melanchthon agreed, but justification takes place when the righteousness of Christ, both God and man, is credited to the believer.

Only one of the many groups that offered judgments on Osiander's position was even mildly favorable to him. Johannes Brenz, since the Smalcaldic War advisor to the dukes of Württemberg, had worked with Osiander on a number of occasions. He tried to put the best construction on his friend's views by pointing out that Osiander did not exclude faith or Christ's human nature from his doctrine even though he did not emphasize them. Brenz and his colleagues at the ducal court in Stuttgart labeled the dispute in Könisberg a war of words and urged moderation and accommodation on both sides. This only aroused the distrust of the Saxons.[34]

Osiander died in the midst of the controversy, Oct. 17, 1552. But a small party of his followers in Königsberg and similar groups in other Evangelical areas, particularly Nuremberg and Pomerania, continued to teach his views. Osiandrism would not have survived its founder's death in Prussia had not Duke Albrecht himself held to Osiander's doctrine. Of course, as a prince, he found at least some clerical and lay advisors who thought he was right, though a surprising number of the men he hired to administer his lands and his church opposed the religious views their duke shared with Osiander and they expressed their opposition publicly. In such a position an aging prince is likely to attract scalawags, and the shenanigans of two in particular, Johannes Funck and Paul Scalich, precipitated pressure from the estates that sent Scalich scurrying away from Königsberg in secret in 1565 and sent Funck to the executioner's block in 1567.[35]

The sharp polemic that Osiander used and to which he was subjected made this dispute a particularly bitter one, in part because of Osiander's own personality, in part because the Wittenberg Reformation felt its cardinal doctrine, the heart of its faith, threatened by Osiander's understanding of Christ and his righteousness. Osiander did not set out to attack Melanchthon for some personal reason; they fell to fighting because they came to realize that their soteriological views differed significantly. Not just Melanchthon's most loyal followers but also his Gnesio-Lutheran foes saw quite quickly that there was more objectionable in Osiander than just a newcomer's irritatingly swift rise to prominence in Königsberg. Gnesio-Lutherans and Philippists alike recognized a foreign philosophical base with far-reaching implications that led to non-Biblical conclusions about the nature of justification. Even his friend Brenz refused to defend Osiander's position but instead tried to present it in a different light. Had not he addressed the central issue of the Wittenberg Reformation, Osiander might have been forgotten after this death. As it was,

40

his position remained a concern for Lutherans until the Formula of Concord rejected his views.

Controversies over the Lords' Supper and Christology

Controversy over the Lord's Supper had plagued the Evangelical Reformation since its beginnings. Luther debated with Carlstadt, Zwingli, and Oecolampadius over the real presence of Christ's body and blood in the elements of the sacrament of the altar. His close friend Amsdorf became suspicious that their "sacramentarian" views might be creeping into Lutheranism, especially through Melanchthon when Philip did not stress this doctrine in the constitution for the church of Cologne which he and Martin Bucer composed in 1544. Luther's *Brief Confession* of 1544 reaffirmed his earlier position on the real presence against the Zwinglian views of Heinrich Bullinger and others in German-speaking Switzerland, but tensions within the Wittenberg Reformation between Melanchthon and those who shared Amsdorf's suspicions did not surface for some time.

After Luther's death Joachim Westphal, a pastor in Hamburg who had studied and taught in Wittenberg in the late 1530s, became alarmed at the rapid advance of Calvin's understanding of the spiritual presence of Christ in the Sacrament. The "Zurich Consensus," a joint confession that aligned Calvin's church in Geneva with Bullinger's in Zurich, was published in 1549; in 1552 its appearance in London, edited by the Polish Zwinglian John Lasco, aroused Westphal's concern that Luther's understanding of the Sacrament was not receiving sufficient public explanation and defense. He wrote his *Farrago of the Confusing Opinions which Differ with Each Other on the Lord's Supper, Collected from the Books of the Sacramentarians* in 1552. This work set out to demonstrate the contradictory nature of sacramentarian arguments against Luther's position and named Calvin as a prominent leader of the sacramentarians. The following year Westphal's *Correct Belief concerning the Lord's Supper* provided exegetical studies of the words of institution and passages from 1 Corinthians relating to the Sacrament. Calvin began his counterattack with his *Defense of the Correct and Orthodox Doctrine of the Sacraments and*

Their Nature, in which he did not mention Westphal by name but belittled those who held his position.[36] On the Reformed side Bullinger, Lasco, and finally Beza were drawn into the dispute, while Johann Timann of Bremen and others supported Westphal with tracts. This debate touched on the Christological presuppositions behind its participants' understandings of the real presence but dealt largely with the interpretation of the words of institution. Westphal and Calvin both failed to understand each other's position. Westphal accused Calvin of regarding the sacramental elements as mere symbols, although Calvin insisted on a spiritual presence of Christ and on the reception of Christ through faith in connection with the reception of the elements. Calvin called Westphal's definition of Christ's presence in the sacrament consubstantiation, a crude kind of local inclusion of Christ's body and blood, whereas Westphal insisted that the presence of the body and blood be defined as sacramental. Their debate ended after a number of fruitless exchanges, and the dispute over the real presence continued in other locales within the Evangelical churches.

Johann Timann's *Farrago of Consonant Views on the True and Catholic Doctrine of the Lord's Supper,* published in 1555, not only reinforced Westphal's efforts against foreign sacramentarians but also precipitated a dispute within the church of Bremen. This dispute had been brewing since Albert Hardenburg arrived in the city to serve as preacher at its cathedral in 1547. Hardenburg had been trained by the Brethren of the Common Life in the late medieval reform-minded spirituality of the *devotio moderna* and had absorbed the spirit of Erasmus during his studies at the University of Louvain. After receiving his doctorate in theology from the Catholic faculty at the University of Mainz, he became an Evangelical, studied briefly in Wittenberg, and joined with Melanchthon and Bucer in asssisting Archbishop Hermann von Wied in his attempt to introduce the Reformation in the archbishopric of Cologne. Hardenburg's friendship with the Zwinglian Lasco and his comments on the nature of the sacraments in lectures he delivered in 1548 aroused concern over his theology in Bremen. However at that time the city officials were satisfied with

Hardenburg's confession that he believed that Christ is present in the Supper with his benefits—forgiveness and strength for the believer. In discussions that followed the publication of Timann's *Farrago*, Hardenburg set himself at odds with the city ministerium by taking exception to the doctrine of the omnipresence of Christ's human nature, as Timann and Johann Bötker expressed it: that Christ's human nature shares fully the attributes of His divine nature because of the union of the two natures in His person. Hardenburg countered with his opinion that the body of Christ is at the right hand of God, to which He ascended 40 days after the resurrection. In the course of the argument, which Hardenburg tried to avoid, parties formed within the city behind each theological position. Citizens joined these factions in part because of the theological issues involved, in part because of the political situation of the city. As late as 1530 there had been a major attempt to broaden the franchise of the aristocratic constitution of Bremen, and feelings of division among the citizens remained. Furthermore, Hardenburg, as a member of the cathedral staff, was under the jurisdiction of the archbishop, still nominally a Catholic. The city council could hardly favor continuing such an arrangement, with its limitations on the council's power in Bremen, especially as Hardenburg's presence increasingly became an embarrassment to the city. Hardenburg's opponents also called the city's legal-religious status into question by pointing to the requirement of the Religious Peace of Augsburg that permitted only the faith of the Roman Pontiff and that of the Augsburg confession in the German empire; Hardenburg's Zwinglian position had not won legal status in the Peace. As a result of the dispute, neighboring Gnesio-Lutheran governments put pressure on Bremen. Denmark suspended the exemption from certain tolls that Bremen merchants had previously enjoyed, the first use of such measures in an Evangelical dispute, but Hardenburg rejected the cathedral chapter's suggestion that he go to Denmark to answer charges against him.

Hardenburg did journey to Wittenberg to solicit support for his position, but the memorandum that the Wittenbergers sent to Bremen did little to settle the dispute because it did not face squarely the specific issues under debate. Instead, the matter was taken before the meeting of the principalities and cities of Lower Saxony held in Lüneburg in 1560. The session appointed a commission to investigate the Bremen dispute and then followed the commission's recommendation that Bremen be urged to remove Hardenburg from his office. That was accomplished in 1561. Simon Musäus, a Gnesio-Lutheran professor at Jena, was called as superintendent of the city's churches, but he left after a short term under pressure from the Hardenburg party, led by Daniel von Buren, who had studied at Wittenberg under Melanchthon and who had served as mayor of the city. Marcus Mening, a Philippist, replaced Musäus as ecclesiastical superintendent in Bremen. Although he resisted both the Gnesio-Lutheran and the Zwinglian elements in the city throughout his tenure, the city became officially Calvinist in the 1580s when Mening was replaced by a former professor from Wittenberg, the crypto-Calvinist Christoph Pezel.[37]

Among those who reacted against Hardenburg's position was a young pastor in the Lower Saxon city of Braunschweig, a former student of Melanchthon's, Martin Chemnitz. His *Repetition of the Correct Doctrine of the Real Presence of the Body and the Blood in the Supper* of 1561 defended a literal interpretation of the words of institution. To it he added a discussion of the communication of the attributes of the human and the divine natures of Christ.[38]

At almost the same time that the Hardenburg affair climaxed in Lower Saxony another phase of the debate over the real presence was beginning in the Palatinate, the electoral principality in south central Germany. The Palatinate did not become officially Evangelical until after the Religious Peace of Augsburg, and its Reformation was really undertaken by the cultured Ottheinrich (1502—59; elector 1556—59). In 1558, not long before his death he called one of Melanchthon's favorite pupils. Tilemann Hesshus, to be pastor and professor of theology at Heidelberg as well as president of the church council and general ecclesiastical superintendent of his lands. Hesshus had arrived in Wittenberg shortly after Luther's death, and a strong bond of friendship formed between Melanchthon and this brilliant Rhinelander. After being exiled from the cities of Goslar and Rostock for his condemnation of the life-styles of prominent citizens, Hesshus received Melanchthon's recommendation to become leader of the new Evangelical church of the Palatinate.

Ottheinrich had been a commited Lutheran himself, but he had not distinguished carefully between various streams of reform sentiment in selecting his ecclesiastical advisors, and Hesshus joined a varied group of men on the Heidelberg ecclesiastical scene. It included committed Philippists and Calvinists, as well as the Zwinglian secular counselor Thomas Erastus and his party. Initially Hesshus got along with his colleagues quite well; the new Evangelical ecclesiastical establishment united to oppose and condemn the views of a disciple of Caspar von Schwenkfeld. But a dispute arose out of the memorandum issued by Hesshus against the Schwenkfelder, Bernhard Herxheimer. A deacon in the congregation of which Hesshus was pastor, Wilhelm Klevvitz, objected to Hesshus' approval of the Lutheran formulas which taught that the body and blood of Christ are received by the mouth in the Lord's Supper *(manducatio oralis)* and that also the unbeliever receives Christ's body and blood in the sacrament *(manducatio impiorum).* The faction headed by Erastus encouraged and supported Klevvitz in his opposition to Hesshus, and the Erastus party used the incident to force Hesshus out of the decision-making processes of the university. Hesshus deposed Klevvitz as deacon and then excommunicated him for his Zwinglian position, but the government of the new elector, Frederick III, opposed Hesshus' efforts and temporarily maintained Klevvitz in his office.

Frederick III, a distant cousin of Ottheinrich, assumed the electorate in early 1559, in the middle of the dispute in Heidelberg. Frederick III would introduce Calvinism into his lands within four years, but in 1559 he was just beginning to move the confession of his lands in that direction. At the time he satisfied himself with an initial action officially aimed simply at ending an unseemly squabble. He removed both Klevvitz and

Hesshus from their offices and asked them both to leave the Palatinate.

As the dispute simmered in Heidelberg, Frederick sent his personal secretary to Wittenberg to ask Melanchthon's opinion on how to proceed. Melanchthon obviously got something less than an objective account of the matter from this personal emissary of the elector. Though friendly correspondence between preceptor and pupil had continued into the months in which the dispute in Heidelberg was taking place, Melanchthon had apparently felt that Hesshus was deviating from his own views of the Lord's Supper as the controversy developed, and their correspondence had come to an end. In his formal response to Frederick's query Melanchthon approved the exile of the disputants and advised that the formula of Paul (1 Cor. 10:16), "the bread which we break is a communion in the body of Christ," be recognized as a sufficient definition of the real presence. He further urged that more emphasis be placed on the use and the benefits of the Sacrament than on the mode of the presence of Christ. He specifically rejected transubstantiation, and he feared that this concept of Christ's presence lurked dangerously close to expressions such as that of the confession of the Bremen ministerium, "the bread is Christ's substantial body," and also to that of Hesshus, "the bread is the true body of Christ." Hesshus was alienated by Melanchthon's rejection and became a stalwart Gnesio-Lutheran. Under the leadership of Caspar Olevianus, who had studied in Geneva, and Zacharias Ursinus, who had studied in Wittenberg, the church of the Palatinate became Calvinistic. These two composed its basic definition of its faith, the Heidelberg Catechism, which was published in 1563.[39]

Developments in the ecclesiastical life of the Palatinate were viewed with some alarm in neighboring Württemberg, whose duke, Christoph, was a convinced Lutheran and also a promoter of Evangelical political unity in the face of the opposition of Catholic princes within the Empire and outside it. In 1559 his own church had addressed the doctrine of the real presence in a synod called to Stuttgart because of the views of Christoph Hagen of Dettingen, a pastor inclined toward

46

Calvinism. As a favorite of the dowager duchess Sabine, Hagen had significant support. However, he denied that unbelievers receive Christ's body and blood, and he appealed to Melanchthon's commentary on Colossians, published in 1559, in his argument against the omnipresence of Christ's human nature as a basis for the defense of the Lutheran view of Christ's real presence. The doctrine of the omnipresence (called "ubiquity," particularly by its foes) of Christ's human nature formed an important part of the Christology of Duke Christoph's leading ecclesiastical advisor, Johann Brenz, and in a synodical decision this doctrine was declared an integral part of the confession of the church of Württemberg. Though Brenz's friend and lieutenant Jakob Andreä had earlier flirted with Calvinism, as the chairman of the official examination of Hagen he defended Brenz's view at Stuttgart.[40]

The publication of the Heidelberg Catechism attracted the attention of Duke Christoph's theologians, who met in autumn 1563 to compose a critique of it, which Christoph forwarded to Frederick III. As a result, Andreä led a delegation of Württemberg theologians that met with Ursinus and others from the Palatinate in a colloquy at Maulbronn in April 1564. An attempt to separate the discussion of the Lord's Supper from the question of the omnipresence of Christ's human nature failed, and the two sides came to an impasse over the meaning of the personal union of Christ's human and divine natures in his person. The Palatine delegation refused to acknowledge that the two natures share their attributes in any way while the Württembergers insisted that though the natures remain distinct from each other, they cannt be separated and they do communicate to each other attributes unique to each in itself. The colloquy brought no narrowing of the gap between their positions.

Christoph invited the theological faculty at Wittenberg to comment on the protocol of the colloquy of Maulbronn and on Andreä's disputation on the majesty of Christ as man. The Wittenbergers objected to his position and indicated that they could not share the view of Brenz concerning the omnipresence of Christ's human nature.[41]

The Christological aspect of the debate on the Lord's Supper loomed ever larger in discussions of the Sacrament within the Evangelical churches. Chemnitz composed a statement of his position, *On the Two Natures in Christ, Concerning Their Hypostatic Union, the Communication of Attributes, and Other Related Questions* in 1570. He paid less attention than did Brenz to the absolute omnipotence and the general omnipresence of Christ. Instead, Chemnitz stressed that the human nature may be present wherever Christ wills since his person is omnipotent by virtue of its divine nature.[42]

As Chemnitz composed the first edition of his work on Christology, events in electoral Saxony were beginning to move toward the political climax of the debate within German Lutheranism on the Lord's Supper and related questions of Christology. Throughout the 1560s the theological faculty at Wittenberg had experienced some tension over the doctrine of the Lord's Supper between moderates, led by Paul Eber, and the party led by Melanchthon's son-in-law, the lay theologian Caspar Peucer. Peucer, the personal physician of Elector August, taught first mathematics and later medicine at Wittenberg. Peucer's theological leadership demonstrates not only his own brilliance but also the mediocrity and inexperience of the several theologians at Wittenberg at this time. Peucer went beyond his father-in-law's position in his understanding of the real presence. Supported by the young theologian Christoph Pezel and other electoral Saxon theologians and pastors, he developed an interpretation of the real presence that would safeguard the distinction between spirit and matter; this interpretation emphasized the benefits of the Sacrament and tried to avoid connecting those benefits directly with the reception of the elements.[43]

The Peucer party's understanding of the relationship between spirit and matter, between the Creator and the created, had been learned from the study of the classics of Greek philosophy. Inherent in this understanding was a rejection of Brenz's concept of the "ubiquity" of the human nature of Christ by virtue of its sharing the attributes of his divine nature. This position was written into a set of 130 theses composed for disputation at the doctoral promotion of six canditates in early 1570. Jakob Andreä visited Wittenberg shortly after the publication of these theses and took offense at the 30th thesis, which rejected the ubiquity of Christ's human nature. His colleague in the temporary employ of Duke Julius of Braunschweig-Wolfenbüttel, Nikolaus Selnecker, had been one of the candidates promoted to the doctorate in the disputation, and the duke asked Selnecker and Andreä to ascertain just what the Wittenbergers were teaching on the subject. In late July 1570 the theological faculty at Wittenberg assured Selnecker and Andreä that they confessed two natures of Christ united in one person. Their explanation of that brief confession satisfied Andreä and Selnecker. Each of them wrote an account of their agreement with the faculty and published it. These accounts displeased the Wittenbergers because they felt that Selnecker and Andreä were ascribing to them a position they did not hold.[44] But they did not want to rock their own boat. For their prince, Elector August, was a somewhat simple but very zealous disciple of the hero of his childhood years, Dr. Martin Luther, and neither he nor his pious Lutheran wife, Anna of Denmark, would tolerate any departure from Luther's teachings.

On the first day of 1571 a new catechism was issued for use in the schools of electoral Saxony; it was designed as an upper level text for pupils who had completed their study of Luther's Small Catechism. The catechism taught that Christ's human nature remains forever at God's right hand in heaven and that the Lord's Supper "is the communion of the body and blood of our Lord Jesus Christ . . . . In receiving it the Son of God [note, not the whole Christ or his human body] is truly and substantially present and shows that He brings His benefits to those who believe." The Wittenberg Catechism was attacked immediately by a number of Gnesio-Lutherans. The theologians of the University of Jena objected not only to its positions on Christology and the Lord's Supper but also to its definitions of Baptism, the Gospel, and discipline. They criticized above all its ambiguity.[45]

In the swirl of controversy the Wittenbergers did issue a defense of their Catechism and its position. The prime author of the Catechism, the young theologian Christoph Pezel, wrote his *Firm Foundation of the True Church, Concerning the Person and Incarnation of Our Lord Jesus Christ.* In it he attacked the "Flacians" and the "Brenzians." He emphasized the function rather than the nature of the person of Christ. He was concerned that the divine nature not be mixed with—or perhaps contaminated by—the human nature of Christ, and he suggested that the two natures were not so much united as federated by virture of the assumption of the human nature by the divine. On the Lord's Supper the *Firm Foundation* taught that Christ's body is received in the Sacrament but not through the elements; it is received rather by faith through the act of eating. A dualistic anthropology distinguished reception of the elements by the recipient's mouth from his soul's reception through faith of Christ's benefits.[46]

In late 1571 the Wittenberg faculty moved to counter the growing uneasiness over its position within electoral Saxony by requesting Elector August to call a synod of ecclesiastical officials and the theologians of his other university, at Leipzig, to review the Wittenberg Christology and the faculty's position on the Lord's Supper. At Dresden a *Consensus* was drawn up on the doctrines under discussion.[47] This document only got the Wittenbergers into more trouble, for the regent of the Palatinate, the Calvinist Johann Casimir, wrote to August, stating that the position of the electoral Saxon theologians agreed with that of the Heidelberg theologians, who were widely known as Calvinists. August asked his theologians to provide him with a firm rebuttal of this allegation, and their ambiguous replies angered him. However, the superintendent of Pirna, Johann Stössel, did present him with a brief, clear critique of the Heidelberg Catechism; that mollified the prince for a time.[48]

After a comparatively peaceful year the electoral Saxon ecclesiastical situation was badly shaken in early 1574 when copies of an anonymous work, *A Perspicuous and Quite Complete Exegesis of the Controversy on the Holy Supper,* were found in Wittenberg. This work attempted to delineate clearly the differences between Luther's polemical utterances on the Lord's Supper and Melanchthon's sacramental doctrine. The

50

fact that the book was printed with French type on French paper suggested a foreign origin, but the Wittenberg faculty was supected of introducing the work into Saxony. A governmental investigating task force could produce no evidence of the faculty's complicity, but it discovered that a printer in Leipzig, Ernst Vögelin, was responsible not only for the distribution but also for the actual printing of the book. He named the author, a Silesian medical doctor who had studied at Wittenberg under Melanchthon, Joachim Curaeus, who had died the previous year. His rejection of elements of Luther's teaching on the Sacrament revealed a Philippist position that could hardly be defended against the charge that it was similar to that of the Calvinist faculty at Heidelberg.[49]

About the same time a misdelivered letter brought the carefully and delicately constructed shelter under which the Wittenberg Philippists had lived for a decade crashing down around them, trapping some in its wreckage. Johann Stössel wrote a letter to his close friend Christian Schütz, one of two court preachers in Dresden. In it he complained about the power of women at court (a reference to the Electress Anna) and about the hypocrisy of the theologian Paul Crell and other members of the Meissen consistory who refused to support the doctrines of the Peucer-Pezel party. A woman from Stössel's congregation was entrusted with the letter, which was addressed simply to "the wife of the court preacher." She delivered it to the home of Schütz's colleague, Georg Listenius, an opponent of the Peucer group. Listenius revealed its contents to his elector, and August ordered the arrest of four men implicated by the letter, Stössel, Schütz, Peucer, and the chancellor of August's government, Georg von Cracow.[50] The latter three were among August's most trusted advisors and closest associates. Peucer not only served as August's personal physician but also as a counselor for education and governmental affairs and was the baptismal sponsor of one of August's children. In the subsequent interrogation of these four August became convinced that they had attempted to alter the theology of electoral Saxony against his wishes and behind his back. In addition to his own strong commitment to his childhood hero, Luther, August was influenced by the same, equally strong commitment of his wife. He must have been stung by the fact that there appeared to be real substance to the charges of "crypto-Calvinism" hurled at his church by the Gnesio-Lutherans, who had pestered him and his brother for 20 years. He was concerned to keep his lands within the provisions of the Religious Peace of Augsburg by keeping them loyal to the Augsburg Confession, lest he act against the laws of the empire. Above all, August was deeply hurt and angered by what he considered the deceit and betrayal of his closest advisors and friends. His new resolve to purge his lands of this crypto-Calvinist menace was strengthened not only by committed Lutherans among his theologians but also by prominent citizens and men at court who had opposed Georg von Cracow's efforts to strengthen the developing absolutism of the prince of Saxony.

In May 1547 August summoned his theologians to Torgau, where a series of positive and negative articles concerning positions on Christology and the Lord's Supper were drawn up and offered for subscription to the theologians of the electorate. The Torgau Articles affirmed the sacramental union of the elements and Christ's true, substantial body and blood. It rejected transubstantiation on the one hand and any symbolic or spiritual interpretation of the words of institution on the other. Crell and Major of the Wittenberg theological faculty subscribed; Christoph Pezel and three other theologians, Frederick Widebram, Caspar Cruciger the younger, and Heinrich Möller, along with an arts professor, Esrom Rüdinger, refused to subscribe. They were detained at the Pleissenburg, a castle near Leipzig, and, after intense argument with Crell and others, they signed the Torgau Articles with the proviso that they accepted them only insofar as they agreed with the Dresden *Consensus* and the *Corpus doctrinae Philippicum,* the standard of doctrine in electoral Saxony since 1566. They were released and left for other parts; Widebram and Pezel became prominent leaders of the German Calvinist movement.

Release was not so easily obtained by the four who, August felt, had betrayed and abused his trust and made a fool of him as well. Selnecker and Andreä met with Peucer in his prison cell, and electoral Saxon theologians met with him and the others a number of times in vain attempts to persuade them to abandon their views, but they refused. Both Cracow and Stössel died in prison, in March 1575 and March 1576 respectively. Peucer was released shortly before August's death in 1586 and Schütz three years later. They were replaced as the key counselors of the electoral government by other students of Melanchthon who found no problems in Luther's understanding of the real presence of Christ. The fall of the Saxon "crypto-Calvinists" helped pave the way for agreement on the doctrine of the Lord's Supper and the Person of Christ among a majority of German Lutherans, though some of those who refused to subscribe to the Formula of Concord did so because they had Philippist reservations in these areas of doctrine.

The Controversy on Election

The doctrine of election was not a major issue in the debates between Philippists and Gnesio-Lutherans or among any other groups within German Lutheranism, though the doctrine was treated in connection with the dispute over the role of the human will in conversion. The occasion for the 11th article of the Formula of Concord arose out of a debate within the church of Strasbourg between the Lutheran Johann Marbach and the Reformed theologian Jerome Zanchi.

Marbach came to Strasbourg as a Wittenberg graduate in 1545, and after Martin Bucer was driven from the city because of the Augsburg Interim, Marbach became a leader in the city's ecclesiastical life. He did not side openly with the Gnesio-Lutherans during the Interim period but instead dealt with the realities of church life under imperial pressure, regulated as it was in southwestern Germany at the time by Spanish troops. But Marbach did work to heighten Lutheran consciousness in the city as soon as he could and urged that the city accept the Augsburg Confession as its doctrinal standard, replacing Bucer's *Confessio Tetrapolitana,* which has been submitted to Charles V at Augsburg in 1530 along with the confession of the Lutheran princes. But Strasbourg's civic leaders were still striving to follow a middle path between Lutherans and Reformed in the early 1550s, and in 1553 the officials of the famous Strasbourg Academy hired Jerome Zanchi as professor of theology at the school. Zanchi was an Italian exile, schooled in the revived Thomist scholasticism of the mid-16th century before his conversion to Protestantism in the 1540s.

Zanchi had aroused Marbach's suspicions when in his inagural address he pledged himself to take insights from Zwingli and Calvin as well as Luther, so long as they were in accord with the Scriptures. Later in the 1550s tensions arose between Marbach on the one side and Zanchi and his supporters at the academy on the other over a number of issues, including clergy influence over the school, which Marbach, as ecclesiastical superintendent, was eager to increase. When Marbach attempted to publish Tilemann Hesshus' *De praesentia corporis Christi in Coena Domini* in Strassburg in 1560, Elector Frederick III of the Palatinate prevailed on Zanchi and others in the city to oppose Marbach. The two also fell into debate over a number of issues, including the question of the perseverance of the saints, whether a believer can lose God's grace. This issue and the Lord's Supper formed the foci of the dispute which finally caused the city council to call on outside arbitration for settlement of the dispute.

Marbach and Zanchi did not disagree on the doctrine of election itself but rather on how the believer can be assured that he is elect. Zanchi based that assurance on the a priori decision of God in eternity to choose His own, while Marbach stressed that the believer's assurance is based upon his a posteriori reception of the promise of forgiveness and the benefits of Christ's death and resurrection through Word and Sacrament. Marbach expressed his concern that an undue emphasis on the secret will and decree of God would obscure the importance of the means of grace as real vehicles that convey grace. Zanchi defended his position with quotations from Luther's *De servo arbirtrio* and Bucer.

The city council invited representatives from Württemberg, Basel, and Zweibrücken to come to Strasbourg to work out a settlement in the spring of 1563. Andreä was a member of this arbitration team though its statement on predestination was probably written by Cunmann Flinsbach of Zweibrücken, who had studied at Strasbourg and Wittenberg. The Strasbourg Concordia of 1563 contained two articles. The first accepted the Wittenberg Concordia of 1536, worked out between Bucer and other south Germans with Luther and the Wittenbergers, as a sufficient statement on the Lord's Supper. The second article of the Strasbourg Concordia formulated specific answers to a series of problems related to the doctrine of election. The Concordia affirmed that God chose certain human beings to be his own in eternity, not because he foresaw any merit in them but because of the merits and the work of Christ. Predestination should never be considered apart from Christ. At the same time the Concordia affirmed the universality of the promise of grace. It addressed the mysteries connected with election without trying to answer them and to place the doctrine in a system of logical explanation: God does not will sin but hates it even though he permits it; he does not create vessels of wrath for destruction; why some are saved and others are not cannot be ascertained, but the question should not trouble consciences, which must be directed to Christ alone. The authors of the Concordia were concerned that the teaching of predestination not conflict with the doctrine of repentance, encouraging those who regarded themselves as elect to sin as they please, and they were also concerned that it should not deprive troubled consciences of consolation and hope by making them feel that their faith might be of no avail if they were not elect. The Concordia stated that the doctrine of election should help believers see the grace of God and the impotence of human beings and thereby give them comfort by placing them in the hands of a loving Savior.

The pastoral orientation of the Strasbourgh Concordia reflects the Lutheran concern for meeting practical, pastoral problems, whereas the scholastically trained Zanchi, though concerned about the consolation of troubled consciences, felt that he had to work such a concern into a logically coherent system. However, Zanchi could accept the position of the Strasbourg Concord, to which he subscribed "as I understand it," and the arbitrators worked out a personal reconciliation between him and Marbach. Under pressure Zanchi did resign his position at the Academy within a few months, however, and he left for a pastorate in Chiavenna. Andreä carried the position of the arbitration team with him into the efforts that resulted in the Formula of Concord a decade later.[51]

The Controversies over the Descent into Hell

Another controversy that had commanded little attention within the Lutheran churches was that over Christ's descent into hell. Though Evangelical theologians interpreted the Creed's confession, "He descended into hell," in different ways, controversy over this doctrine broke out in only three places among German Lutheran theologians during the years preceding the composition of the Formula of Concord. The most significant of these controversies took place in the city of Hamburg, for that dispute commanded wider attention than the other two.

Johann Aepinus, Hamburg's ecclesiastical superintendent, received his doctorate from the University of Wittenberg in 1533 and took with him to Hamburg what he had learned from Luther and Melanchthon. He passed their ideas on to the pastors in Hamburg through lectures to his ministerium. Commenting on Psalm 16 in 1542 or 1543, he presented his understanding of Christ's descent into hell: Christ completed his suffering for mankind by bearing the ultimate to which sinners are condemned when He entered hell and suffered its agony. Though details of the genesis of the controversy within the Hamburg church remain unclear, it was not until 1548 that his view was attacked publicly by a few of his fellow clergymen in the city. The city council solicited memoranda on the issue from a number of north German theologians, among them Aepinus' fellow Gnesio-Lutherans as well as Melanchthon and others on the Philippist side. The council wanted civic peace above all and called on participants to desist from public controversy. Aepinus complied; his opponents did not, and they were exiled from the city after a series of consultations in 1551.

Aepinus had tried to repeat Luther's understanding of the descent into hell, but he failed in part, as did other Gnesio-

Lutherans in respect to certain other points of doctrine, for he did not grasp the full radicality of Luther's break with the scholastic teaching of the late Middle Ages. Luther taught Christ suffered hell for sinners and that He triumphed through His suffering for them. That understanding was reflected in the memorandum that the Hamburg council received from the Gnesio-Lutheran Flacius. Melanchthon, on the other hand, stressed only one part of Luther's understanding and excluded the other. Melanchthon's view that Christ's descent into hell was a triumphal victory march separated His victory from any suggestion of suffering.

The reasons for the treatment of this doctrine in the Formula are not clear, since it appears for the first time in the Torgic Book, near the end of the process of the composition of the Formula. Several of the authors of the Formula, notably Selnecker, had received their instruction on the descent into hell from Melanchthon and had adopted his position. In spite of the fact that Andreä following his mentor Brenz, taught a position closer to that of Luther, the formulators favored Melanchthon's position by including in the Formula a statement which referred to Luther's "Torgau" sermon. As prepared for print by his students Georg Rörer and Anton Poach, that sermon dwelt on Christ's victory over Satan and hell.[52]

The Unity of Evangelical Churches and Pure Doctrine

No one had sought, planned, or welcomed the disruption that ripped through the German Evangelical churches as a result of the two Interims of 1548 and subsequent controversies on the various issues discussed here. The events associated with these Interims effectively destroyed the friendly cooperation and harmony that Lutherans had enjoyed with one another during the first generation of the Reformation. All Evangelicals viewed that loss of unity as a detrimental and harmful catastrophe, and all were eager to restore it. There were two primary reasons for this. The first was theological; they believed that Christ wanted His church to be one, filled with harmony as it preached His Word. Second, even in the best political situation that the Evangelical estates obtained during the second half of the 16th century, concerns for their security prompted Evangelical princes to work for a united front against Roman Catholic forces.

Not only did all sides in these intra-Lutheran disputes agree on the necessity of unity within Evangelical Christendom—each also agreed that unity must be founded on the pure doctrine of the Holy Scriptures, and each shared a common dedication to the defense of pure doctrine against papists on the one side and "raving" sectarians on the other.[53] What divided Gnesio-Lutherans from Philippists and Osiander from both groups was not a lack of commitment to Evangelical unity or of zeal for pure doctrine. They differed in the way they thought unity should be established; furthermore, each party criticized the way the other party interpreted and expressed the pure doctrine of the Scriptures and the way it presented its message to the public.

Quite consistently throughout the three decades between the Leipzig Interim and the Formula of Concord, the Gnesio-Lutherans called for a special group of experts, e.g., a synod of theologians, to meet to determine the proper expression of pure Lutheran doctrine; through its decisions, such a synod would establish Lutheran unity. The Philippists, especially Melanchthon, thought that theologians should settle the theological issues themselves, but they did work in consort with their princes and helped produce confessions within the context of the assemblies of the Evangelical princes and towns. If the Gnesio-Lutherans were correct in suspecting that a meeting of princes could not produce a theologically respectable document, the Philippists were also correct in sensing that in 16th-century Germany Lutheran unity depended on princely support.

Furthermore, the two sides differed on more than the agency for achieving unity. The Philippists contended that unity could best be reached by a relatively brief and general declaration on disputed points, while the Gnesio-Lutherans insisted on a thorough examination of those points, accompanied by a condemnation of errors that had arisen in the course of the dispute. The Philippists advocated the principle of "amnesty" in the settlement of the disputes: names of individuals should not be mentioned in any confessional document, and old

58

disputes should simply be forgotten, not dredged up again, they insisted. The Gnesio-Lutherans called for public condemnation of those who had taught error as well as the errors themselves, though they often tempered their demand for a rite of public penance from those who had taught falsely to a mere insistence on public rejection of former errors.

Even in the initial stages of the conflict over the Interims a concern for unity is evident in one of the stock exchanges between Magdeburg and Wittenberg. The Philippists charged that the Magdeburgers were seditious, disruptive rebels who were maliciously and unfairly attacking them, thus destroying Evangelical unity. Flacius and his colleagues replied that unity had been destroyed by the Philippists when they forged their compromise with the pope, thus betraying Luther's cause and splitting off from it.

The political situation in which such exchanges took place did not remain static. Rather quickly after the composition of the Interims, the edifice of power that Charles V had erected with his victory at Mühlberg began to crumble. Several of the Evangelical princes who had lent him support, beginning with Margrave Hans of Brandenburg-Küstrin, became disaffected and left the imperial camp. Elector Moritz was persuaded to join these princes in a movement against the Hapsburgs during 1551, and in 1552 his alliance of German princes, supported through treaty commitments by Henry II of France, won concessions from the Hapsburgs in the Truce of Passau. The truce permitted the practice of the Evangelical faith until a final religious settlement could be negotiated.

Although Charles V opposed any conciliation, his brother and heir, Ferdinand, recognized that the Hapsburgs would not be able to impose their religion upon their empire. At the diet of Augsburg in 1555 extended negotiations produced the Religious Peace of Augsburg, which granted legal though inferior status to the faith of the Augsburg Confession within the German empire. One of the leaders in the Evangelical party during these negotiations was Elector August of Saxony, who had succeeded his brother Moritz in 1553 after Moritz's death on the field of battle at the hands of one of his Evangelical confederates in the

Smalcaldic War, Margrave Albert Alcibiades of Brandenburg-Kulmbach. August and Elector Joachim of Brandenburg pursued a conservative course in the negotiations at Augsburg. Because of this conservative stance, the Evangelicals exacted from Ferdinand only a minimum of concessions, the most important of which granted secular princes the right to determine that their lands would be Evangelical *(cuius regio, eius religio)*.[54]

Already before the diet at Augsburg the Evangelical princes had addressed themselves to the problem of theological disunity in their ranks. In working out their approach to the Hapsburgs, representatives of Hesse and electoral Saxony met at Naumburg in May 1554 and issued a statement that tried to establish a united position. Their proposal did not meet the requirements set down in a call for unity issued the previous year from Magdeburg. In it Flacius and Gallus had urged that a committee of 10 or 20 clerical and lay Lutherans be convened to deal with specific issues at the heart of the Saxon ecclesiastical strife.[55]

After 1555, as before, the problem of Lutheran unity could not be separated from the larger problem of the unity of Western Christendom. Once the Religious Peace of Augsburg legalized Lutheranism, a new era of struggle between the Evangelicals and the Roman Catholics in Germany began. The desire for reconciliation between the two confessions had been severely dampened in most quarters by the collapse of the colloquy at Regensburg in 1541 and by the events surrounding the Smalcaldic War. But Ferdinand was still eager to achieve religious accord through dialog, since he had failed to do so through the sword. In such a situation the Evangelicals recognized the necessity of a common front. Led by Duke Christoph of Württemberg, one of the most devout, zealous, and energetic of the Evangelical princes, the Lutheran party began immediately to try to solve the doctrinal issues under dispute within its own ranks. In early 1556, in cooperation with Elector Frederick II of the Palatinate, Christoph sent a delegation to the court of John Frederick the Middler and Weimar to work out an accord with the ducal Saxon theologians. His mission failed because agreement could not be reached on the condemnation of adiaphorism, Majorism, and synergism, as demanded by the Gnesio-Lutherans in addition to the rejection of the teachings of the Papalists, Zwinglians, Osiandrians, and Schwenkfelders.

Another initiative for unity came in May 1556 from Flacius. He sent his "Gentle Proposals" for the settlement of differences between the Magdeburgers and the Wittenbergers to Paul Eber, an arts professor in Wittenberg. He asked the Wittenbergers to join him in recognizing the pope as anti-Christ and in condemning the Council of Trent, the Augsburg Interim, and anything that had lent support to that Interim, as well as the errors of the Zwinglians. With that the Wittenbergers could probably have concurred. But they stumbled at his proposal to condemn all compromise with the anti-Christ, not because they did not agree but because they knew that Flacius thereby was asking them to condemn their own actions in preparing and defending the Leipzig Interim, which they still believed had been necessary. Worse yet, Flacius proposed that both sides affirm that temporal government ought not introduce changes in ecclesiastical ceremonies without the consent of the church and that princes do not have the right to compromise with godless persecutors. Not even Flacius' demand that they reject the idea that good works are necessary for salvation, and thus sacrifice their colleague Major, was as difficult for the Wittenbergers to accept as his condemnation of Moritz's role in the difficulties of the Evangelical churches. They ignored Flacius' "Gentle Proposals."[56]

After a number of mutual friends had tried and failed to bring Flacius and Melanchthon together, Flacius asked the pastors of the Lower Saxon cities, Lübeck, Lüneburg, Hamburg, and Braunschweig, who had cordial relationships with the Magdeburgers, to serve as intermediaries between himself and the Wittenbergers. In January 1557 Flacius, Wigand, and others from Magdeburg traveled to the town of Coswig to meet representatives of the towns, among them the Gnesio-Lutherans Joachim Westphal of Hamburg and Joachim Mörlin of Braunschweig. Accompanying Mörlin was his colleague Martin Chemnitz. The Lower Saxon delegation shuttled back and forth between Coswig and Wittenberg, exchanging messages between the two parties. Again, the Magdeburgers invited the Wittenbergers to find unity in the doctrine of the Augsburg Confession and the Smalcald Articles and in the condemnation of papists interimists, Anabaptists, sacramentarians, and those who teach that good works are necessary for salvation. Melanchthon offered clarification of his position on the controverted issues and counterattacked with charges of antinomianism and misinterpretation of the Biblical concept of the Son of God as Word, the latter charge aimed specifically at Flacius. He asserted that he could not in good conscience bow publicly before a scurrilous rascal like Flacius. The intermediaries worked on adjusting the Magdeburgers' formula for agreement to some of Melanchthon's suggestions, but Melanchthon still had reservations, and the Magdeburgers stood fast on their position. For 10 days the Lower Saxon pastors pursued their shuttle diplomacy as they carried an exchange of views between Coswig and Wittenberg, but in the end nothing came of their efforts.[57]

The Evangelical estates did not want to lose what seemed like momentum toward unity. Duke Johann Albrecht of Mecklenburg intervened within a month of the collapse of the Lower Saxon effort. He sent emissaries from his staff to Wittenberg and Magdeburg with articles formulated by his own theologians. Since their sharply worded critique of the debate over adiaphora was as strong as any authored by Flacius, the Wittenbergers could not accept their document, and in Magdeburg the Mecklenburgers did not receive the full cooperation which the Lower Saxon pastors had. Their attempt at forging unity also failed.

But Evangelical unity was sorely needed. Emperor Ferdinand was determined to push ahead with plans for reconciling the two confessions of his empire through dialog. The Roman Catholics were reluctant and not optimistic as they accepted Ferdinand's summons to colloquy at Worms, and the Evangelicals were distressed over their own continuing divisions. In June 1557 their princes met in Frankfurt and tried to end disunity by fiat, on the basis of a brief confession, but that action brought no real results.

The colloquy of Worms began in September 1557. When representatives from both electoral and ducal Saxony joined those from south Germany, including Hesse, Württemberg, and the Palatinate, in Worms, tensions within the Evangelical camp could do nothing but mount. During the colloquy, which lasted into December, other princes kept up pressure on Duke John Frederick to bring his theologians (led by Dietrich Schnepf and Victorin Strigel) into line, but they, along with men from Braunschweig (Joachim Mörlin) and Mansfeld (Erasmus Sarcerius), refused to declare their unity with Melanchthon, Brenz, and other Evangelicals because they believed that they should first resolve their differences. Conferences in Worms failed to produce accord. Schnepf tried to bring Brenz to his point of view, but Brenz refused to condemn Osiander, felt time was too short to work out an adequate condemnation of Zwinglianism, and stated that the Württemberg church need not declare itself on adiaphorism and Majorism since those problems had not plagued the church in south Germany. Similar differences separated Schnepf from the electoral Saxon theologians. Melanchthon presented a formal statement of the differences between the Evangelicals and the Roman Catholics to the Jesuit Peter Canisius, a participant in the colloquy. Melanchthon's statement displeased the Gnesio-Lutherans, who sent along their own appendix, a condemnation of the adiaphorists and the Majorists. Under pressure they later withdrew this document, but they did continue to express their concern over these issues. Canisius exploited the Evangelical divisions, presenting his views of Osianderism and Majorism to the assembled colloquants. The ducal Saxons and Mörlin stood fast, Melanchthon showed a willingness to agree with them, but Brenz refused to condemn Osiander by name. Without that kind of condemnation the Gnesio-Lutherans felt that they must separate from the other Evangelicals. The chairman of the colloquy, the Roman Catholic bishop Julius von Pflug, insisted that the colloquy could not allow a third party; the Evangelicals either had to unite or had to exclude those who would not cooperate. After intense negotiations by princes and theologians failed to bridge the gap within the Evangelical delegation at

Worms, the Gnesio-Lutherans left the colloquy. It limped along for more than a month; in mid-November the Roman Catholic representatives told the emperor that it was pointless to continue what they had known would be a futile effort. Within weeks the colloquy collapsed.[58]

Its collapse only stimulated the Evangelical princes to work harder toward unity. The king of Denmark joined in the search for a formula for concord and asked Melanchthon to compose such a document in late 1557. This document provided the basis for discussion when the Evangelical estates met in Frankfurt am Main in early 1558. Their meeting occurred as the result of suggestions from Philip of Hesse and others; Christoph of Würtemberg again led the efforts to organize this peace conference. On March 18, 1558, the electors of the Palatinate, Saxony, and Brandenburg, along with Christoph of Würtemberg and representatives of Philip of Hesse and Wolfgang of the Palatinate signed the "Frankfurt Recess." The Recess treated four points of dispute. Without mentioning Osiander by name, it affirmed that believers are justified through Christ's blood and obedience, through His imputed righteousness. It taught that new obedience is necessary for the Christian and that good works must result from faith. On the Lord's Supper, Melanchthon wrote that Christ is present in the sacrament and gives the Christian His body and blood to eat and drink there. He rejected emphatically all papal abuses connected with the Lord's Supper. The recess finally stated that the use and practice of adiaphora dare not conflict with the pure Gospel.[59]

The princes of the Frankfurt Recess sent a diplomatic mission to Weimar and exerted pressure on Duke John Frederick the Middler, but he refused to accept the Recess and had the estates of his dukedom reject it as well. Instead, at the advice of counselors close to Flacius, he decided on another course. Flacius himself attacked the Frankfurt Recess in an unpublished critique, his "Refutation of the Samaritan Interim, in Which True Religion Is Perniciously and Maliciously Confused with Sects and Corruptors." Flacius objected particularly to the absence of specific condemnations in the

64

Recess, and he found its doctrinal definitions not specific enough to resolve the issues it addressed.

Therefore Duke John Frederick countered the unity program of Frankfurt with proposals of his own, suggested by Flacius and others at his court or on his ecclesiastical staff. He announced that he would play host to the Evangelical estates in the city of Magdeburg in May 1558. The meeting there would draw up a confutation of all errors and thus establish Evangelical unity. Philip of Hesse and August of Saxony in particular were incensed, and August used diplomatic pressure to dissuade the city council of Magdeburg from permitting the meeting in the city. August and Melanchthon were determined not to expose their position to the wrath of the Gnesio-Lutherans in an open synod.

John Frederick proceeded with his plans for confutation in spite of this reversal and in spite of the opposition of some of his leading counselors, including Victorin Strigel and Erhard Schnepf. The circumstances surrounding the composition of John Frederick's *Book of Confutation* have been sketched above. The *Book* which resulted from the extensive revisions by Flacius and his comrades was published in 1559.[60] It condemned specific errors advanced by Servetus, Schwenkfeld, the antinomians, the Anabaptists, Zwingli, Osiander, Stancarus, Major, and the adiaphorists, as well as errors on the freedom of the will. It offered correct answers to the doctrinal questions raised by these errorists. The *Book of Confutation* did not serve as a basis for furthering Lutheran unity. It only angered princes and theologians alike who opposed its method and its tone.

At about this same time the Gnesio-Lutherans tried again to promote Lutheran unity through a *Supplication*, presented to the Evangelical estates in the name of 51 theologians, led by Amsdorf, Flacius, Gallus, and other Gnesio-Lutherans. The *Supplication* spelled out at length the issues that cried for resolution and the method which a synod should use for discussing and determining these issues. When the *Supplication* fell on deaf ears, Flacius attempted to appeal directly to Christoph of Württemberg, and in 1561 the *Supplication* was reissued and directed to the Evangelical princes as they assembled in Naumburg.[61]

The princes hoped to establish Evangelical unity at Naumburg by resubscribing the Augsburg Confession as had the previous generation of Evangelical rulers in Augsburg in 1530. However, debate broke out among them over the proper version of the Augustana to use. Elector Frederick III of the Palatinate, well on his way toward Calvinism by this time, insisted on using the altered version of 1540, while Dukes John Frederick the Middler and Ulrich of Mecklenburg refused to countenance its indefinite language on the Real Presence. Furthermore, they could not accept the new preface which the majority of princes proposed as an expression of their position on issues raised since 1530. The two dukes walked out of the assembly, and this ended its hopes of effecting unity.

Representatives of princes gathered for discussions of religious differences during the 1560s, for example in Erfurt later in 1561 when they met to decide on a common approach to the final session of the Council of Trent. But the avenue toward concord by way of the assembly of the Evangelical estates seemed blocked, and new ways to establish peace among the Lutherans needed to be developed.

In 1568 a grand attempt to achieve Saxon Lutheran unity was initiated by Duke John William of Saxony and Elector August. John William had succeeded his devout, zealous, but rather foolish brother, Duke John Frederick the Middler, after the latter had been imprisoned by Emperor Maximilian II for his futile attempt to support the knight errant, Wilhelm von Grumback. John Frederick had hoped to use Grumbach's feud against the bishop of Würzburg to his own advantage, but August executed an imperial ban against the duke and Grumbach in 1567, and John Frederick spent the rest of his life jailed in Vienna. John William and August promptly moved to open negotiations between their theologians, aimed at resolving the bitter quarrels between the Philippists and the Gnesio-Lutherans. Their secular counselors met to establish the ground rules for a colloquy, and the formal opening of the colloquy took place October 21, 1568, in the town hall at Altenburg with speeches by John William and Laurence Lindemann, one of August's key counselors. Paul Eber led the electoral Saxon theologians, Heinrich Salmuth, Caspar Cruciger, Christian Schütz, and others, while the ducal Saxon theologians were headed by Johann Wigand, who had been restored to favor and recalled to Jena by John William just shortly before the colloquy opened. He was assisted by Johann Friedrich Coelestin, Christoph Irenaeus, Bartholomaeus Rosinus, and Timotheus Kirchner.

The opening speeches by Eber and Wigand echoed the noise of battle of the previous two decades, set the tone for the encounter at Altenburg, and sounded the colloquy's final defeat. Eber appealed to the days of friendship enjoyed by representatives of the two parties at old Wittenberg and called for a common front against the spreading anti-Trinitarian menace. He pointed to their common commitment to the Word of God, the ancient symbols, the Augsburg Confession, its Apology, Luther's writings, and the Corpus Doctrinae Philippicum. The last confession, a collection of Melanchthon's writings, was not accepted by the ducal Saxon representatives as a doctrinal standard. Wigand replied, averring his side's commitment to unity and truth, and criticizing the electoral Saxons for tolerating and defending corruptions of pure doctrine for 20 years. The conference then turned to its agenda, which included discussions of justification, the necessity of good works, free will, and adiaphora. The first two items were discussed together; the colloquy broke up before the last two subjects could be treated.

The two sides had quarreled primarily over the relationship of good works and faith in regard to justification in the early stages of the controversy, but at Altenburg a whole series of criticisms of the other side were launched by each concerning what all regarded as the heart of the Lutheran faith. The two sides were divided not only by differences in terminology but also by differing attitudes or emphases in the way they described the relationship between God and his human creatures. These differences were cultivated into arguments over substantive issues and interpretations, and each side reverted to putting the worst construction on the other's position. The Philippists from Wittenberg smeared the professors from Jena with the epithet "Flacianist," though Wigand and Flacius were on the verge of a personal break over original sin. The Wittenbergers implied that the ducal Saxons were teaching the doctrines of both papists and "raving" radicals by equating passive justification with the infusion of grace. At the same time, in the presentation of their own counterpositions, they struggled to maintain the psychological participation of the believer in the process of salvation with less clarity than vehemence. The Gnesio-Lutherans, on the other hand, hammered away against the concept of the necessity of good works for salvation that the Philippists defended, and they stressed the importance of the word "alone" in connection with grace and faith, charging that the Philippists had soft-pedaled the exclusive nature of grace and faith in discussing soteriology at the time of the Interims.

Sessions were held in October and November and at the end of December 1568; in mid-January 1569 the talks resumed, and the reading of statements of position and rebuttal continued. After another recess the colloquy opened again in early March, but the frustration of the electoral Saxon theologians grew, and they unilaterally broke off the colloquy on March 6 by leaving town. Among the reasons they gave were the ducal Saxons' failure to abide by the provisions of the regulations laid down for the colloquy, their personal attacks (in which both sides actually indulged), their failure to recognize Melanchthon's writings as confessionally authoritative, and their rejection of fellowship with the Philippists.

The ducal Saxon theologians published reports on the colloquy, and the electoral Saxon delegation replied with the publication of *Complete and Unfalsified Documents and Transactions of the Colloquy between the Electoral and Princely Theologians of Saxony on the Article of the Righteousness of Man before God* in an effort to counter the accusations of the Gnesio-Lutherans. The Jena faculty in turn issued its corrections and objections to the electoral Saxon report on the colloquy.[62] The attempt to establish unity at Altenburg had only provoked more polemic and intensified old animosities.

68

The Road to Concord

While the electoral Saxon theologians were arguing with their ducal Saxon opponents in Altenburg, a theologian from Swabia visited Wittenberg. Jakob Andreä, ecclesiastical counselor to Duke Christoph of Württemberg and chancellor of the University of Tübingen, had been sent by his prince to a number of cities and principalities to assist in Evangelical reform. In 1568 Christoph had loaned Andreä to his cousin, Duke Julius of Braunschweig-Wolfenbüttel, who had just inherited the lands of his arch-Romanist father, Duke Heinrich. Julius wanted to reform the churches of his lands, and Andreä helped conduct a reforming visitation of those churches. Christoph urged Andreä to draw Julius and the Lower Saxon theologians of his area into Christoph's program for Lutheran unity. Julius agreed, and in 1569 supported and subsidized a tour of Evangelical cities and lands by Andreä.[63]

As he visited Wittenberg and other cities and princely courts Andreä presented a "Confession and Brief Explanation," which dealt with issues under dispute by contemporary Lutherans. He had composed this "Confession" as a means for the solution to disputes in five areas of doctrine: justification (on Osiandrism), good works, conversion, adiaphora, and the Lord's Supper. His motives were attacked on all sides, and his text was rejected as inadequate for different reasons by both the Philippist and the Gnesio-Lutheran camps. His journey in search of unity did anything but provoke a groundswell of approval for his program. However, he was able to induce Landgrave Wilhelm of Hesse, Chrisoph's son-in-law, and Duke Julius to invite a number of Evangelical princes and cities to send theologians to meet at Zerbst in Saxony, to affirm to establish Evangelical unity. Disagreement between the electoral Saxon delegation and the Lower Saxon representatives, who tended to be sympathetic to the Gnesio-Lutheran positions, surfaced during the course of the meeting even though the most strident critics of the electoral Saxon position, the theologians from Jena in ducal Saxony, were not present. The "Recess" agreed upon by most of the delegates at Zerbst did not meet the full approval of the electoral Saxons, though they did not enter a major protest at the meeting itself. However, when Andreä published the "Recess" with elaborate explanation a few months later, they did protest, for the "Recess" implied that everyone present, even the electoral Saxon delegation, accepted Andreä's doctrine of the ubiquity of Christ's human nature. The reaction to the publication of the "Recess" revealed the failure of Andreä's first attempt at bringing Saxon Lutherans together through his "Confession" and the synod at Zerbst. The storm of criticism from both electoral and ducal Saxony sent Andreä back home to Württemberg. However, he did not give up his hope for Lutheran unity. Three years later he published his *Six Christian Sermons on the Divisions That Have Continued to Surface Among the Theologians of the Augsburg Confession from 1548 Until This Year 1573.*[64] These sermons treated the subjects already dealt with in the "Confession" of 1569 along with disputes over Law and Gospel and over the person of Christ. Each section was greatly expanded from the brief statements of the "Confession," criticized for their brevity by the Gnesio-Lutherans. These sermons presented details of the two or more sides represented on 10 specific issues controverted at the time. Particularly the section on the Lord's Supper transformed into a discussion of the person of Christ and the ubiquity of his human nature, received expanded attention. The *Six Christian Sermons* represent a different approach to achieving Lutheran unity than did the "Confession." The Confession's brevity and vagueness were designed to bring about compromise through a general statement that sidestepped the specific points at issue and that ignored the related polemic of an entire generation. It was a document formulated along lines which the Philippists and princes had followed in the past. The *Six Christian Sermons,* on the other hand, reviewed specific positions and, although its text does not generally name names in connection with these positions, the names of representatives of both the correct and the condemned positions appear in the margins alongside the text.

Not only in form but also in content the *Six Christian Sermons* indicate that Andreä was attempting a rapprochement with the main body of Gnesio-Lutherans. It is true that Flacius

70

is condemned for his view of original sin, but in so doing Andreä was simply affirming, as he indicated in the margin, his support for the position of other Gnesio-Lutherans such as Wigand and Hesshus. Furthermore, Andreä made no effort to hide the conclusion he had come to after the synod at Zerbst: the Wittenbergers were teaching false doctrine in regard to the person of Christ. He condemned them by name in the text of his discussion of ubiquity as well as in the margin at other points. In contrast, the main body of Gnesio-Lutherans were often mentioned as those who had upheld the proper doctrinal position.

The *Six Christian Sermons* received criticism from the electoral Saxon theologians and from Flacius, but in other quarters reaction was favorable. However, prominent northern German theologians who liked Andreä's new approach had one major criticism of the *Sermons.* Andreä had written it for "simple pastors and common Christian lay people" and had based his critique of the disputed positions on the catechism. Theologians such as Chytraeus of Rostock and Chemnitz of Braunschweig favored a more carefully argued, theologically respectable document as the basis for further negotiations aimed at establishing Lutheran unity upon a firm settlement of doctrinal disputes. They asked Andreä to convert his *Six Christian Sermons* into that kind of document.

Andreä set to work during the winter of 1573-74 to formulate another document of harmony on the basis of his *Sermons,* taking into account the suggestions of north German theologians who approved his basic concepts. By spring the document was ready, and Andreä sent copies first to Duke Julius and to Martin Chemnitz.[65] He wrote them both that this new text was still designed for lay consumption. Theologians, Andreä somewhat naively believed, could work with briefer discussions, but the simple pastors and lay people for whom he had written his *Six Christian Sermons* needed fuller explanations for the disputes that were troubling their churches. Actually, it had been the brevity and generality of his "Confession and Brief Explanation" that had aroused suspicions of Andreä that still refused to die among Lower Saxon theologians. He may have been explaining why he had not prepared a document consisting of simple theses and antitheses. Andreä did not comply with the Lower Saxons suggestions in another way as well. It had been suggested that Andreä not submit the revision of his *Sermons* in his own name but rather in the name of the Tübingen theological faculty or of the theologians of the duchy of Württemberg. He did present his new text to the ducal ecclesiastical staff and won the approval of its members, but he sent his "Swabian Concord" to Julius and Chemnitz accompanied by letters over his own signature.

Andreä retained the German language for his new "Concord" because he did believe it was just as necessary to help lay people find answers to the questions raised by the feuding theologians as it was to provide the theologians themselves with a formulation of the disputed doctrines on which they could agree. He did move toward formulating his statement in theses and antitheses, as had been suggested, but as he explained to Duke Julius, he still found it necessary to expand his confession well beyond brief thetical statements so that those who would read the document could better understand the doctrinal issues in their context. Thus, he avoided strictly syllogistic argumentation, used by some of his contemporaries, and presented his materials in a more rhetorical way. He did, however, clearly define the points he affirmed and the points he rejected and condemned. In so doing he scrapped many sermonic elements from the *Six Christian Sermons* and recast the form in which he had presented his material there. The author's dialogs with the questioning lay person are not found in the "Swabian Concord," and some homey illustrations vanished as well. In the *Six Christian Sermons* Andreä had created such dialogs to present Scripture passages that each side in a dispute had used to defend its position; after such a review the author then pointed out on the basis of the catechism which side was using Scripture properly. In the "Swabian Concord" Andreä did not discuss the Scriptural defense of those whose positions he was rejecting, and the catechism no longer provided final arbitration of the differences under discussion. Instead, he reviewed passages that clearly taught the position he was presenting, and he made

Scripture the final arbitrator in all the disputes he treated. Since he was no longer analyzing the Scriptural dimensions of the controversies, Andreä could omit explanations of problem passages he had included in the *Six Christian Sermons*. He introduced patristic support for his position on the Lord's Supper into the "Swabian Concord" and cited Luther more often and from a wider range of his writings than he had in the *Sermons*.

The "Swabian Concord" treats the issues with which the *Sermons* dealt, original sin, the freedom of the will, justification, good works, Law and Gospel, the third use of the Law, necessity and freedom in regard to good works, adiaphora, the Lord's Supper, and the Person of Christ; in addition, it treated election and listed errors of certain sects, e.g., the Anabaptists, the Zwinglians, the Schwenkfeldians, the "new Antitrinitarians." Andreä's succinct condemnations of the views of these groups are based largely on a series of 33 sermons he had preached in 1567 on the differences between Lutheran teaching and the doctrines of the Roman Catholics, Zwinglians, Anabaptists, and Schwenkfeldians.[66] His article on the Lord's Supper used the argument for the real presence based on the ubiquity of Christ's human nature. His article on election drew arguments from the Strasbourg Concordia of 1563, in the composition of which he had played a role, and from the work of Martin Chemnitz, the friend with whom he had worked closely in Braunschweig. Other articles of the "Swabian Concord" show signs of improvement, produced in reaction to the comments and criticisms which the publication of the *Six Christian Sermons* had elicited. For instance, Andreä's treatment of Law and Gospel uses material from the church constitution that Chemnitz had prepared for the duchy of Braunschweig-Wolfenbüttel.[67]

In late March 1574 Andreä dispatched copies of his new formula for concord to Julius and to Chemnitz. Andreä had been working rather intensively for Lutheran concord for six years, and he must have agonized over the slow pace at which his brothers in the north took up his new formulation and worked with it to cultivate formal harmony. In May he wrote again to Braunschweig, urging action, and the Tübingen theological faculty supported his appeal for action.[68] Chemnitz had delayed pursuing the matter because of his own feeling that Andreä's "Concord" was not fully acceptable to his friends in Lower Saxony and because of the unfolding events in electoral Saxony, where Elector August had just become aware of the "crypto-Calvinistic" tendencies of many of his advisors. At conferences among the Lower Saxon churches and through correspondence during the summer and autumn of 1574 Chemnitz circulated Andreä's "Concord" and worked on revising it to meet the concerns of the north Germans. The following year the theological faculty at Rostock, under the leadership of David Chytraeus, also set about reworking its text with additions and improvements. Conferences between the Mecklenburg theologians, led by the Rostock faculty, and representatives of several cities and principalities in Lower Saxony, refined the text of Andreä's "Swabian Concord" into a document called the "Swabian-Saxon Concord," which was sent to Andreä and his colleagues in Würtemberg in September 1575.

The leading theologians who contributed to the composition of the "Swabian-Saxon Concord" were Martin Chemnitz and David Chytraeus of Rostock. By background and in talents and abilities these two men were somewhat different from Andreä. Andreä, a Swabian by birth, had remained in that area of Germany, studying theology only at Tübingen and then faithfully serving the dukes of Württemberg as a local ecclesiastical superintendent, a roving ecclesiastical diplomat, a university professor and administrator, and a counselor of high standing. He was more a man of action than of thought; his theology reflected the strong influence of his friend and mentor, Johann Brenz. As a south German he had gotten first hand acquaintance with the strife between Gnesio-Lutherans and Philippists only when his missions for his dukes had brought him into other principalities.

In contrast, Chemnitz and Chytraeus lived in the area in which the two Saxon parties were struggling, and though neither could be properly labeled either Philippist or Gnesio-Lutheran in a strict sense, both exhibited certain characteristics of each party. Both were more familiar with the issues and the

74

personalities behind the northern German Lutheran controversies that Andreä had been.

Chemnitz, a Saxon by birth, studied liberal arts at Wittenberg under Melanchthon, who recommended him as librarian and astrological consultant to the duke of Prussia. Chemnitz left Königsberg in the midst of the Osiandrian controversy and returned to Melanchthon's fold to study theology. He accepted a call to serve as pastor and assistant to a friend from his Königsberg days, Joachim Mörlin, now superintendent in the city of Braunschweig, in late 1554, and he served the city and later Duke Julius of the duchy of Braunshweig-Wolfenbüttel for the rest of his career. Chemnitz published occasional pieces that dealt with the specific doctrinal discussions of the Lower Saxon church during the 1550s, 1560s, and 1570s, prepared *Loci communes* for lecture (published posthumously), and composed a massive critique of the theology of the Council of Trent.[69] Already in the "Swabian Concord" signs of his influence on Andreä can be detected, and the "Swabian-Saxon Concord" and subsequent stages of the development of the text of the Formula of Concord are even more directly the work of his hand.

His friend and colleague Joachim Mörlin, a Gnesio-Lutheran, influenced Chemnitz to a certain degree. Chemnitz never became a partisan of Flacius; like Mörlin, Wigand, Hesshus, and other Gnesio-Lutherans he attacked Flacius' views of original sin. Indeed, the imprint of Melanchton's instruction never disappeared from its prominent place in Chemnitz's theology. Nonetheless, Chemnitz did share certain positions and attitudes with the Gnesio-Lutherans that put him at odds with the Philippists and shaped his reactions to the events of the 1570s. Early on, in 1561, he opposed the Philippist understanding of the Lord's Supper, and his massive study of the Scriptural and patristic doctrine of the person of Christ was written to counter the Philippist theologians at Wittenberg in 1570.[70] He had joined with others in opposing Philippist adiaphorism in the 1550s, and he attacked Majorism in 1567. Later, in 1578, he displayed an attitude toward his prince characteristic of the Gnesio-Lutherans. Like them, Chemnitz always welcomed princely assistance for the Evangelical church, but also, like them, when the prince strayed, he did not hesitate to criticize and break with his prince, Duke Julius, regardless of personal cost. Julius had his son, Heinrich Julius, consecrated as Roman Catholic bishop of Halberstadt in 1578; Andreä, as Württembergers were generally wont to do, did not take exception to the prince's decision, but Chemnitz denounced it as apostasy and thus alienated Julius, as a number of prominent Gnesio-Lutherans had done in battles over principle with other rulers or city councils.

David Chytraeus had also studied under Melanchthon, had lived in his home, and throughout his life wrote and thought under his preceptor's influence.[71] As a 13-year-old master of arts, he had left the University of Tübingen for Wittenberg, where he immediately impressed Melanchthon with his learning. He became professor of liberal arts at the University of Rostock in Mecklenburg in 1550 and soon assumed teaching duties in theology as well. Primarly an exegetical theologian, he, like Chemnitz, displayed impressive gifts as a thinker and writer. He never lost a basically Melanchthonian approach to learning and theology, yet he criticized the tendency of the Philippists at Wittenberg to generalize and compromise on disputed issues. He censured Melanchthon's "Frankfurt Recess' without knowing that his beloved friend and preceptor had written it. Though a close friend of the Gnesio-Lutherans Hesshus and Wigand during their Mecklenburg careers, he never shared their party spirit and their joy for disputation. Like Chemnitz, Chytraeus' relatively irenic manner seems to distinguish him from the Gnesio-Lutherans quite radically, but his viewpoint did coincide with theirs at important points.

The text of the "Swabian-Saxon Concord" stems from the hands of Chytraeus and Chemnitz although much of Andreä's "Swabian Concord" remained after their reworking. Chytraeus rewrote the sections on the free will and the Lord's Supper with only little assistance from Chemnitz, and he also reshaped Andreä's article on adiaphora to some extent. Chemnitz's influence was particularly prominent in the treatments of original sin, the righteousness of the sinner before God, good works, the person of Christ, and election.

By the time the northern German theologians had completed their work on the text of the Swabian-Saxon Concord, events in the electorate of Saxony had once again taken the direction of German Lutheranism out of the hands of the theologians and placed it firmly in the grip of one prince, Elector August of Saxony. In 1573 his cousin, Duke John William of ducal Saxony, had died, and August assumed guardianship of his children, exercising power in their lands. August had despised the Gnesio-Lutheran theologians at John William's University of Jena for years because of their persistent attacks on his own theologians at Leipzig and Wittenberg. Therefore, as one of his first acts as overlord of ducal Saxony, he ousted the Gnesio-Lutheran theological faculty, Tilemann Hesshus, Johann Wigand, and their colleagues, thus destroying the single most important center of Gnesio-Lutheran activity. Early the following year August discovered that some of his most trusted advisors had been working to advance a spiritualistic interpretation of the real presence of Christ's body and blood in the Lord's Supper, and he purged his theological staff and faculties of several leading young members of the Philippist party's "crypto-Calvinist" wing. Having struck out against the leadership of both theological parties in Saxony, August was determined to reconstruct the theological basis of his church along strict Lutheran lines. To do that he consulted with those among his own theologians who had repudiated the spiritualizing wing of the Philippist party, and he also enlisted the aid of prominent Lutheran theologians from outside his own domains. As August moved ahead with efforts to define the faith of his church, other princes were also trying to bring the German Lutheran churches to an agreement on a common statement of belief in regard to the disputed issues that were dividing them.

In November 1575, at the wedding of Duke Ludwig of Württemberg to Dorothea Ursula, daughter of Margrave Karl of Baden-Durlach, Count Georg Ernst of Henneberg, Ludwig's brother-in-law, joined these two princes in a new effort toward concord. Their theologians conferred and recommended the formulation of a new document defining solutions to the Lutherans' doctrinal disputes. The two Henneberg theologians, Adam Scherdinger and Peter Streck, and Rupert Dürr of Baden delegated to Balthasar Bidembach and Lucas Osiander of Württemberg the task of implementing the group's recommendations. Both Württembergers had studied at Tübingen and were serving as court preachers and ecclesiastical counselors in Duke Ludwig's court at Stuttgart. Osiander was Jakob Andreä's brother-in-law. They incorporated south German criticisms of the form and style of the Swabian-Saxon Concord into the formula they produced. The Württembergers had found no serious doctrinal error in the Swabian-Saxon Concord, which Duke Julius had forewarded to them the previous September. In a formal review of the document in October Ludwig's theologians had objected to its use of technical Latin terms that would make the document difficult for the laity to understand; they criticized its length and its reference to other theologians beside Luther, particularly its citations from Melanchthon's works. Osiander and Bidembach composed their statement and presented it for approval by the theologians from Baden, Henneberg, and Württemberg at a meeting held Jan. 19, 1576, at Maulbronn in Württemberg; hence the document was named the Maulbronn Formula. It presented definitions of the issues at hand (original sin, the person of Christ, justification, Law and Gospel, good works, the Lord's Supper, adiaphora, the freedom of the will, and the third use of the Law) in relatively short statements. Its authors strove for straightforward terminology, and they cited Luther at length but appealed to no other theologian as an authority.

Count Georg Ernst of Henneberg, who had long warned his friend August of Saxony about the errors of the Saxon Philippist theologians, sent the Maulbronn Formula to the elector, who had already received a copy of the Swabian-Saxon Concord. August consulted with other Lutheran princes, with Jakob Andreä, and with his own theologians regarding the best way to proceed toward an official formulation of doctrine that would replace the official statements adopted by the Saxon church in recent years, particularly the *Corpus doctrinae*

Philippicum, a collection of Melanchthon's writings, and the spiritualizing Dresden *Consensus.* Establishing an official statement of doctrine for electoral Saxony was August's first concern; his second was to offer all Lutheran churches a formula for concord.

The princes whom August consulted urged that a small group of theologians, rather than a larger synod such as had assembled at Zerbst six years earlier, be charged with the task of composing the formula. Landgrave William of Hesse promoted this idea, and his suggestion was supported by Georg Ernst of Henneberg, Elector Johann Georg of Brandenburg, and also by Margrave Georg Friedrich of Brandenburg-Ansbach, whose own diplomatic missions in behalf of Lutheran unity had collapsed in 1575.

August's theologians also supported the concept of a select committee of prominent theologians meeting to compose a definitive statement of Lutheran teaching. At a convocation at Lichtenberg in mid-February 1576 12 theologians replied to questions on method and procedure from the elector and thus launched the final stage of the development of the text of the Formula of Concord.

Most prominent among the electoral Saxon theologians at Lichtenberg was Nikolaus Selnecker. Melanchthon had befriended Selnecker during his student days at Wittenberg and earned his undying devotion. At Melanchthon's recommendation he became a court preacher at Dresden in 1558 and two years later assumed duties as tutor for Elector August's four-year-old son, Alexander, who died in 1565. In that year Selnecker was forced out of his position in Dresden; the immediate cause for his departure was his fiery denunciation of nobles' practices on the hunt, but it was also suggested that he had run afoul of certain theologians whose spiritualizing views of the real presence he did not share. Although a zealous member of the Philippist party, he had defended Luther's view of the Lord's Supper in print. After two years service at the University of Jena, which Duke John Frederick the Middler had purged of Gnesio-Lutherans during the Strigel affair, Selnecker was removed from his professorship by the succession of the

Gnesio-Lutheran Duke John William in 1568. He then succeeded Strigel at the University of Leipzig and became superintendent of the city's churches as well. Elector August granted him a leave of absence in 1570 so that he could accept a call from Duke Julius to serve as court preacher in Wolfenbüttel and general superintendent for the church in his lands. During his three-year tenure in Braunschweig-Wolfenbüttel Selnecker worked closely with Martin Chemnitz and Jakob Andreä. When, in the wake of the colloquy at Zerbst, suspicions about the electoral Saxon theologians' understanding of the person of Christ arose in Duke Julius' mind, he sent Selnecker and Andreä to Wittenberg to obtain a clarification of the Wittenbergers' position. Both men published favorable reports of their conversations with the theologians there, but Selnecker's former colleagues attacked him and Andreä for misrepresenting their position in these reports. Selnecker returned to his positions in Leipzig in 1573. Somewhat alienated from the Peucer wing of the Philippist party already, he became a leader in August's attempts to rid his church of the "crypto-Calvinists" the following year.[72]

Selnecker and his colleagues at Lichtenberg cleared the way for the formulation of a new confessional statement for electoral Saxony by announcing that the *Corpus doctrinae Philippicum* was salutary for reading but inadequate as a confessional definition of the princedom's faith. They also urged August to call Jakob Andreä to the vacant city pastorate of Wittenberg so that he might assist in restoring a strong Lutheran position to the churches and schools of August's lands. Finally, they set forth procedures for a meeting of a select committee of prominent Lutheran theologians to assist them in the composition of a new confessional norm, a formula for concord.[73]

In late May 1576 this committee assembled near the Saxon town of Torgau. The electoral Saxon theologians who had met at Lichtenberg were joined by Andreä, Chemnitz, Chytraeus, and two representatives sent by Elector Johann Georg of Brandenburg, Andreas Musculus and Christopher Corner. Both Brandenburgers were professors at the University of Frankfurt an der Oder and ecclesiastical counselors on Johann Georg's staff. Musculus, though not an intimate associate of Flacius and the Magdeburg group of Gnesio-Lutherans, shared their viewpoint to a large extent. Locked in dispute with his colleague Abdias Praetorius over the role of good works in the Christian life, Musculus had advanced propositions which Andreä had condemned in the *Six Sermons*.[74] Musculus' penchant for disagreement—if not disagreeableness—made him the most irascible of the committee. Nonetheless, the entire group went to work on the document they were commissioned to prepare. With intense debate on some points, including Law and Gospel and the person of Christ, they combined sections of the Maulbronn Formula with the definitions of the Swabian-Saxon Concord; from these two documents they constructed a statement on the issues which stood before them. The committee also added a brief article on Christ's descent into hell.

The Swabian-Saxon Concord formed the basis of the new document, called the Torgau Book; the formulators also used sections from the Maulbronn Formula, particularly in treating the freedom of the will, Law and Gospel, the Lord's Supper, the person of Christ, and adiaphora. They also revised or added material to the statements of these two documents in completing the articles on Law and Gospel, adiaphora, and especially on the person of Christ. Because of the length of the document Andreä composed a "Brief, Summarized Excerpt of the Articles . . . Composed at Torgau," for Elector August; this summary became know as the Epitome of the Formula of Concord. It reflects Andreä's own understanding of the formula he and his colleagues had prepared.[75]

Elector August circulated the Torgau Book among all Lutheran estates of the empire, and most returned memoranda from their theologians on the contents and form of the Torgau Book. Andreä and Chemnitz visited a number of principalities and cities in efforts to explain and attract support for the book. Representatives from Württemberg, Baden, and Henneberg approved the Torgau Book at a meeting at Maulbronn in September, a month after electoral Brandenburg's key theologians had reported favorably on the book. In a series of meetings Lower Saxon cities and Braunschweig-Wolfenbüttel registered their support, and Mecklenburg, under Chytraeus' guidance, also approved the book. Opposition to it came from two sides. The Gnesio-Lutherans Wigand and Hesshus dominated the church of Prussia; they and their colleagues praised the doctrinal position of the book but objected to the absence of condemnations of false teachers by name. The hostility of the Gnesio-Lutherans toward Andreä because of his earlier compromising stand in relation to the Philippists affected the Prussian evaluation. On the other hand, the rejection of some Melanchthon's positions implicit in the Torgau Book offended the theologians of Pomerania, Hesse, Holstein, Anhalt, and the several counties of the Palatinate, and the Torgau Book's use of the concept of the omnipresence of Christ's human nature aroused objections in Philippist quarters, as well as among some others.[76]

After negotiations with Elector Johann Georg of Brandenburg, August of Saxony arranged for Chemnitz, Andreä, and Selnecker to meet at the monastery at Bergen, near Magdeburg in March 1577. They took in hand the memoranda received from the theologians of Lutheran estates from all areas of Germany, and on the basis of these critiques worked out a final form on which they believed Lutheran concord could be established and Lutheran doctrine determined. In May they returned to Bergen to review their revisions with Chytraeus, Musculus, and Corner, and this group of six completed the formulation of the document known as the Bergic Book, which became the Solid Declaration of the Formula of Concord. The most extensive revisions at Bergen were made in the articles on the person of Christ and the descent into hell; some changes were also made on the articles on the freedom of the will and on good works. Not all the members of the committee were happy with the Bergic Book's final form; Musculus' objections to passages on the third use of the Law were apparently met, but Chytraeus believed that the concept of the omnipresence of Christ's human nature still loomed too large in the book's treatment of the Lord's Supper. Nonetheless, the committee presented the Bergic Book to their fellow Lutherans as a statement of faith which, they believed, should draw all

82

Lutherans together in theological agreement. They had incorporated the criticisms of the Evangelical churches into their new book as best they could, and they believed that it was the instrument of unity for which they and many others had been searching for years. So they urged that further debate on their text be avoided and that Elector August forward the Bergic book to other Evangelical princes, asking that they collect the subscriptions of individual pastors in the parishes of their lands.[77]

During the succeeding months of 1577 the parishes and schools of electoral Saxony were visited by a commission consisting of Andreä, Selnecker, and Polycarp Leyser, Andreä's nephew and newly installed professor of theology at Wittenberg. Through sermons and personal discussions they induced subscriptions to their Formula of Concord. For many of the Saxon clergy the article that dealt with the person of Christ was still troublesome, and the Bergic Book's discussion of the definition of the Gospel and its description of the role of the will in conversion also attracted criticism from the Philippists. However, the Saxon commission met little stiff resistance to their efforts, apart from the party's leadership at Wittenberg and Leipzig.

In Brandenburg Musculus and Corner headed a similar commission that visited the churches of the elector's lands; Chemnitz performed a similar task in Braunschweig and the Lower Saxon cities. In other lands, including Brandenburg-Ansbach, Oldenburg, Mecklenburg, Baden, Henneberg, the archbishopric of Magdeburg, and finally also in Prussia princes circulated the Bergic Book and solicited signatures from all pastors. Some refused, but only a very few were so strongly opposed to the text of the Bergic Book that they risked—and suffered—deposition. Criticisms from Gnesio-Lutheran followers of Flacius offered objections to the book's doctrine of original sin,[78] but they swayed no prince into opposition to the Book.

However, theologians sympathetic to Melanchthon's views, particularly on the person of Christ, supported and influenced their government's rejection of the Bergic Book in several areas, among them Bremen, Nuremberg, Anhalt, and Pomerania, while in other areas personal differences between local theologians and the formulators at Bergen seemed to play the decisive role. The rejection of the book of Holstein, under the leadership of Paul von Eizen, seems to be an example of this personal motivation.[79]

The forces opposed to the Bergic Book were led by Landgrave William of Hesse, who organized a league to counteract the drive toward concord based on the Bergen formula in the autumn of 1577. Among the theologians who urged this course was Christoph Pezel, the exiled "crypto-Calvinist" of Wittenberg. This movement was supported by warnings from Queen Elizabeth of England against any attempt to isolate Lutheran Evangelicals from Reformed Evangelicals. In late 1577 Count Johann Casimir of the Palatinate also moved to counteract the Lutheran coalition growing up around the Bergic Book by summoning a conference of representatives of Reformed communities from eastern Europe, Switzerland, Holland, France, and Germany.

The pressure exerted by these groups and individuals caused Elector August of Saxony to rethink his commitment to the Bergic Book and so he called a conference of theologians and counselors from his government and that of Elector Johann Georg of Brandenburg to Tangermünde in March 1578. There the theologians resisted August's suggestion that their formula for concord be revised further to meet the objections of William of Hesse and others. The theologians, under Andreä's leadership, resisted such compromises, and August backed down. Instead, a conference between the governments of Saxony and Hesse, with some of William's allies also present, was arranged for Langensalza in March 1578. This meeting, and a similar one in August with representatives from Anhalt, produced no understanding between the two sides. In spite of such setbacks the formulators continued to enhance their Formula's authority.

In December 1578 Andreä set about the task of composing a preface for a publication that would include not only the Formula of Concord composed at Bergen but also the three ecumenical creeds and the documents that 16th-century Lutherans had come to regard as authoritative interpretations of their faith: the Augsburg Confession, its Apology, Luther's two catechisms, and the Smalcald Articles. The preface was laid before Chemnitz, Chytraeus, Musculus, Corner, and Selnecker at a meeting at Jüterbogk in January 1579. After extensive reformulation by the Saxon counselor Hartmann Pistorius, it was reworked into its final form at Bergen the next year by Andreä, Chemnitz, and Leyser. Elector August circulated it among his fellow princes, soliciting their personal subscriptions. In the principalities and cities where the Bergic Book had found acceptance, princes and councils, except in Braunschweig, subscribed the preface.

The Lutheran Elector Ludwig of the Palatinate, who had succeeded his Reformed father, Frederick III, in 1576, had at first sided with the landgrave of Hesse and others in opposition to the text of the Bergic Book. Through the diplomatic activity of other Lutheran princes, however, Ludwig was won over for the Formula of Concord and subscribed the preface in the summer of 1579, thus bringing all three secular electors of the empire into line behind the Concordia project.

Andreä's plans for the publication of the Formula of Concord and the other confessions of the Lutheran churches—begun in 1578—proceeded during 1579, and the entire Book of Concord appeared in the booksellers' stalls at the same time in Dresden and Tübingen, on June 25, 1580, the 50th anniversary of the presentation of the Augsburg Confession to Emperor Charles V.

The Book of Concord provided the historical definition of Lutheranism as it faced issues raised in the second half of the 16th century. Some Evangelical churches that did not accept it remained Lutheran in basic commitment, and some of these did come to accept the Concordia later. In Braunschweig Duke Julius had become alienated from Chemnitz in the course of the dispute over his plans to have his son, Heinrich Julius, consecrated bishop of Halberstadt according to the Roman Catholic rite. He did so in order to assure the incorporation of these church lands into his domain, and he specifically stated that his son would not leave the Lutheran faith. Although Andreä was unwilling to protest the prince's course, Chemnitz criticized the ceremonial subservience to the Roman pope so fiercely that he and Julius were never reconciled. Julius therefore withdrew from the Concordianist movement in which he had invested so much money, time, and energy, and his lands did not accept the Book of Concord.

Other Evangelical churches in Germany turned away from this specific Lutheran confession to the Reformed faith. From the Reformed camp came a number of attacks on the Formula of Concord in particular, and one, the *Neuburg Admonition* of 1581, induced Chemnitz, Selnecker, and Timotheus Kirchner to compose an apology to the Formula of Concord in 1583.[80] This apology dealt above all with the doctrine of Christ's person and the omnipresence of his human nature. Gnesio-Lutheran supporters of Flacius' view of original sin, gathered chiefly in Austria, continued to attack the Formula after its 1580 publication, but their movement lacked strong princely support and disappeared in the early 17th century. Within Lutheranism the theology of the Formula of Concord became dominant.

The Formula of Concord introduced a new period in the life of the Lutheran churches of central Europe; it marks the end of the era in which Luther's heirs debated the meaning of his legacy, and it points the way toward the Lutheranism of the early modern Orthodox period of Western Christendom.

The Formula of Concord is sometimes called a compromise. It certainly was not a document that merely sought to stand on middle ground on every issue—though, indeed, emphases from various disputing groups found a place in the Formula. Andreä's *Six Christian Sermons,* the earliest version of the Formula, affirmed the views of the main body of Gnesio-Lutherans regarding issues involving free will, good works, the Lord's Supper, and adiaphora, while condemning extreme Flacianists and a Gnesio-Lutheran like Musculus on the one hand and rejecting Philippist positions across the board on the other. Some Philippist concerns were met, but by and large the condemnations of the Formula are directed against Philippist positions, not against those of most members of the Gnesio-

Lutheran movement, even if its statements were tailored to take account of the positive viewpoints of the Philippist party. On the doctrine of Christ's person, the Württembergers' emphasis on the omnipresence or ubiquity of Christ's human nature had raised the hackles not only of committed Philippists but also of Concordianists like Chytraeus, and so the theologians at Torgau and Bergen had to formulate a common position that incorporated the concepts of both the northern German and the southern German interpretations of Luther, those of Melanchthonians of both Gnesio-Lutheran and Philippist parties on the one hand, and those of Brenz and his followers on the other. The Formula of Concord failed to meet all the concerns of some northern Germans who accepted its text—Chytraeus among them—on the doctrine of the person of Christ. Nonetheless, the Formula of Concord succeeded in ending 30 years of rancor and dispute; it succeeded in establishing agreement among a majority of Luther's followers and heirs on what it meant to be Lutheran.

The success of the Concordianist movement stems in part from the political support it received from princes, to be sure. However, its success as a confession of faith arises from its authors' concern for a confession that was true to Scripture and which spoke to the laity with answers for the doctrinal problems besetting them in the midst of controversy. Their dedication to the goal of creating harmony based upon the Scripture, as Luther had taught its message to his followers, produced the Formula of Concord.

LOOKING AT THE FORMULA TODAY

Wilbert H. Rosin

*A*n age that contends not only for freedom but insists on an equal hearing for all ideas cannot understand, much less accept, the concept of a confessional church that draws its statements of belief together in a formal document and seriously subscribes to them. For decades higher education has been touting the philosophical proposition that a primary function of a college or university is to present forcefully and impartially all sides of any issue. To encourage certain values and discourage others is thought to be unnecessarily restrictive, a violation of personal rights, and harmful to the integrity of the individual.

Reared in the Jeffersonian tradition, Americans resist regulation and regard submission to the opinion of others as an unwise bowing to the will of fallible men. The fallacy in this line of reasoning is that in reality no one thinks independently. If nothing else, we select from the ideas of others. Even the basis for our selection is not without influence. Nevertheless, we idolize "independent thinking" and "value-free" education without sensing that agnostic philosophy has for many Americans become an "objective" approach—not to mention collectivist economics, situational ethics, and other ideas of fallible men.

Historians of recent decades have been more forthright than most defenders of their vocation. By actively seeking new interpretations of history they acknowledge that they are in a never-ending pursuit of objectivity. Edward Hallett Carr in *What Is History?* likens the historian's art to fishing: he says much depends on what part of the lake you fish, the kind of fish you wish to catch, the time of the day, and the kind of bait you choose.

Granted that man must make decisions, evaluate his past, and choose from among alternatives and that in so doing he is influenced by fallible men, must he be consigned to relativism and an uncomfortable feeling that what he knows is qualified by uncertainty? Although he must make decisions and will do so imperfectly, are there no reliable guidelines, no absolutes, no central controls? Is there no true compass or gyroscope to hold man in balance?

Until the 18th-century philosophic movement called the Enlightenment, the world, at least the Christian portion, took for granted that the Bible was indeed such an infallible guide. The Lutheran fathers of the Formula of Concord spent no time debating the authority of the sacred Scriptures. The Christian Church had always assumed it. Martin Luther's emphasis on *sola scriptura* had not been weakened since his death in 1546. His emphasis had been on *sola,* not on whether the Bible was an authority, or even an infallible authority.

It remained for the post-Enlightenment era to question the divine role in the writing of the Bible and, therefore, its reliability. Unfortunately, the means for questioning—the human mind—was unequal to the task. According to the Bible, man's reason no longer was capable of making the kind of evaluation envisioned by unbelieving scholars. The mind of man had been impaired by the fall. The mistake of the Enlightenment was to assume that, given the time, man by means of his intellect could arrive at a complete understanding of the universe. In the words of orthodox Biblical theologians, a magisterial use was assigned to the mind. Since the fall it could properly be accorded only a limited ministerial function.

The thinking of the Enlightenment logically led to a series of philosophical schemes in subsequent centuries, many of which had as their common core the relativity of human understanding. One could not *know* anything as absolutely true. Some took the next step to declare that absolute truth does not exist, or that, if it does, we can never know it. Those assumptions—note that they are assumptions—introduced not merely honest respect for divergent opinions but tolerance of all opinions as being of equal merit. All ideas deserve a hearing because there is no final authority for judging them, so the argument went.

If that kind of reasoning is valid, then confessional statements have no place in the church, other than to be a common rallying point not to be taken seriously. Lutherans, however, have consistently taken the position that truth is not "plucked from the inner consciousness of man," as 19th-century transcendentalists held, nor arrived at by a pragmatist trial-and-error process. Religious truth is ascertainable because God has revealed Himself, though not exhaustively, in the sacred Scriptures.

Numerous ideological variations have supported anticonfessionalism. All of them ultimately owe their origin, at least indirectly, to the Enlightenment, as well as to the earlier Renaissance movement, in which man became the measure of all things. The division is between humanistic thought and divinely given revelation. The 16th-century fathers of the Formula recognized that difference, though obviously from a different perspective, since the Enlightenment and its progeny followed later. The 16th-century Lutheran leaders contended for the authority of Scripture as opposed to the authority of the church, its traditions, and the writings of the church fathers. These three sources, or standards, represented a somewhat modest humanist

90

trend, as compared with the later Enlightenment, but, even, so they were unacceptable to Lutheran scholars.

Among the more penetrating anticonfessional influences that have prevailed in America is a distortion of democracy that has affected other institutions as well as the church. The student of American history knows that neither Thomas Jefferson, John Adams, nor the other Founding Fathers believed in absolute equality, as though there were no differences among people. Jefferson led the attack against an artificial aristocracy, transplanted from Europe, based on birth and wealth. He built his political philosophy on the belief that a natural aristocracy based upon talents would emerge if society provided the means whereby it could develop naturally.

Since the Declaration of Independence in 1776, however, Americans have made of Jeffersonian democracy a leveling process rejecting anything that is beyond the grasp of anyone else. According to this reasoning, every individual is entitled to a college education, pass/fail grading has often replaced traditional evaluation, every American is entitled to a degree of material wealth if not affluence, and a kind of Jacksonian democracy is practiced, with the result that mediocrity prevails in political elections. A corollary of that mind-set is the conviction that religious truth can be and must be arrived at individually. Confessionalism implies religious conformity to specific beliefs. Confessionalism is therefore undemocratic and is to be shunned. Lutherans, however, object to this humanistic view because God has revealed His will and way with man. For them religious truth is not a matter of open debate, though an understanding and application of it is quite another matter and requires much discussion for fallen man.

Christians of every age, in seeking to meet the problems and challenges of the day, find it necessary and useful to formulate credal statements. Properly formulated, they are only restatements of Biblical doctrine. Therefore Christians can still assent to the confessional statements of an earlier day, such as the Apostles' Creed, the Nicene Creed, and the Athanasian Creed. Today Lutherans subscribe not only to the ecumenical creeds of all Christendom, but also to the Formula of Concord, the Small and Large Catechisms, the Augsburg Confession, and the other portions of the Book of Concord of 1580.

Just as the Scriptures do not describe God exhaustively, so confessional statements do not present all truths contained in the faith. Therefore Lutherans today might profit from an attempt similar to that of the late 16th century if they wish to halt the present-day erosion of Biblical doctrine. During the 20th century many Protestant theologians have verbalized Christian theology in a way that is nontraditional and, to all appearances, at times non-Biblical. Their names are known to all theologians and most laymen: Rudolf Bultmann, Karl Barth, Reinhold Niebuhr, H. Richard Niebuhr, Paul Tillich, and many others. Roman Catholic theologians who fall in the same category include Pierre Teilhard de Chardin, Karl Rahner, and Johannes Metz. These and others believed that Christian doctrine is largely achieved through interaction with the cultural milieu and develops through time. The effect has been to cut away at the very foundations of the faith.

The polarity between this type of humanistic theology and revealed theology is evident today. The extreme representatives of the latter type have been loosely categorized as "Fundamentalists" because of their emphasis upon fundamental doctrines and their tendency toward anti-intellectualism. To be sure, the 20th century theological scene cannot be described in these few lines. It is, however, reasonably accurate to state that Lutherans have tried to steer between the rationalistic extremes of humanistic theology and the simplistic tendencies of fundamentalism by relying on the Reformation principle of *sola Scriptura,* the Bible as the only source and norm of faith and life.

The case for confessionalism, unfashionable though it may be today, is based on sound logic. Some of the mainline churches have unwittingly become the victims of agnostic philosophy. While their pulpit rhetoric seems to articulate basic Biblical beliefs, their discussions with peers and their scholarly writing at best give evidence of a serious erosion of what have traditionally been considered the fundamentals of the faith.

The Biblical and confessional view, however, is based on

the concept of God—a God with more than superhuman attributes, a God who could create a world more complex than man could completely understand, a God who could become man and redeem mankind, and a God who could do all the other things attributed to Him in the Scriptures. Such a concept of God is logical. It assumes that God would not and did not reveal Himself exhaustively. Yet He reveals Himself to be a God of order, the Creator of an orderly universe with a unified body of knowledge, so that man can in part understand his world. The Christian, whom the Holy Spirit has brought to faith, deepens and reenforces his faith and his understanding of God as he discovers that what he learns about his world through the use of reason agrees (though superficially) with what the Bible teaches about God. This kind of corroborative and supplementary mutuality strengthens the Christian's faith in the unseen and in the incomprehensible acts of God.

Not having been exposed to the Enlightenment, the Christian of 1580 was not dependent on rational reenforcement of his faith. There was little need for Christian apologetics. How different from the 20th century! This places the Christian today into a world of instant communication dominated by skepticism, agnosticism, and rationalistic thought. Hence every Christian craves a rational justification for his confessional position.

The Lutheran Christian regards confessional statements as a systematized compilation of Biblical principles of faith, the decisional premises for life, rather than a restrictive straitjacket. The anticonfessional Christian seeks the broadest base for agreement and cannot understand the need for delineating doctrine in clear detail. To him a simple assent that Jesus is Lord (some would say "Savior and Lord") is sufficient. To that the response of the confessional Lutheran is threefold: (1) The Lutheran Confessions are a summary of Biblical doctrine and of official doctrine of the church, more than a mere statement of what is necessary for salvation. (2) Those who preach and teach in the church need more than the minimum if they are to serve responsibly. (3) Simple assent that Jesus is Savior and Lord is not sufficient for the Christian as he confronts the complex problems of life and the need to distinguish justification and sanctification or Law and Gospel.

Clarifying doctrine and reaffirming the Lutheran Confessions belong not in the realm of unnecessary theorizing or much ado about nothing. Proper systematic theologizing is in a different category from medieval scholastic speculation. The truth is, the Lutheran Confessions provide a positive platform for Christian witnessing and for a satisfying understanding of God and His ways with man in the 20th-century world.

RULE AND NORM OF DOCTRINE IN THE FORMULA OF CONCORD

H. Huth

*T*hose who are within the Church do not inquire about the authority of Scripture, for this is their starting-point. How can they be true disciples of Christ if they pretend to call in question the doctrine of Christ? How can they be true members of the Church if they are in doubt concerning the foundation of the Church? How can they wish to prove that to themselves which they always employ to prove other things? How can they doubt concerning that whose efficacy they have experienced in their own hearts? The Holy Spirit testifies in their hearts that the Spirit is truth, *i.e.,* that the doctrine derived from the Holy Spirit is absolute truth." [1]

In these words, written less than four *decades* after the publication of the Book of Concord, Gerhard not only reflects faithfully the attitude of the Lutheran Confessions toward the Sacred Scriptures but still speaks for all true Lutherans a full four *centuries* after the publication of the Book of Concord.

Implicit in the above citation from Gerhard there is a very important distinction that 17th-century Lutheran dogmaticians made when they discussed the authority of the Scriptures. The power of the Holy Scriptures to call sinners to saving faith in Christ through the Gospel which is revealed in them the dogmaticians called the *causative* authority of the Scriptures. The authority of the Scriptures that belongs to them as the Word of God to be the rule and norm of doctrine the dogmaticians called the *normative* authority of the Scriptures.

David Hollaz describes the authority of the Scriptures as follows: *"(a) Causative authority,* by which the Scriptures create and confirm in the mind of man assent to the truths to be believed. *(b) Normative or canonical authority,* by which authentic Scripture is distinguished from other writings and versions, and that which is true from that which is false."[2]

These technical dogmatical terms are not found in the Formula of Concord, but that for which they stand is found from the first paragraph of the Epitome to the closing paragraphs of the Solid Declaration.

The Formula affirms the *causative* authority of the Scriptures when it teaches that fallen man "is and remains an enemy of God, until he is converted, becomes a believer . . ., is regenerated and renewed, by the power of the Holy Ghost *through the Word"* (FC SD II 5, Triglot) and emphatically declares, "by this means, and in no other way, namely, *through His holy Word,* when men hear it preached or read it, and the holy Sacraments when they are used according to His Word, God desires to call men to eternal salvation, draw them to Himself, and convert, regenerate, and sanctify them" (II 50. Emphases added).

The Formula affirms also the *normative* authority of the Scriptures.

The Formula emphasizes the normative authority of the Scriptures for doctrine because without the guidance of divine revelation "blind reason, in matters pertaining to God, gropes

96

about" in soul destroying error and delusion (SA-III, III 18). It was by the light of God's Word that "the doctrine concerning the chief articles of our Christian religion [was] explained and purified again" which for centuries "had been horribly obscured by human teachings and ordinances" (FC SD, Preface, 1.). The depth of man's depravity "no reason knows and understands, but . . . it must be learned and believed from the revelation of Scripture" (FC SD I 8; cf. 60); the magnitude of God's grace can be known only when "we truly learn to know Christ, our Redeemer, in the Word of the Gospel" (III 11); concerning the hidden counsels of God "we should accustom ourselves not to speculate" (XI 13), but "adhere to His revealed Word" (XI 55) and carefully distinguish between what is revealed and what is not revealed (XI 52).

"Articles of faith must be judged only from God's Word" (II 8). "The Word of God alone should be and remain the only standard and rule of doctrine" (Comprehensive Summary [Rule and Norm], 9). When controversies occurred among the adherents of the Augsburg Confession about the central and other fundamental articles of faith, the Formula of Concord was produced not only to explain the true meaning of the Augsburg Confession relative to the disputed issues, but above all to examine the conflicting positions and settle the dissensions according to *God's Word* (II 6; III 8; IV 6; VIII 5). The Formula fully subscribes Luther's rule: "The Word of God shall establish articles of faith, and no one else, not even an angel" (SA-II II 15).

Now a basic question emerges that is crucial to a discussion of the topic, "Rule and Norm of Doctrine in the Formula of Concord." The question is this: What does the term "Word of God" mean in the contexts of the Formula that deal with the rule and norm of doctrine?

The term "Word of God" has various referents in the Formula. At least eight times the term "Word of God" refers to the Law (FC SD I 3, 25, 61; II 17; IV 7; VI 3, 20; XI 75). In more than 80 instances it refers to *Gospel* (Ep II 4, 13, 19; XI 6, 12; SD II 2, 5, 19, 26, 36—37, 50, 52, 54, 71, 80, 89—90; III 11, 59; IV 37; V 19; VII 62; X 10; XI 10, 21, 34, 39, 41—43, 59, 69, 78, 88,

91; XII 7, 16; et al.). In at least a dozen places the term refers to the words of institution of the sacraments (Ep VII 13; SD VII 1, 9, 20—27, 32, 39, 74, 96, 102, 108, 112, 128). In still other contexts the term "Word of God" refers to the Second Person of the God head (VIII 75), the Catechism (Ep XI 22), Sermons (Ep II 4; SD II 50, 55, 71, 89—90; VIII 94; XI 39, 65, 76), the Old Testament (XI 64), revelations to the patriarchs (VII 46), and divine communications to Pharaoh (XI 83).

While the term "Word of God" has several meanings in the Formula, one thing is perfectly clear. Whenever the Formula refers to the Word of God that is the rule and norm of doctrine it means the Holy Scriptures, the prophetic and apostolic writings of the Old and New Testaments in toto. *Scriptura* in *sola Scriptura* is *tota Scriptura*.

This can be documented with more than 50 references in the Formula. In the interest of brevity only the main arguments will be presented here.

1. There are passages in the Formula that expressly declare that the *Scriptures* (and Scriptures are by definition *writings)* of both Testaments are the rule and norm of doctrine. "We believe, teach, and confess that the sole rule and standard according to which all dogmas together with [all] teachers should be estimated and judged are the prophetic and apostolic *Scriptures* of the Old and of the New Testament alone" (Ep, Summary Content, 1). "The *Holy Scriptures* alone remain the only judge, rule, and standard, according to which, as the only test-stone, all dogmas shall and must be discerned and judged, as to whether they are good or evil, right or wrong" (Ep, Summary Content, 7). This *sola Scriptura* principle is demonstrated in the many instances where such phrases as "the Scriptures testify," "the Scriptures inculcate," and the "Scriptures teach" occur (SD 1 34, 43, 45—46; II 87; III 30; VIII 50—51, 53, 55, 58; XI 2—3, 12, 32). The *sola Scriptura* principle is affirmed also by the frequent repetition of the motto, "It is written" (SD III 20, 57; VI 9; VIII 6; X 8; XI 7).

2. Additional evidence that in the Formula the Word of God that is normative for doctrine is the Sacred Scriptures lies in the fact that the terms "Word of God" and "Holy Scriptures"

98

are used interchangeably in the contexts that discuss the rule and standard by which teachers and teachings are to be judged. The SD says: "The *Word of God* alone should be and remain the only standard and rule of doctrine" (Comprehensive Summary [Rule and Norm], 9). The corresponding paragraph in the Ep says: "*Holy Scriptures* alone remain the only judge, rule, and standard" (Summary Content, 7).

3. A factor that is significant is that very often when the German text reads "God's Word" the Latin translation of the Formula renders it "Sacra Scriptura" or "sacrae litterae." Already in the passage of the SD, Comprehensive Summary [Rule and Norm], 9, in which German text says "God's Word" the Latin text says "sacrae litterae." This occurs regularly throughout the entire Formula. Compare the German and Latin texts in the following instances: SD, Preface, 3; Comprehensive summary [Rule and Norm], 3, 9; II 28; IV 35; VII 107; 43. On at least two occasions when the German text reads "Holy Scripture" the Latin translates "Word of God" (Comprehensive Summary [Rule and Norm], 17; VIII 60). and that the terms "Word of God" and "Holy Scriptures" were not first used interchangeably in the period when the Formula was written, but already in the earlier Symbols, is established by comparing the German and Latin texts of the AC XVIII 35; Ap XXIII 4; SA-II II 14.

4. Finally, in two instances where the Formula says that it will substantiate its position from *God's Word* it proceeds to quote passages of the *Holy Scriptures* (SD II 8-10, 48—51).

The Formula maintains that the Scriptures are the rule and norm of doctrine because it regards the Scriptures as God's Word. In addition to the evidence submitted above, there are other statements that need to be considered. SD, Comprehensive Summary [Rule and Norm], section 16, speaks of God's Word of the prophetic and apostolic Scriptures; section 9 clearly distinguishes between the Scriptures and the writings of men, thereby necessarily implying that the writings that are normative for doctrine are not human writings; the Scriptures are called "holy, *divine* Scriptures" (SD II: 45); errors are rejected because they are contrary "to God's Word, the doctrine of the prophets and apostles, and our Christian faith" (SD III 59), "contrary to the pure Word of God, the Scriptures of the holy prophets and apostles, and our Christian faith and confession" (SD, VIII 96). The Preface to the Book of Concord refers to the norm that would regulate the doctrine taught in Lutheran lands, territories, schools, and churches as "the Holy Scriptures *of God."*[3]

The authors of the Formula purposed in their confession to adhere to the Augsburg Confession "in accordance with the pure, *infallible,* and unalterable Word of God" (Tappert, p. 8). They hoped that their confession would lead others to "turn to the *infallible* truth of the divine Word."[4] In these contexts "Word of God" refers to the *Scriptures* on which all the articles of the Formula are founded, including the articles on Original Sin, Free will, and Third Use of Law, and therefore cannot be arbitrarily limited to the Gospel content of the prophetic and apostolic writings. These references to the infallible Word must therefore be understood as affirmations of the infallibility of the Scriptures. In determining the meaning of the term "infallible" the Apology of the Augsburg Confession, which the Formula subscribes without reservation, must be consulted. Ap XXIV 95 clearly says that Lutherans appeal to the Scriptures in support of their doctrine and not to the fathers, since the fathers were men who could err and be deceived. The implication is inescapable. The Scriptures are not the writings of men who could err and be deceived. The infallible Word that is rule and norm for the Formula is the *Scriptures,* in which are not found the dissimilarities, contradictions, and errors that sometimes occur in the writings of the fathers.

The Formula regards the *Scriptures* as the inerrant Word of God, which is rule and norm of doctrine. The Formula therefore bases its doctrine on "the foundation of the Scriptures" (SD XI 3 Triglot), believes and teaches "according to the Scriptures" (SD VIII 60) rejects errors because they "are contrary to the Scriptures" (SD I 44) or are "without any ground in the Holy Scriptures" (SD VIII 28).

SD VIII 53 makes it very clear that the Formula regards the Scriptures as the *absolute* norm of Doctrine from which there is no appeal. "Now, everything for which we have in this instance clear, certain testimonies in the Scriptures, we must simply believe, and in no way argue against it." When the Formula calls the Scriptures the sole and only *judge* of doctrine it at the same time rejects all approaches to the Scriptures that reduce them to mere witnesses or even to the role of defendant whose truthfulness and authority must be vindicated by some other criterion.

Even when the Formula endorses the earlier Lutheran Confessions it does this only because these symbols are in full agreement with the Scriptures. "We confess also the First, Unaltered Augsburg Confession as our symbol for this time, not because it was composed by our theologians, but because it has been taken from God's Word and is founded firmly and well therein . . . . We unanimously confess [the Apology] also, because not only is the said Augsburg Confession explained as much as is necessary and guarded . . . , but also proven . . . by clear, irrefutable testimonies of Holy Scripture" (SD, Comprehensive Summary [Rule and Norm], "The rule is to be that nobody's power or authority is to avail more than the Word of God" (SD X 21).

Since no other authority is to avail more than God's Word, the Formula in its Solid Declaration says: "No one should assume lordship or authority over the church, nor burden the church with traditions" (X 21).[5] Not even "the consensus of . . . many nations" (X 22) is definitive for church doctrine and practice, but the Scriptures alone. Human reason also is rejected as an authority in matters that pertain to God and spiritual things. "Man's reason . . . is so ignorant, blind, and perverse that when even the most gifted and the most educated people on earth read or hear the Gospel of the Son of God and the promise of eternal salvation, they cannot by their own powers perceive this, comprehend it, understand it, or believe and accept it as truth" (II 9). All the arguments of human reason against the true persence of Christ's body and blood in the Lord's Supper are overthrown and refuted by the testimony of Scripture (VII 106). "Nor dare we permit any objection or human contradiction, spun out of human reason, to turn us away from these words [of Scripture], no matter how appealing our reason may find it" (VII 45). Concerning eternal

101

election "we should not pass judgment on the basis of our reason" but "we must heed the revealed will of God" (XI 26). We must not pry presumptuously into the mystery of the personal union of the two natures in Christ with human reason, but take our intellect captive to obey Christ (VIII 96) and believe the Scriptures (VIII 53, 60). The doctrine that man has no free will in spiritual matters is contrary to proud reason and philosophy (II 8); reason and philosophy cannot lead to a right understanding and give a correct definition of original sin, for Scripture alone can do this (I 60).

Because the Formula based doctrine on the inerrant, objective norm of "divinely delivered truth" (Preface to the Book of Concord, Latin text),[6] its authors could refer to it as a "true norm and declaration of pure doctrine" (Preface to the Book of Concord, Latin text),[7] as the "simple, unchanging, constant truth" (FC SD, Comprehensive Summary [Rule and Norm], 20), and as "an altogether uncolored declaration of pure truth" (Preface to the Book of Concord, Latin text).[8] The Formula, therefore, is called a "norm" (Preface to the Book of Concord)[9] by which "all other writings are to be approved and accepted, judged and regulated" (FC SD, Comprehensive Summary [Rule and Norm], 10), which "is called and also is [Latin text: 'both is called and forever will be']" the confession of all Lutherans (Preface to the Book of Concord),[10] and which "must [or should; Ger.: *solle;* Latin: *debeat*] remain the unanimous understanding and judgment of our churches" regarding the articles treated (FC SD, Comprehensive Summary [Rule and Norm], 16).[11]

102

Article I
The Formula of Concord

ORIGINAL SIN

R. Klann

*T*he theme of Article I is the effect of original sin on the relationship God intended to have with man according to the terms of His creation. The confessors of the Formula of Concord did not intend to offer a comprehensive description of the origin and effect of evil in this world. Hence the topic is not the question, "Why does God permit evil and the consequences of evil to exist in the world?" Such an approach actually includes the hidden agenda of the inquirer to make himself the judge of God and to reduce God the Creator to the status of a defendant charged with a universal crime. That would be a demonic reversal of roles.

The Christian church has always derived its singular understanding of sin and its origin and consequences from the Scriptures. Biblical teaching on sin functions as a correlative to the Biblical teaching on salvation, because man would not need salvation if he had not fallen into sin.

This Biblical understanding of sin is necessary for

Christians in order to perceive the greatness of their salvation.

Repentance means contrition and faith, according to the Scriptures. No one will be sorry for his sins, unless he understands the meaning of sin. But the meaning of sin, according to the Scriptures, is not comprehended merely by an effort of the mind. As he is now constituted, fallen man is unable to understand himself objectively. Only the Holy Spirit is able to convict man of sin, of righteousness, and of judgment (John 16:8). When it occurs, the event is comparable to a new spiritual vision, the result of a new spiritual life or spiritual birth.

A study of the Biblical doctrine of original sin must therefore be undertaken in the firm confidence that the teachings of the Scriptures are God's own revelation regarding man's sin as well as His judgment of sin. Such a study rejects the focus of the mystic, of neurotic or egocentric introspection of a lost past, the focus of scientific analysis, regardless of the degree of objectivity claimed for it. The point here is not how man understands himself, but what man is in the judgment of God. Unbelievers are necessarily excluded from such an understanding (1 Cor. 2:14).

Article I treats the question of the dimension of the fall of man. Is man's fall total or does he retain some spiritual capability that enables him, in however slight a measure, to make a contribution or a determination regarding his spiritual relationship to God?

Original sin became an extremely important doctrine in Luther's debates with the theologians of the medieval church as well as among some theologians of the Reformation. The reason for this development is the fact that the Biblical doctrine of salvation will be distorted unless it is taught in tandem with the Biblical doctrine of man. This is necessary for the proper Scriptural understanding of the Christian teaching of God the Creator, Judge, and Savior.

When someone asked our Lord Jesus Christ, "What good deed must I do, to have eternal life?" he was given the answer, "Keep the commandments" (Matt. 19:16-17 (RSV). Since no man can do that, according to the Scriptures, the Savior is necessary. Leaning on their own interpretation of terms like

104

"fallen man" or "lost sinner", some Christian theologians assumed a picture of man's condition that permitted them to assume that the sinner had retained some spiritual abilities to contribute to his own rescue. Article I on Original Sin totally rejects the possibility of the smallest contribution by the sinner. Original sin is a teaching that declares fallen man, the sinner, to be spiritually dead. A denial of this teaching withholds from God *all* credit and glory for man's salvation by diminishing the severity of God's judgment, the atoning work of Jesus Christ, and the regenerative work of the Holy Spirit.

The Christian trusts in the promise of God's mercy because he also believes the threat of God's judgment. Fear, love, and trust in God are the means of Christian perception and action.

A Question of Man's Ability to Cooperate with God

The years of the Interims had shaken the confessional foundations of the Lutheran churches. In southern Germany more than 400 pastors had been driven from their parishes. While the churches in northern Germany were not similarly devastated, the theological confusion caused by Philipp Melanchthon and his followers was not soon removed.[1] A fundamental issue was the doctrine of man, which has a very long history.

Since the time of Pelagius' flight to Carthage in 409 A.D., the Western church, under leadership of Augustine, Bishop of Hippo, had wrestled with the question of what capacities a human being possessed for the attainment of his own salvation. Pelagius had denied original sin, and thereby also questioned the necessity of Christ's redemptive work. His governing theological thought was the omnipresence of God's justice. When seen from this perspective, Pelagius concluded, God could not possibly require man to do the impossible. Such a rational or philosophical concept of the will or disposition of God made the Biblical doctrine of sin irrelevant. Pelagius believed that Christ had redeemed mankind from the habit of sinning, by which he meant and said that man could thus be saved by faith alone. But this faith was directed to the expectation of being rewarded for his good works, and not the person and work of Jesus Christ.

Pelagius' denial of original sin, and therefore of sin in the Biblical sense, led to an individualistic moralism, an exclusive concern for a righteous self-discipline, and indifference to the means of grace. The direct implications of Pelagius' teaching were a reduction of the Christian faith to the level of an ethical humanism. Since his time, the Christian church has never ceased to be afflicted with teachers who advocated a humanistic or philosophical view of man, assigning to fallen man spiritual and ethical abilities whereby he could work out his own salvation or at least make some contribution to its attainment.

It was the achievement of Aurelius Augustinus, then Bishop of Hippo in North Africa, to provide the effective Biblical evidence and theological formulations for the repudiation of this heresy in the West. In its proper or essential sense, so Augustine taught, sin is the basically hostile structure of man's will against God. It shows itself in *superbia* (pride, the overweening arrogance of the creature who wants to be like God) and *amor sui* (love of self) which is the rejection of God as the highest good. *Concupiscentia* (ardent desire, like sexual love) for the objects whereby fallen man expects to achieve self-fulfillment. Since man is a creation of God, sin always entails guilt deserving God's inevitable judgment.[2]

After Augustine, the theologians of the Western church diminished considerably the content of his teaching on original sin and original guilt. Anselm of Canterbury denied the imputation of Adam's guilt to his descendants; Abelard would concede no more than inherited punishment; Duns Scotus and his followers thought of original sin and guilt as the loss of the gift of original creation, and not as the corruption of the human nature, nor as genuine sin, but as a condition in which a human being becomes a sinner when a sinful action is willingly undertaken. Thomas Aquinas and his followers were much closer to the position of Augustine: original sin was concupiscence in the material sense (content), and showed itself in its formal sense as the loss of original righteousness.

Session VI of the Council of Trent gave the Roman Catholic dogma an original sin its final form: Adam lost his original holiness and righteousness by his disobedience, which placed him under the wrath of God and the dominion of death and Satan. As a consequence, the inclination of Adam toward evil is conveyed to his descendants by propagation. The original sin of Adam is therefore the sin of each of his descendants. Since this sin is not a matter of mere imitation, but an inherited condition, the consequences of sin are removed only by the death of Christ, whose merits are applied to the sinner in baptism. Not only does baptism convey the forgiveness of original sin, but actually removes it. The remaining concupiscence is not actual sin, but merely inflammable material *(fomes),* which inclines the Christian toward sin. The Council of Trent met intermittently from 1545—63. Its dogmatic formulations precede those of the Formula of Concord by as much as 30 years.

Luther's Teachings

In the Smalcald Articles (III I) Luther states his summary position about sin from the Biblically theocentric perspective:

> Here we must confess what St. Paul says in Rom. 5:12, namely, that sin had its origin in one man, Adam, through whose disobedience all men were made sinners and became subject to death and the devil. This is called original sin, or the root sin.
>
> The fruits of this sin are all the subsequent evil deeds which are forbidden in the Ten Commandments, such as unbelief, false belief, idolatry, being without the fear of God, presumption, despair, blindness—in short, ignorance or disregard of God—and then also lying, swearing by God's name, failure to pray and call upon God, neglect of God's Word, disobedience to parents, murder, unchastity, theft, deceit, etc.
>
> This hereditary sin is so deep a corruption of nature that reason cannot understand it. It must be believed because of the revelation in the Scriptures (Ps. 51:5; Rom. 5:12 ff.; Exod. 33:20; Gen. 3:6 ff.). What the scholastic theologians taught concerning this article is therefore nothing but error and stupidity, namely,

1. That after the fall of Adam the natural powers of man remained whole and uncorrupted, and that man by nature possesses a right understanding and a good will, as the philosophers teach.

2. Again, that man has a free will, either to do good and refrain from evil or to refrain from good and do evil.

3. Again, the man is able by his natural powers to observe and keep all the commandments of God.

4. Again, that man is able by his natural powers to love God above all things and his neighbor as himself.

5. Again, if man does what he can, God is certain to grant him His grace.

6. Again, when a man goes to the sacrament there is no need of a good intention to do what he ought, but it is enough that he does not have an evil intention to commit sin, for such is the goodness of man's nature and such is the power of the Sacrament.

7. That it cannot be proved from the Scriptures that the Holy Spirit and his gifts are necessary for the performance of a good work.

Such and many similar notions have resulted from misunderstanding and ignorance concerning sin and concerning Christ, our Savior. They are thoroughly pagan doctrines, and we cannot tolerate them.[3]

The Cause of Divine Wrath According to Luther.

In his preaching, Luther stressed the chasm of enmity between God and man. Man cannot prevail against God, because he cannot maintain a claim of independence against the Creator (Sermons of 1527 for Ascension Day and Pentecost). This is the proper way of thinking about man theologically. In his introduction to Ps. 51 Luther writes that the proper subject of theology is man the lost sinner and the justifying God. Whatever is sought or disputed apart from subject in theology is error. Whatever is discussed in theology in disregard of this central or basic subject is error. Before God, man cannot stand as an independent entity; he is by his fallen nature in a state of total spiritual corruption. The reality of man the sinner before God who is Creator, Judge, and Savior is the basis for Christian theology.

Luther's meaning and intention becomes even clearer when he distinguished Biblical theology from other branches of knowledge which also deal with the question, "What is man?" The philosopher thinks of man as "rational animal"; the jurist deals with man in his capacity as "possessor and lord of his own things"; the physician looks at man according to his health or the lack of it; but "the theologian speaks about man the sinner."

Since ancient times, philosophers demanded with Socrates that man begin with self-knowledge—"know thyself." The ignorance admitted by Socrates about himself applies to every man because the demand cannot be fulfilled. At the same time, having man as rational animal in the center of their thinking, they do not think of man in the presence of God. St. Augustine made the methodological shift in the history of Christian thought from the Hellenistic demand for self-knowledge as the point of departure *(terminus a quo)* to the first goal of knowledge *(terminus ad quem)* for the theologian. The argument of Augustine, that in his research for self-knowledge man would find the truth about himself in his self-confession as sinner, would have been incomprehensible to the Greek philosopher. It remains incomprehensible to the modern philosopher.

Luther did not imitate Augustine's theological-apologetic method. He recognized fully, as he made it plain in his writing against Erasmus *(The Bondage of the Will)*, that he will not think of man philosophically, man-as-he-is-in-the-world or phenomenologically, but as man-as-he-is-before-god.[4] Man cannot know or understand himself at all, according to divine revelation, except "in some measure" pertaining to the material things of this world.

Luther's exposition of Genesis 3 is a marvelously perceptive discussion of the fall of man into sin.[5] Before his fall, man's "reason or intellect was sound, so that what God wanted or said, man also wanted, believed, and understood the same thing. The knowledge of all the other creatures necessarily followed this knowledge; for where the knowledge of God is perfect, there also the knowledge of the other things that are under God is necessarily perfect." (p. 141). But now after the fall of man, Luther continues (p. 143), "let us maintain that reason in men is most hostile to God, and that the respectable will is most opposed to the will of God."

The first sin totally corrupted man's will and intellect. But how did this come about? After all, for Luther the story of the fall of man was no saga or mythical discourse but a "historical event of which Moses gives us an account in this present chapter" (p. 144). Luther interprets the story as a turning away from or as a fall from the grace of God, and points to the basic elements of the story. God had given His clear and express command to Adam not to eat of the tree of the knowledge of good and of evil: death will be the consequence of his trespass.

But Satan takes note of the apparent incongruity between the gravity of the threat of punishment and the apparent insignificance of the forbidden trespass. An inquiry directed through the serpent to the woman appeared to be a request for further information regarding the dimensions of the divine prohibition. Actually, the serpent's question was calculated to elicit a contradiction from Eve. Luther's comment continues:

> The beginning is rather favorable: she makes a distinction between the remaining trees and this one, and she quotes God's command. But she begins to waver when she comes to the mention of the punishment. She does not mention the punishment as God had stated it. He had simply stated (Gen. 2:17): 'On whatever day you will eat from it, you will surely die.' Out of this absolute statement she herself makes one that is not absolute when she adds: 'Lest perchance we shall die.'
>
> This is a striking flaw, and one that must not be overlooked; for it shows that she has turned from faith to unbelief. For just as a promise demands faith, so a threat also demands faith. Eve should have main-

tained: 'If I eat, I shall surely die.' On this faith Satan makes such inroads with his crafty speech that Eve adds the little word 'perchance.' She had been persuaded by the devil that God was not so cruel as to kill them for eating the fruit. To this extent Eve's heart was now poisoned with Satan's venom.

For this reason our text here, too, has been poorly translated. It reads as though Eve were quoting her own words; actually, she is quoting God's words, and on her own she is adding to God's Word the little word 'perchance.' And so the deceit of the lying spirit met with success. What he sought to achieve above all—to lead Eve away from the Word and faith—this he has now achieved to the extent that Eve distorts the Word of God; that is, to use Paul's language, he has turned her away from the divine will, so that she goes after Satan (1 Tim. 5:15). But it is the beginning of one's ruin to turn away from God and to turn to Satan, that is, not to remain constant in the Word and in faith. When Satan sees these beginnings he now exerts himself with his utmost power, as though against a leaning wall, in order to overwhelm her altogether.[6]

At this point the serpent unreservedly contradicts God's original threat, "On whatever day you will eat of it, you will surely die." Satan provocatively interprets the threat as a prohibition of interest only to God who selfishly seeks to keep man from knowing good and evil and thereby becoming like God. Sin is the rejection of God's will for man, or of His created order. Desire and reason acting together provide the motivating power toward the goal of achieving independence, the absolute dominion over the life received as a gift from the Creator.

The story continues to make the point that revolt against God does not depose or abolish the Creator, who demands of man the sinner to give God an accounting. The Apology (II 9) contrasts original sin with original righteousness: "To be able to love God above all things by one's own power and to obey His commandments, what else is this but to have original righteousness?" Again (II 17, 18):

So original righteousness was intended to involve not only a balanced physical constitution, but these gifts as well: a surer knowledge of God, fear of God, trust in God, or at least the inclination and power to do these things. This the Scripture shows when it says that man was created in the image of God and after His likeness (Gen. 1:27). What else is this than that a wisdom and righteousness was implanted in man that would grasp God and reflect Him, that is, that man received gifts like the knowledge of God, fear of God, and trust in God?

Original Sin According to the Lutheran Confession

The Lutheran Confessions reflect a consistently clear understanding of the meaning of sin in terms of original sin. As a consequence of the fall of man into sin, the human nature has lost "the gift and capacity to produce the fear and trust of God"; that is "the continual inclination of nature" (Ap II 3). The reference here is to the basic description of human existence presented in the Augsburg Confession (II 1—2):

It is also taught among us that since the fall of Adam and all men who are born according to the course of nature are conceived and born in sin. That is, all men are full of evil lust and inclinations from their mothers' wombs and are unable by nature to have true fear of God and true faith in God. Moreover, this inborn sickness and hereditary sin is truly sin and condemns to the eternal wrath of God all those who are not born again through Baptism and the Holy Spirit.

The continuity of the original sin of man in all descendants of the first man and woman is far more than a mere biological phenomenon. To be sure, the loss of the likeness of God had instant biological consequences that culminate in the threat and sentence of death (Gen. 2:17 and 3:19). But original sin controls the entire structure of human existence and demonstrates its presence in the terrors of conscience, when the voice or word of

112

God is heard, just as Adam confessed his awareness of terror after his sin (Gen. 3:10).[7]

These terrors of conscience are the point where fallen man meets his Creator in the destroying thunderbolt and crushing hammer of His Law and will, so that "Rom. 3:19, 20, the whole world may be held accountable to God, for no human being will be justified in His sight'" (SA-III III 1—2). "For the Law works wrath; it only accuses; it only terrifies consciences" (Ap IV 257). In this confrontation fallen man today, like Adam before him, knows himself to be "a lost and condemned creature" (SC II 4). A fuller statement appears in the Formula of Concord (SD I 6):

> Dr. Luther calls this sin "nature-sin" or "person-sin" in order to indicate that even though a man were to think no evil, speak no evil, or do no evil—which after the Fall of our first parents is of course impossible for human nature in this life—nevertheless man's nature and person would still be sinful. This means that in the sight of God original sin, like a spiritual leprosy, has thoroughly and entirely poisoned and corrupted human nature. On account of this corruption and because of the fall of the first man, our nature or person is under the accusation and condemnation of the law of God, so that we are "by nature the children of wrath," of death, and of damnation unless we are redeemed from this state through Christ's merit.

Against the humanist view of man, the confessors write, "This damage is so unspeakable that it may not be recognized by a rational process, but only from God's Word" (FC Ep I 9). It is a position repugnant both to renaissance and modern humanist thought. As Paul argued in 2 Cor. 3:15-17 (RSV), the "veil" that prevents fallen man even to sense his condition before God is his false opinion about himself (Ap IV 133—134). The "magnitude of sin" (Ap IV 135, Latin text) cannot be perceived by means of ethical, philosophical, psychoanalytical, biological, or any other socalled scientific method of inquiry. By its deceiving consequences, sin has so blinded the understanding and perverted the will of fallen man that he cannot know the meaning of God's judgment upon him (Rom. 1:18-24).

The Christian doctrine of sin is an article of faith. The Spirit of God must liberate fallen man from the bondage of his own false opinions regarding himself: "But this veil is removed from us, and this error taken away, when God shows us our uncleaness, and the greatness of our sin" (Ap IV 135).

"Unbelief is a root and fountainhead of all culpable sin" (FC SD V 17). God opposes the unbelief or rebellion of fallen man by the condemnation of the Law. Quoting Luther, the Formula of Concord (SD V 12) reads: "Everything that preaches about our sin and the wrath of God, no matter how or when it happens, is the proclamation of the Law. . . . In fact, where is there a more earnest and terrible revelation and preaching of God's wrath over sin than the passion and death of Christ, His own Son?"

The condemnation of the Law addresses the sin and guilt of man, which always has its roots in the original unbelief of man. The consequence of this encounter is the sinner's terrors of conscience, which claim him entirely and seize him for judgment. FC SD I 8—9:

> Thirdly, reason does not know and understand the true nature of this inherited damage. As the Smalcald Articles point out, it is something that has to be learned and believed from the revelation of the Scriptures. The Apology summarizes the matter under these heads:
> 1. That this inherited damage is the reason why all of us, because of the disobedience of Adam and Eve, are in God's disfavor, and are children of wrath by nature, as St. Paul says (Rom. 5:12).

Terrors of conscience are the realities of man's existence in his confrontation of judgment and death beyond the capacity of his damaged reason. Beyond the merely obvious meaning of physical death, the awareness of the coming divine judgment on sin, from which there is no escape, the imminence of eternal death—that, and not thoughts about death as mere extinction of physical life, is the cause of the sinner's terrors of conscience.

The issue demands a depth of perception that fallen man in his spiritual blindness does not have. He will not see, unless his eyes are opened, that the verdict of God has compressed his entire existence into a dimensionless point. Here Luther spoke of *angustia (Angst),* the sense of being caught and threatened with death. But this is not the end. A spiritual perception of the meaning of original sin opens the vision for the sinner that he is caught and subjected to the power of the devil's kingdom. (FC SD I 13)

Original sin is the name for the teaching that the human nature in its entirety is controlled by unbelief, disobedience, and hostility to God unexceptionally in all respects. This is the spiritual death of the creature and entails all the corruptions of active or specific sins in life.

A Sequence of Events

"On Original sin" is listed as the first of the 12 topics comprising the Formula of Concord. The historical sequence of the doctrinal controversies following the military defeat of the Lutheran territories must rank the Adiaphoristic Controversy first. In began in 1548 as a result of the imposition of Roman liturgy on Lutheran congregations. As noted before, Melanchthon and his friends defended the Leipzig Interim on the supposition that liturgical changes of the kind imposed by the Interim did not not entail doctrinal changes. A group of ardently faithful students of Luther opposed the Interim as offensive to the Christian faith because false doctrines were being imposed on the evangelical churches under the pretense that only ceremonies were being changed. The leader of these staunch defenders of Luther's doctrine was Matthias Flacius Illyricus (1520—75), possessed of a magnificent education, a former protégé of Luther, and professor of Hebrew at Wittenberg University in 1544.[8] His theological axiom, which genuine Lutherans will defend at all times, succinctly stated the main point: "Nothing is an adiaphoron in case of confession and offense." But the authors of the Formula of Concord treated the adiaphoristic issues near the end of the Formula, in Article X.

The reason for such an arrangement was clear to them 30 years after the controversy had started: the essential issues were triangular (1) Man the sinner, (2) the person and work of Jesus Christ, (3) the application of salvation to man. Accordingly, this article became the first of the series.

But the incident that led to a profoundly serious controversy about the nature of fallen man began with a previous dispute between Victorin Strigel and Matthias Flacius. In 1560 all parties agreed to attempt a settlement by means of a public disputation or debate in the manner of the universities at that time. The procedure was that both parties would set up theses for debate or discussion on the basis of clear Scripture texts. In order to minimize the implications of his synergistic position, that man had the ability to contribute something to his own conversion, Strigel argued that original sin was a mere accident, with the implication that fallen man had not totally lost his original spiritual capacities. Against this, Flacius replied that original sin was not so insignificant as all that. On the contrary, in fallen man original sin had become the substance of his nature. Flacius had meant by that term to point to the total devastation of the spiritual capacity of man as the immediate consequence of Adam's disobedience (Gen. 2:17). Unfortunately, Flacius' good theological intention was soon displaced by academic pride. Taken literally, Flacius' expression, that original sin was now the substance of man, placed him among the Manichaeans. Despite the entreaties of his friends, he was too stubborn to correct himself. Strigel and his friends took advantage of Flacius' blunder by publicizing his error, an action that provoked Flacius to defend his untenable position as though it had been Luther's. The outcome was a personal tragedy for both Flacius and Strigel: both were banished; Strigel died in 1569 in Heidelberg as a Reformed professor; Flacius wandered from place to place until he finally died in Frankfurt in 1575.

The Point of the Initial Error

The error of Flacius began with a linguistic excess. He failed to analyze and expose Strigel's ambiguous use of the term

116

"accident," and thereby illustrated the imprudence of debating an issue on one's opponent's terms. For Strigel, "accident" meant in this context that after the fall man retained the capacity to assent to his own conversion. Initially, Flacius meant to point to the totality of man's original fall which stripped him of all of his concreated spiritual endowments, with the result that fallen man is spiritually dead in trespasses and sin. But the term "substance," while a seemingly convenient opposite to "accident," as Strigel used the term, was nonetheless an erroneous description of the condition of man after his fall. To identify the substance or nature of man with original sin, as Flacius and his followers had done, would assume sin to be a substance, with the consequence that the polarities of sin and righteousness would necessarily become substantialized on the order of the Manichaean notion that evil is a material reality.

The orthodox Christian and Lutheran position maintains the distinction between God's created work—man—and the corruption of man. Another way of stating the matter would be to say that sin and righteousness are attributes of the substance, nature, or essence of man. For this reason also the "other party" of theologians correctly

> maintained that original sin is something in man's nature, in his body, soul, and all his powers, and that it is an abominable, deep, and inexpressible corruption thereof, in the sense that man lacks the righteousness in which he was originally created, that in spiritual matters he is dead to that which is good and is turned to everything evil, and that, because of this corruption and this inborn sin which inheres in his nature, all actual sins flow out of his heart (FC SD I 2).

The Truth About Original Sin

The confessors are explicit in affirming that the source and root of all sins is the corrupted nature of fallen man. There can be no "actual sins" or trespasses without the all-pervasive original sin. Its core is unbelief active in disobedience to the will of God and hatred of all that God is and does. Now fallen man continually repeats in all of his sinning what he did when he

117

first sinned: he converts the truth of God into a lie (Rom. 1:25). The story of the fall (Gen. 3) turns upon this primal unbelief and its consequent actions.

Such an understanding of original sin necessarily elevates this article of faith to a level of highest importance. The Biblical doctrine of man is central to the proper understanding of the Christian faith, because the redemption of the sinner stands revealed as a superior correlative to his fall (Rom. 5). For this reason the confessors continue (I 3):

> This controversy concerning original sin is not a useless contention about words. On the contrary, when it is presented clearly from and according to the Word of God and is purged of all Pelagian and Manichaean errors, then (as the Apology declares) we are led to understand better and to magnify more fully Christ's benefits, His precious merits, and the Holy Spirit's gracious activity. Furthermore, we are extolling God's honor properly when we carefully distinguish His work and creation in man from the devil's work, the corruption of the human nature.

The human nature of fallen man is still human. But sin has so entirely corrupted it that the human being is spiritually dead in the moment of his conception (Ps. 51:5). This means far more than mere "alienation" from God. Man and God have become mortal enemies in a warfare necessarily ending in the destruction of the creature on the day of doom. "Dead through . . . trespasses and sins . . . by nature children of wrath, like the rest of mankind" (Eph. 2:1, 3)—an accurate description of the condition of man in consequence of the command and threat of God before man's fall (Gen. 2:17). The first disobedience became the perpetual state of rebellion of all human beings subsequently and functions both as everyman's accusation and condemnation.

Scripture is cited because fallen man does not have the spiritual resources, which were utterly devastated by his fall, to understand the damage he has suffered. Reason, understood as the sum of man's perceptive capabilities, can only produce the fear of a personal doom (Gen. 3:10), without conveying to man the meaning of his condition and fatal predicament. Even when the Scriptures reveal the enormity of sin to man, the terrors of his soul at the prospect of God's certain judgment convey not understanding but confusion and shame. Beginning with the first sin, the original sin, the human nature lost its concreated righteousness and holiness and suffered the total corruption of its natural reason and physical powers. This deprivation has been part of Christian teaching since the beginning (John 3:6; Rom. 5:12). "All men are full of evil lust and inclinations from their mothers' wombs and are unable by nature to have true fear of God and true faith in God" (AC II 1, German text). But the Formula of Concord (SD I 11—12) carefully and distinctively offers a compressed description:

> Original sin in human nature is not only a total lack of good in spiritual, divine things, but . . . at the same time it replaces the lost image of God in man with a deep, wicked, abominable, bottomless, inscrutable, and inexpressible corruption of his entire nature in all its powers, especially of the highest and foremost powers of the soul in mind, heart, and will. As a result, since the Fall man inherits an inborn wicked stamp, an interior uncleaness of the heart and evil desires and inclinations. By nature everyone of us inherits from Adam a heart, sensation, and mind-set which, in its highest powers and the light of reason, is by nature diametrically opposed to God and His highest commands and is actually enmity against God, especially in divine and spiritual matters. True, in natural and external things which are subject to reason man still possesses a measure of reason, power, and ability, although greatly weakened since the inherited malady has so poisoned and tainted them that they amount to nothing in the sight of God.

Care must be taken to repeat the confessional emphasis that God is not the cause or author of sin. His integrity is such that He never is, nor can be in contradiction with Himself at any point whatsoever. All sin is sin against God. Still, the ultimate source of sin against God is not explained. Conforming to their own Scriptural principle, *sola Scriptura*—the Scriptures alone as the source and norm of Christian truth—the confessors of the Book of Concord limit their statement to the Biblical description: "The devil has sinned from the beginning" (1 John 3:8 RSV; cf. Rom. 5:12). The cause and process of sin are not even mentioned beyond those Biblical references.

Like a victim of leprosy and blindness from birth, unable to compare his condition to a perfectly healthy person, and therefore bereft of the ability to understand what is happening to him unless a skilled physician informs him of his afflictions, so every human being is blind and insensitive to the devastations of original sin. God only can fully describe fallen man's condition. For this reason, the confessors repeat in summary form (FC SD I 13 14) what Christians before them have confessed on the basis of the Scriptures:

> The punishment and penalty of original sin which God imposes upon Adam's children and upon original sin is death, eternal damnation, together with other bodily, spiritual, temporal, and eternal misery, the tyranny and dominion of the devil, so that human nature is subject to the devil's dominion, abandoned to his power, and held captive in his servitude. He misleads many influential and wise men of the world with terrible errors and heresies, strikes them with other kinds of blindness, and drives them headlong into all sorts of vice.

> This inherited damage is so great and terrible that in baptized believers it can be covered up and forgiven before God only for the Lord Christ's sake. Likewise, only the Holy Spirit's regeneration and renovation can heal man's nature, which original sin has perverted and corrupted. Of course, this process is only begun in this life, not to be completed until the life yonder.

Since the cause of sin is not God, who creates and preserves nature, but "the will of the wicked, that is, of the devil and ungodly men" (AC XIX), the Christian doctrine of original sin provides a general and comprehensive interpretation for all issues arising from the fallen human condition. Subjected to a critique based on the Biblical teaching of original sin, all political theories, economic plans, recommendations for social peace, all scientific and artistic endeavors exhibiting man's aspirations toward self-perfection must end in failure. There can be no progress out of the fallen state of man; he lives in the world without God and without hope (cf. Eph. 2:12); his thoughts and works have no enduring value, and his end on earth means his return to the dust from which he was taken. But the horrible calamity of the fallen human conditions is sharpened by the fact that man does not even understand his condition and its implications as the consequences of his creaturely rebellion against God.

No one but God can rescue fallen man. The confessors write from the knowledge of the Gospel that God had done so when He assumed the human nature in the person of Jesus Christ, who, as the "second Adam," reversed the human condition (cf. Rom. 5).

FREE WILL, OR HUMAN POWERS

Eugene F. Klug

$\mathcal{T}$he question of the human will and its freedom is an old one, at least as old as man himself. Involved are questions of moral choices, of God's providential rule, and the contingency of human actions or decisions, not to mention human responsibility, under and before God.

Philosophical opinion runs the gamut between extreme fatalistic determinism, which denies all freedom to man, and logical positivism and idealism, which posit man's total freedom as lord over his own destiny. Neither is true, and life's experience confirms that this is so.

The formulators of the Formula of Concord began at the right place when they asked, *Which* man? Are we talking about man before the fall, after the fall, after regeneration, after translation into heaven? They narrowed the field to the obvious focus, man after the fall as he now is by nature. What freedom does *that* man have?

But even then one has to divide the field, or the question, for the sake of clarity. Are we talking of temporal affairs, the mundane realm over which God placed man in dominion, the secular realm, or are we referring to the realm of spiritual matters? With good reason the Formula singles out the latter, because this was the "hinge," as Luther wrote against Erasmus, "on which our discussion turns," namely, "what ability 'free-will' has," that is, in things spiritual. "How it stands related to the grace of God," this is the crucial question, said Luther.[1] In achieving righteousness before God the so-called free-will of man is unable to advance itself even a little, stated Luther, not even "a little imperfect something."[2] But neither Luther nor the Confessions of the Lutheran Church ignored or denied the fact that in matters that are beneath him man continues to have a large measure of freedom, making many choices day in, day out.[3]

First Aspect—In Temporal Matters

Like Luther, the Lutheran Confessions do not minimize the human volitional capacity in life's routine affairs. They spend little time on this, however, becaue it was not contested. The Augsburg Confession, quoting Augustine, notes "that all men have a free will, free, inasmuch as it has the judgment of reason," and that man thus decides of himself "to labor in the field, to eat and drink, to have a friend, to clothe himself, to build a house, to marry a wife, to raise cattle, to learn divers useful arts, or whatsoever good pertains to this life." This the Augsburg Confession terms the "liberty to choose civil righteousness." At the same time it notes that man perversely often chooses to commit the unrighteous or evil act. In the same context it affirms vigorously that the human will "has not power, without the Holy Ghost, to work the righteousness of God, that is spiritual righteousness." (XVIII 4—5, 1, 2, this quotation and those that follow in this chapter are from the Triglot.)

In the Apology of the Augsburg Confession (XVIII 4; Triglot section 70) Melanchthon underscores the same truth, that the human will "can to a certain extent render civil righteousness," because "the carnal nature, that is, reason," is able to choose or make "judgment concerning objects subjected to the senses."

Man thus has freedom, or is the moving agent in the routine, ordinary affairs of life. He wills to do many things and he is responsible for what he does.

But even though this brief is made here for human freedom, there is a dimension that, as Luther points out, must not be overlooked. From the side of God, under His all-encompassing providence, there is a certain necessity, or immutability of events, that rules out the notion that things happen accidentally, or apart from God's overseeing purpose and power. Luther reminds Erasmus that he (Luther) did not say by "necessity of *compulsion*"; for then man would be no longer responsible.[4] The world continues to exist, and creatures in it, because God so wills. "In Him we live and move and have our being," Paul said to his audience on Mars' hill at Athens (Acts 17:28; this quotation and those that follow in this chapter are from the KJV unless otherwise indicated. The sparrow falls to the ground, and God not only knows about it, Jesus points out, but this happens under or by the will of God (Matt. 10:29). Thus everything has a certain inevitability or definiteness about it, and is not simply fortuitous, when viewed from the side of God. God alone is free, Luther insists, as befits the Creator, and free will is rightly only a divine attribute or prerogative.[5] Under Him all creatures and all secondary causes are subject.

Viewed from this perspective, from the side of God, as Scripture does in treating of God's sovereign rule over all things, there is but one conclusion, and that is that God alone is able to will all things freely. That observation led Luther to say, and he did so on solid Biblical grounds, that even in his pristine state of purity man could not be described as a free agent, for he was the dutiful servant of his Creator. This was a position Luther articulated very clearly already in his Heidelberg Theses in 1518. In Thesis 15 he stated: "Nor could free will endure in a state of innocence, much less do good in an active capacity, but only in its passive capacity."[6] Particularly after man's fall into sin, free will must be seen as a "name only," an empty thing, stated Luther in his 13th thesis at Heidelberg.[7] The principle simply

124

was that "you would not call a slave, who acts at the beck of his lord, *free.*"[8]

Man knows within himself that he is a morally responsible being, free of coercion (Acts 17:31; Rom. 1:32; 2:15), and yet at the same time he senses very definitely that there is a certain inevitability of things happening in line with an overarching divine ordering.

Scripture, of course, cements this all very tightly together, as Luther observes. The "omnipotence and foreknowledge of God . . . utterly destroy the doctrine of 'free-will,'" he states.[9] How could you trust any of God's promises, if this were not so, Luther asks? Moreover, the idea of allowing two totally free agents to stand side by side, in other words *"both* the foreknowledge of God *and* the freedom of man" would create a totally "insoluble" situation.[10] So the Reformer simply lets stand whatever difficulty the human mind might have in trying to reconcile the necessity of things happening immutably under the providential purposing of God, and the parallel teaching of human contingency of action according to which man is totally and alone responsible for all that he does. He studiously avoids the dualistic philosophical trap of asserting absolute, unrestricted freedom for both.

A special problem in this connection arises on the question of evil and God's participation in it. Does God concur in the evil that men do, in the sordid tale of wickedness left in the wake of each day's passing?

Luther's answer to this question was to cite that flat principle attested by Scripture concerning the utter rightness of all that God does or purposes. In no way is God the prompter or designer of evil, like some angry, evil-minded innkeeper against his guests, says Luther.[11] God does not plot the evil that men do. For Luther the basic rule of thumb here was to say: "It is not lawful to ask," or to speculate further in an insolent inquisitive sort of way about these things, like the Scholastics.[12] Luther was not dismissing the fact that God is operative throughout His universe at all times and in every place, also in the evil that men do. But the Reformer simply refused to play God and try to give

125

answers beyond his capacity or right to do so. He knew that there was no need to make excuses for God for anything, or to accuse Him of any wrongdoing. If in His unsearchable wisdom God deigned to maintain this old wicked world, He was beyond all reproach.[13] We can only speak of God's goodness, rightness, kindness, in maintaining the world, wicked though it is.

The evil of an act like Judas' betrayal could only be laid at the betrayer's own door. Yet without God's supportive hand Judas would not have had the rational capacity to do his planning, no strength to lift his hand to take the 30 pieces of silver, no energy to move his legs to guide the enemy to Christ, not even the ability to purse his lips to plant the traitorous kiss. Judas remained Judas, a morally responsible soul, not God's puppet. His deeds were contingent on his own evil will and decision, uncoerced by God. Luther knew that these actions were somehow out of the purview or eternal purposing of God would be to deny God's very deity. Scripture, as a matter of fact, clearly attests that God had foretold by sure prophetic word what would transpire. So, from Judas' side, it must be stated that he acted voluntarily and of his own evil will; but from the side of God's omnipotent and omniscient will, it must be affirmed just as certainly, Luther held on Scripture's basis, that if the Lord Himself was not to be deceived, Judas could not have acted differently than he did.[14]

So what if this conundrum was mind boggling! It must simply be left to stand, said Luther. On the one hand, there was absolutely no other way for man to look at this than to see that he himself, like Judas, is responsible for every evil act. On the other hand, there is absolutely no way to rule God out of *any* event or happening in this world, for He is Lord of all. Why did He not destroy the wicked world at the first inception of evil? Or why does He uphold it now as it continues its evil course? These things we will never know this side of eternity, Luther held. All we can see or say is that God graciously permits the world and men to go on, as He meanwhile accomplishes His *gracious* purposes. It is not for us to know the reasons why for God's ways and judgments (Rom. 11:33—36). Suffice it to say, they are right, true, and just, always and in every way.

Second Aspect—In Spiritual Matters

"Without me ye can do nothing." This saying of Jesus is no mere boast or idle platitude on the part of one of history's great moral teachers. When He said, "I am the Vine, ye are the branches. He that abideth in Me and I in him, the same bringeth forth much fruit; for without Me ye can do nothing" (John 15:5), He spoke as the Savior of all mankind. He only is able to knit a man to Himself in faith and bestow on him the forgiveness of sins, life, and salvation, and then equip him for fruitful Christian living. In matters of the spirit, concerning a man's faith and the fruits of faith—love, obedience, and right attitude towards God—man does not possess in himself, or in his will, the power to approach, to hold on to, or to serve God. At Augsburg (1530), the confessors had stated: "Man's will . . . has no power, without the Holy Ghost, to work the righteousness of God, that is, spiritual righteousness" (AC XVIII 1). This truth the "theologians of the Augsburg Confession" (FC SD II 1) were at pains to articulate very clearly in Article II of the Formula of Concord (1577), for they well realized that this article on free will (along with the first article on original sin) was the opposite side of the coin of the article on justification *sola gratia/fide*.

Let us attempt an illustration and an analogy by citing the example of three men who became Christian believers. How do we explain the fact that they are friends of God? The first was baptized as a child, was taught from youth on the elements of the faith by devout parents, and continued under the benign influence of home, church, and fellow believers to live as a true child of God. The second, after years of what might be called decent, but godless, living, came to read the Bible and to take seriously his need for Christ, was converted to faith in his Savior, was baptized, and thus became a Christian like the first. The third had neither love for God nor for decent, respectable living, but he was led through God's mysterious ways and a strange confluence of happy circumstances to faith, baptism, and fruitful Christian living.

In each case spiritual regeneration can hardly be denied. But how it took place remains somewhat of a mystery, for conversion is not something that lends itself to simple psychoanalytic explanation. The human mind, of course, loves to rationalize and reach for its so-called reasonable answer. Since the mind, reason, will, and emotions of all three were in some way involved, it seems logical to suppose that each reached a decision after due process of thought and weighing of evidence. What took place in their lives was apparently little different from the case of a man who jumps away from a fire that licks at his heels to the safety of the firemen's nets below. There was no other escape. Hence the decision to jump, pressed forth by the dire, threatening circumstances. The simple assumption from the analogy is that this explains the decision—free decision—of a man who leaps into the safety of the Gospel net, pursued by the fiery threats of the Law. He has no alternative. His mind and his will dictate the response.

Logical though the analogy seems—and it passes for the explanation of conversion in many Christian thought systems—it does not hold up in the light of facts taught in Scripture. Man, contrary to the usual opinion, likes to play with fire spiritually; he prefers darkness to light (John 3:19); he is drawn by "the lust of the flesh, and the lust of the eyes, and the pride of life" (1 John 2:16), and tends naturally to "mind earthly things" (Phil 3:19). That is the picture of man as he really is. A truer analogy, therefore, would be that, instead of running from fire, he blunders into it. Even the waiting net of the Gospel, offering safety and respite, means nothing to him. The Gospel is a despised item to self-sufficient and spiritually dead man. Its preaching "rather makes him angry," Walther observes quite rightly.[15] The apostle Paul's analysis is right on target: "The natural man receiveth not the things of the Spirit of God, for they are foolishness unto him; neither can he know them, because they are spiritually discerned" (1 Cor. 2:14). Can a man be convinced of that which he considers folly—when he prefers darkness to light, his own "righteousness" to Christ's righteousness, fire to the safety of the net? "The preaching of the cross is to them that perish foolishness," is the way the apostle Paul accurately pegs the matter in its seriousness (1 Cor. 1:18). The simple truth is that "the carnal mind is enmity against God" (Rom. 8:7).

128

Accordingly, if we want to use an analogy at all, it will be closer to the facts if we picture man's conversion or regeneration taking place when the fireman climbs in after the man who does not realize his danger and, midst protestations and resistance, carefully carries him to safety, with firm reassurance causing the unwilling to become willing, as our Confessions put it. Only when he has his feet on the ground in faith does he see the terrors from which he has escaped and the blessedness to which he has come. At that point, reflecting on how he has contributed nothing to his rescue, he is ready to exult with the apostle Paul: "By the grace of God I am what I am" (1 Cor. 15:10). Only when his feet have been solidly planted on the saving Gospel by faith can he know and appreciate the fact that the apostle's word is true: "By grace are ye saved through faith; and that not of yourselves; it is the gift of God, not of works lest any man should boast" (Eph. 2:8-9) and that in Christ there is power of which he never dreamed—so great indeed that he is now able to exult: "I can do all things through Christ which strengtheneth me" (Phil. 4:13).

Though Scripture is absolutely limpid in its accounting of man's conversion or regeneration in this way, Christian theology has been plagued by synergism's tendency to inject some measure, even just an iota, of human contribution into this remarkable spiritual change or turnabout. Scripture's strong exhortations and evangelical invitations or imperatives, calling the sinner to repentance and faith, are cited as proof that God is appealing to the mind and will of man for a decision, and that it is, therefore, at least partly up to him. The "free decision of faith" is a charmed fixation in man's mind. McSorley, in his critical work on Luther, *Luther: Right or Wrong?,* faults the Reformer for not including it in a man's conversion. He states:

> The fact that Luther excludes man's free coopera-tion, in saving faith makes his teaching on this point unacceptable not only to Trent, but also to the Lutheran confessional statements, as well as to the overwhelming majority of modern Protestant theologians, Lutherans included.[16]

This is a serious charge. It is true that Luther excludes

"man's free cooperation in saving faith." It is also true that Trent stands opposed to Luther on this point. It is likewise, and unfortunately, true that much of Protestant theology and many Lutherans think and talk theologically along the same lines. But it is an unconscionable and totally false charge to set the Lutheran Confessions into tension with Luther on this point. They stand as one, both recognizing that it is the Holy Spirit who uses the divine imperatives and strong invitations of the Gospel—He only works through the means of grace!—in order to draw men's hearts to God in faith, and that man, therefore, does not assist in his conversion but can properly only be called a fit subject for conversion. As Luther says, quoting a proverb, God did not make heaven for geese, but for men.[17] But it is God who breaks down man's resistance through His Word, through the Law, and who also works faith and the acceptance of Christ in the heart through the Gospel.

Man, therefore, is not capable of even assisting in his conversion. In spite of the Pelagian teaching, which is popular with natural man, that man can turn himself to God, or the semi-Pelagian, that man can make a beginning on which the Holy Ghost can then build, or the synergistic, of which there are many shades, that man can in some way cooperate or be less resisting, the fact remains that all of these explanations give man more credit than he deserves or in capable of and all detract from Christ's glorious redemption and God's regenerating grace. Luther rightly asks, "What need is there of the Spirit, or Christ, or God, if 'free-will' can overcome the motions of the mind to evil?"[18] The ugly fact is, as Luther shows on Scripture's basis, that "original sin itself then, does not allow 'free-will' any power at all except to sin and incur condemnation."[19]

This is the truth that human reason and pride find hard to stomach and that philosophy and psychology reject out of hand, because of what it does to the human ego. Natural man cannot in any way either contribute toward or prepare himself for a favorable response to God's grace. This is the truth God's Word teaches. Unsavory though it is to man's ego, it is true none the less. Man's new life is the regenerative miracle of the Holy Ghost, who moves the hearts of sinners to give heed to

130

God's word, enlightens, kindles faith, and causes faith to grow and increase. It is God who opens men's understanding (Luke 24:45), gives repentance (Acts 5:31; 2 Tim. 2:25), works faith (Phil. 1:29), draws us to Christ (John 6:44), creates us new in Christ Jesus (Eph. 2:10), and works in us to will and to do of His good pleasure (Phil 2:13). The more a Christian believer reflects on the greatness of God's gift, the more he agrees with the apostle Paul: "What hast thou that thou didst not receive? Now if thou didst receive it, why dost thou glory as if thou hadst not received it?" (1 Cor. 4:7) Little wonder that St. Augustine felt constrained to say, and the Formula of Concord authors felt constrained to quote him: "I erred when I said that it is within our own power to believe the Gospel and to will; but it is God's work.
" (FC SD II 27)

Article II of the Formula of Concord, "Of Free Will," is surely one of the most brilliant pieces ever written on the subject. Foremost is the fact that it is so totally in tune with the Word of God, Holy Scripture. It comes immediately to the main or principal point, man's spiritual incapacity after the Fall. While some argue for man's innate capacity to prepare himself for grace, and others contend that God works directly on men's hearts without the means of grace, Word and Sacrament, the Augsburg Confession position is, according to the formulators of the Formula of Concord, that man is totally incapable in things spiritual by his native powers, and that it is the Holy Spirit who regenerates the sinner through the Word. Not a spark of spiritual power remains in natural man, and the natural will of man is only hostile and capable of what is contrary to the holy will of God (FC SD II 7).

The case against free will in conversion is very strong. Men simply do not "from their own powers perceive, apprehend, understand, or believe and regard [the Gospel] as true"; they are spiritually defunct and dead (FC SD II 9—10). Scripture presses this fact home at many places, states the Formula (SD II 9—16). Thereupon it reinforces this point still more by showing that even the regenerate man still possesses a natural sinful will that continues in its hostility toward God (SD II 18). Luther described man's spiritual capacities in terms of "a pillar of salt, like Lot's wife, yea, like a log and a stone, like a lifeless statue, which uses neither eyes nor mouth, neither sense nor heart," states the Formula (SD II 20). In a real sense man is even worse than a block or a stone, for he resists aggressively, with his faculties turned against God (SD II 24). Reason and free will have capacity for an outwardly decent life, but not for true, inward, spiritual change that puts a man right with God. Accordingly, "the Holy Scriptures ascribe conversion, faith in Christ, regeneration, renewal, and all that belongs to their efficacious beginning and completion, not to the human powers of the natural free will, neither entirely, nor half, nor in any, even the least or most inconsiderable part, but *in solidum,* that is, entirely, solely, to the divine working and the Holy Ghost, as also the *Apology* teaches" (SD II 25). In order then to confirm what it means to be a Lutheran Christian after the meaning and intent of the Confessions, the Formula in turn quotes the Augsburg Confessions (XX, 29—40), the Apology (XVIII), the Smalcald Article (Part III, I and III), the Large Catechism (Third Article), the Small Catechism (Third Article and Second Petition of the Lord's Prayer) to secure the position that regeneration and the renewal that follows result from the Holy Spirit's gracious working, not from initiative or power in man (SD II 28—41). At the same time, in order to affirm Luther's complete accord with the position taught by the Confessions, the Formula cites significant and salient statements from Luther's great theological pieces, the "Great Confession" of 1528, and the *De servo arbitrio* of 1525, and then underscores his complete consistency on the matter throughout his life by showing how his Genesis Commentary of 1545 accords totally with his earlier statements concerning the bondage of the human will in spiritual matters (SD II 43—44). Likewise the Formula notes how Luther severely scores libertinism of any kind that would cheapen God's free grace in Christ by making a mockery of His great kindness and neglecting the means of grace (SD II 46).

It is because God's promises are sure, not because faith is of a certain intensity or quality, that the believer has assurance of his salvation. A man can make up his own mind to hear the Word of God, and he can in turn determine to close his ears and reject the Word, but if he is converted it is because the "power and efficacy of the Holy Ghost" (SD II 55) have effectively worked in him through the Word. "God does not force man." Rather "God the Lord draws the man whom He wishes . . . to convert, and draws him in such a way that his darkened understanding is turned into an enlightened one and his perverse will into an obedient one" (SD II 60). Man can neither begin nor prepare things for God; but once he is converted the regenerated man wills that which is godly, not by coercion but spontaneously, as one in whom the Holy Spirit lives and reigns. One may properly speak, therefore, of cooperation on the part of the regenerate man, not by natural, carnal powers but to the extent and as long as the Holy Spirit guides and leads him (SD II 65—66).

Thus there is a great difference between a baptized and an unbaptized man, between a regenerate and an unregenerate man, as the combat against the sinful flesh is engaged. In the regenerate man we may now rightly speak of a "liberated will," one that tries to work along with God. But the battle is only begun and continues throughout life, with trough and peak periods, as the Christian struggles against the flesh with the power of the Spirit indwelling (SD II 67—68). Though there be failures again and again, the marks or evidences of his conversion will be present in the fruits of the Spirit, in the fruits worthy of repentance (SD II 69—71).

Conclusion

Having set down "this thorough explanation of the entire doctrine concerning free will," states the Formula, "we can now judge, lastly, also the questions upon which, for quite a number of years, there has been controversy (SD II 73). The erroneous alternatives described are basically three: (1) a sovereign action by God, who by speical grace elects some to salvation and decrees others to reprobation (so, classic Calvinism, and, before that, Manichaean thinking!); (2) Pelagianism and/or semi-Pelagianism, according to which man is the initiator of his own salvation by his own action or by some degree of cooperative assist (so Romanism and a host of natural religions!); (3)

synergism, which flies under many flags, but is always recognizable by its bowing in man's direction, the idea being that God in some way activates or stimulates a man by His enabling grace so that he responds properly by *his own* "free decision of faith."

High in the northern Rockies, in Glacier Park, is Triple Pass, the only point in the North American continent from which rivulets flow in three directions, one to the Atlantic, the other to the Pacific, and the third to the Arctic ocean, but each finally to the sea. Whichever way you go, you finally end in the same massive water system. Many people's thinking corresponds to this theologically: whichever way you go—Pelagian, semi-Pelagian, synergistic, Calvinistic—you finally come out at the same place.

The truth is that each is a dangerous assault on Scriptural truth and a virtual surrender to rationalistic human philosophy. McSorley is right when he claims Trent, Aquinas, all of Protestant theology, also much of Lutheran theology, for what he "innocently" wants to call the "free decision of faith." Human nature inclines just that way. It sees or allows no other explanation for the difference why some men are saved and others are lost except to say that the difference lies in each man's free decision—unless of course one takes Calvin's way out and opts for the double decree.

While Luther was alive he was able to hold theological thinking stricly on beam with Scripture's teaching, "how God in conversion changes stubborn and unwilling into willing men through the drawing of the Holy Ghost," *sola gratia/fide* (SD II 88). This the formulators recognized, as they sought to rid the Lutheran church of the synergistic plague that had swept like a wild fire through the Reformation church from the moment when Melanchthon allowed that, besides the Holy Spirit and the Word, there was also a third cause in a man's conversion, his nonresisting will *(non repugnans voluntas)*. Walther is correct when he notes that "Melanchthon's teaching was the cause why Article II was inserted in the Formula of Concord."[20] Accordingly, after the Confessors had carefully delineated the

134

various false notions about man's conversion, they stated (without mentioning Melanchthon's name):

> When Luther says that with respect to his conversion man is *pure passive* (purely passive), that is, does nothing whatever towards it, but only suffers what God works in him, his meaning is not that conversion takes place without the preaching and hearing of God's Word; nor is this his meaning, that in conversion no new emotion whatever is awakened in us by the Holy Ghost and no spiritual operation begun; but he means that man of himself, or from his natural powers, cannot do anything to help towards his conversion, and that conversion is not only in part, but altogether an operation, gift, and present, and work of the Holy Ghost alone, who accomplishes and effects it by His power and might, through the Word, in the intellect, will, and heart of man. (SD II 89)

That the Lutheran church should itself have been victimized by the synergistic scourge is one of history's ironical twists, in view of Luther's yeoman's work in carefully sifting out of the church of his day the leaven of work-righteousness. It took 30 years of bitter controversy within the Lutheran church before the Formula of Concord was able to set the record straight once more.

But history records that synergism is a besetting, persistent plague that engulfs the church over and over again. The reason is that the Pelagian or synergistic tendencies are part of the fiber of natural man. He can think no other way, or wants to think no other way. Obviously the "free decision" of faith is something that leaves at least a certain amount of respectability for the self, elevates at least slightly his ego, and satisfies his pride that his salvation ultimately did not entirely have to be handed to him. There is no way to cure this pattern of thinking except by the Word of God, which, like a sharp threshing instrument, cuts through all the fibers of man's pretension of righteousness and self-attainment in the matter of his salvation.

In our day the threat of higher criticism has been a lowering cloud that has threatened the church, the Bible, its people. We do not underestimate the potential damage from this sore, troublesome source. But the chief threat to Christianity has always been that it lose the distinction between justification and sanctification, that it somehow return to the fleshpots of natural religion which invariably traces man's salvation to himself. But, if a sinner does not see, understand, and believe with all his heart that Law and Gospel differ from each other as a demand laid upon us differs from a gift given to us, he will tend to move the works of sanctification which he goes under the Spirit's power and prompting into the picture or place of his justification. And, as Luther put it so forcefully in his Galatian commentary, "if the doctrine of justification is lost, the whole of Christian doctrine is lost."[21] When the apostle Paul said, we "know that a man is not justified by works of the law but through faith in Jesus Christ," he wanted the Galatian Christians and us to confess with him: "Even we have believed in Christ Jesus, in order to be justified by faith in Christ, and not by the works of the law, because by works of the Law shall no one be justified" (Gal. 2:16 RSV). The same Gospel that proclaims Christ so winsomely is the Holy Spirit's powerful Word that elicits and draws forth faith in sinners' hearts.

Luther, the Lutheran Confessions, and the Holy Scriptures stand as one on this important truth. The opposite side of the coin on free will is the article on justification *sola gratia/fide!* This is the truth that Christian believers must see and treasure with all their hearts. There are not many ways to salvation, no triple divide to heaven. There is only one way. "If it is by grace, it is no longer on the basis of works; otherwise grace would no longer be grace" (Rom. 11:6 RSV). Our boast is in Christ, not in ourselves, nor in our so-called free decision of faith.

If the Christian faith and truth themselves are not to be lost, then this is where we must stand, this is the distinction we must defend, this is the anchor to which we must hold. By nature we are turned in on ourselves *(incurvatus in se)*, as though our hope lay within but the Gospel turns us *out* of ourselves and gets us to place our trust in Christ.

Article III
The Formula of Concord

THE RIGHTEOUSNESS OF FAITH BEFORE GOD

Henry P. Hamann

$\mathcal{T}$he Third Article of the Formula of Concord is concerned directly with what the Reformation from its very beginnings has regarded as the very heart of the Christian faith, justification by faith. The Formula in Article III makes specific reference to this, quoting the Apology, "the chief article of the entire Christian doctrine," and the sentence of Luther, "Where this single article remains pure, Christendom will remain pure, in beautiful harmony, and without any schisms" (SD III 6; this quotation and those that follow in this chapter are from the Tappert ed.). The teaching of the gifted Andreas Osiander (1498-1552), who is not mentioned by name in the article, was a subtle attack on this central doctrine.

The peculiar feature of Lutheranism's presentation of the Gospel is its emphasis on what I shall call objectivity. Justification or salvation is wholly from God and becomes man's wholly by reception. Faith comes by objective hearing of the Word of the Gospel, faith attaches to the objective signs of the water in Baptism and the bread and wine in the Lord's Supper, which, because of the Word of promise attached to the elements, faith knows to be the body and blood of Christ to be taken and eaten. Whatever happens within the human heart or soul or mind through the Word of God and the Spirit, who accompanies that Word, none of this is what faith is concerned about; its concern is wholly with what comes from outside the human being and its multifarious experiences. Justification is for Christ's sake, because of what He has done, and justification is by faith. These are two sides of one coin. Now Osiander, as will be shown in detail later, had as his chief emphasis in justification a view of righteousness that directed the man of faith to what happened within him when he came to faith.

> The one party contended that the righteousness of faith . . . is the essential righteousness of God (namely, Christ himself as the true, natural, essential Son of God, who through faith dwells in the elect, impels them to do what is right, and is in this way their righteousness) (FC SD III 2).

Osiander was very much one against the world, for contemporary Lutherans of all shades combined in condemning his idea of righteousness, Melanchthon among them. They generally saw a threat to two aspects of the whole justification doctrine that are made much of throughout the Lutheran Confessions: the glory of the work of Christ and the comfort of the distressed conscience or the certainty of salvation. Both of these concerns appear clearly in Article III, the former more directly stated, the latter rather underlying the presentation. But both are stated together in SD III 30: "Not only on this account but also in order to afford saddened consciences dependable and reliable comfort and to give due honor to the merit of Christ and the grace of God . . . ."

1.

A clear picture of the teaching of Osiander is necessary for a true appreciation of the content of the Formula of Concord's article on the righteousness of faith and the method of argumentation. A general view of his teaching may be gained from a writing of the year of his death. It is entitled *Wider den Liechtflüchtigen Nacht-Raben, der mit einem einigen Bogen Papiers einen falschen Schein zu machen unterstanden hat, als solt mein Lehr, von der Rechtfertigung des Glaubens, Doctor Luther's seligen Lehr entgegen . . . sein.* This curious title may be rendered in English: "Against the Night-loving and Light-fleeing Crow, who with one sheet of paper has tried to arouse the false impression that my teaching of justification is contrary to that of the Blessed Doctor Luther." He puts his view of the order of salvation in summary form as follows:

What is true righteousness? I answer like this. (1) From pure grace and mercy God gave His only Son for us. (2) The Son became man under the Law, and redeemed us from the Law and its curse. (3) He took all the world's sins upon Himself, and for them suffered, died, shed His blood, descended into hell, and rose again; and in so doing conquered sin, death, and hell and gained for us forgiveness of sins, reconciliation with God, the grace and gift of justification and eternal life. (4) This is to be proclaimed in all the world. (5) He who believes and is baptized is justified and is saved through such faith. (6) Faith seizes Christ, so that He dwells in our hearts (Eph. 3:17). (7) Christ, dwelling in us through faith, is our wisdom, righteousness, sanctification, and redemption (1 Cor. 1:30; Jer. 23:6; 33:16). (8) Christ, true God and man, dwelling in us through faith, is our righteousness according to His divine nature, as Dr. Luther says: "I am founded on the righteousness, which is God Himself; this He cannot reject. That is the simple and true understanding, and don't let yourself be led away from it."

The significant feature about this list is the emphasis in 6— 8 on the indwelling of Christ through faith. What this significance is becomes plain from a completer statement of Osiander's views in other writings of his, especially *Disputatio de iustificatione* (Disputation Concerning Justification), 1550; *Von dem einigen Mitler Jhesus Christo und Rechtfertigung des Glaubens* (Concerning the One Mediator Jesus Christ and Justification by Faith), 1551; *Widerlegung der unergrundten undienstlichen Antwort Phil. Melanthonis* (Rebuttal of the Unfounded and Unhelpful Answer of Philip Melanchthon), 1552. From these it becomes clear that Osiander distinguished sharply between redemption and justification as two separate works of Christ as Mediator. Redemption he sees as a completely objective action played out between God and Christ, and the reconciliation that results from it is just as objective a matter. Everyone who is baptized has his part in that reconciliation apart from his own subjective attitude and apart from its appropriation through faith. "It is as if a person ransomed a Moor from captivity, by which fact also his descendants are free." But this redemption is by no means our justification, and can't be. For that redemption took place 1,500 years ago, before we existed. Justification, on the other hand, can only be said of a person who is alive, "because it depends on faith." Redemption or the forgiveness of sins is only the objective basis for the accomplishment of righteousness in the individual person, and no more.

> If a person asks what righteousness is, one must reply: Christ living in us through faith is our righteousness according to His divine nature, while the forgiveness of sins, which is not Christ Himself but what has been won by Christ, is a preparation and cause why God offers us His righteousness, which is Himself.[1] But that the fulfilling of the Law and the passion and death of the Lord . . . are our justification or righteousness, this I have never found in the Sacred Writings.[2]

The reason why Osiander took this line is made quite clear by certain statements of his, and their resemblance to those made in modern discussions of justification is quite noticeable. That reason is that no justification can be valid that is not related to some real basis for it in the human being. The imputing of the righteousness of Christ to a person still infected with sin seemed to him to be a contradiction, even an impossibility, for God. That would be the sort of unjust judgment to be expected from a false judge, not from the true God. God does not pronounce innocent one who is not really so. So he can write:

> Their doctrine is colder than ice who declare that we are counted righteous only on account of the forgiveness of sins and not also because of the righteousness of Christ who dwells in us through faith. For God is not so unjust that He should account that man righteous in whom there is no true righteousness at all.[3]

Quite in keeping with this line of thinking is his definition of the verb *iustificare* (to "justify"). "To justify in its proper and primary usage means to make a righteous man of an impious one, that is, to call the dead person to life."[4]

It is plain from what has been shown so far that the real concern of Osiander lies in the last three of the sentences (6—8) from his writing cited above. The righteousness of faith to him is the indwelling righteousness of Christ. What he means by this must be more closely defined, even more closely than in the quotation from the Formula cited above. The indwelling of the Godhead of Christ, with which the whole Triune God dwells in us, is our righteousness before God; or more exactly, "His divine nature is our righteousness."[5] It is quite clear that justification is the regeneration and renewal of man worked by the presence of Christ.[6] When the Scripture makes righteousness depend upon faith, the meaning is that faith is involved inasmuch as it has Christ as its content,[7] i.e., "Jesus Christ, true God and man, who through faith dwells in our hearts."[8] When we are bound to Christ through faith, we are "overwhelmed and filled" with divine righteousness. And though sin still attaches to us, "yet that is only an impure drop of water in comparison with a whole, completely pure ocean, and God will not see it for the sake of Christ who is within us."[9]

It is an important aspect of this teaching that there is

repeated reference to Christ our righteousness *according to His divine nature.* In his work *Concerning the One Mediator,* Osiander sees the divine righteousness as that which made Christ Himself righteous.

> The divine righteousness is that which God Himself has, yes, which God Himself is; this is united, in the incarnation, with His assumed humanity (for the incarnation is the becoming human of this righteousness), and makes that humanity righteous, leads it to total obedience and good works and to perfect fulfilment of the Law."[10]

In the *Disputation* we find a number of basically similar statements: "Only Christ is righteous" (Theses 1, 2, 3, 26); "Nevertheless He is not righteous insofar as He fulfilled the Law, but because He was from eternity the righteous Son of a righteous Father" (Thesis 27); "The righteousness of the Father, Son, and Holy Spirit is the same; and this righteousness is the righteousness of faith" (Thesis 28). This righteousness of Christ according to His divine nature is communicated through the mediation of the human nature, but Osiander does not make the process clear. However, this is not of very great significance, since justification is *always* based by him *only* on the divine nature. One quotation represents all:

> This is now my sincere, accurate, and clear answer, that Christ is our righteousness according to His divine nature, and not according to His human nature, although we could not find nor reach nor seize His divine righteousness apart from His humanity. When He dwells in us through faith, He brings His righteousness, which is His divine nature, with Him into us, and it is then reckoned to us as though it were our very own. Yes, it is even given to us, and flows from His humanity into us, from head to members, and it impels us to surrender to God our Lord our members as weapons of righteousness.[11]

It is not difficult to understand the general condemnation that Osiander's teaching met in his time. Whether the error of

142

Osiander should be described as a "subjectivism which destroys thoroughly the objective ground of salvation of the Lutheran Church, as a mysticism which transforms the Christ for us into the Christ in us" (Frank), may be doubted or rejected, as is done by Reinhold Seeberg. However, it is clear that Osiander's position does make the consciousness of the indwelling righteousness of Christ in His divinity the basis of the sinner's peace with God, even if this was not Osiander's intention. The believer is directly guided to look within to look for the fruits of the indwelling holy Christ. Of this more later. At the moment it is necessary to note in general by way of a résumé of the contents how the Formula dealt with the Osiandrian error, and then to take up certain special matters of the answer for detailed study.

2.

Article III of the Formula introduces the whole subject by a statement of the point at issue, by a reference to the teaching of the Augsburg Confession, and by some observations on the importance of the article of justification and of the necessity of a clear exposition and rejection of erroneous teaching with respect to it (SD 1—7). The positive portion of the article describes what justification is in a general way, without any obvious polemic against the Osiandrian error (SD 8—43).

To be justified is to be absolved from sin, set free from the verdict of punishment, and adopted as a child of God and an heir of eternal life—all this without any human merit or worthiness, only God's grace and the obedience of Christ in life, suffering, death, and resurrection being the ground of such justification. The sinner is offered these treasures in the Gospel and appropriates them by faith, and by faith only. This faith, like everything it receives, is a gift of God (SD 8—16).

At this point there follows a section devoted to definitions of important words and warnings against misunderstandings. The word "justify" is defined as "to declare righteous and free from sins"; "regeneration" is shown to have been more loosely used in at least three senses: (1) as a synonym of justify, (2) as including "both the forgiveness of sins solely for Christ's sake and the subsequent renewal which the Holy Spirit works in

143

those who are justified by faith," and (3) as a synonym of renewal. It is carefully pointed out, on the one hand, that regeneration does not mean that sin is done away with in those who are justified, and, on the other, that true regeneration involves genuine contrition and a real renewal of life, even if this remains imperfect, a beginning rather than a perfect state (SD 17—23).

A more far-reaching distinction is set forth in the rest of the positive exposition, namely the distinction between what invariably is associated with justification and what actually constitutes justification (SD 24—43). It is held that "the only essential and necessary elements of justification are the grace of God, the merit of Christ, and faith which accepts these in the promise of the Gospel" (SD III 25). The concomitants of justification by faith, both those that precede and those that follow, are held to be necessary concomitants but not parts of justification itself. These concomitants, with some overlapping, are: contrition, true repentance, love, good works, renewal, sanctification, and the new obedience. Both Luther and St. Paul are called up as witnesses. An important part of this exposition is the reference to and insistence on the "exclusive terms," terms like "without works," "without the law," "freely," "not of works," "through faith alone." This whole distinction is applied especially to the proper order of faith and good works, in which connection the statements of James 2 are taken up.

The final section (SD 44—67) is devoted to the condemnation of errors contrary to the true exposition of the doctrine. There are two lists of these, 45—51 and 60—65. The first is the more general, while the second is particularly directed against the error of Osiander and the less prominent error of Stancarus, who spoke of Christ as our righteousness only according to the human nature. Osiander's error is particularly dealt with in the condemnatory section also apart from the numbered lists of errors, especially his teaching on the righteousness of Christ as opposed to a true statement of this righteousness. One paragraph (52—53) extends the argument concerning justification to cover also the somewhat wider term "salvation."

The key word in the whole discussion of the Formula with

144

Osiander is "obedience." The thought of the obedience of Christ crops up again and again—more than 20 times all told—and it is found in a number of interesting variations: "obedience" or "perfect obedience" (4, 11, 22, 30); or "entire (total) obedience" (15, 56); or "sole, total, and perfect obedience" (55); or "entire, perfect obedience" (58: the Latin here has "solid, absolute, and perfect obedience"); "obedience and passion" (56) "obedience, passion, and death" (32); "the obedience, the passion, and the resurrection" (14); "the merit of total obedience, the bitter passion, the death, and the resurrection of Christ" (9).

The obedience of Christ is in a number of places expressly defined as His passive and active obedience, as in some of the passages just mentioned. The most deliberate statement is, however, the following (15):

> Since Christ is not only man, but God and man in one undivided person, He was as little under the law— since He is the Lord of the Law—as He was obligated to suffer and die for His person. Therefore His obedience consists not only in His suffering and dying, but also in His spontaneous subjection to the Law in our stead and His keeping of the Law . . .

As the obedience of Christ is described in as wide and all-embracing a way as possible, so there is emphasis on the assertion that none other than the whole person of Christ is involved in and behind this obedience. It is the obedience of the "entire person" (57), the total obedience of "Christ's total person" (56), the obedience of the "person who is God and man at the same time," not the "divine nor the human nature of Christ by itself" (58). Associated with this emphasis on the total person of Christ is that on the fact that the obedience embraces the whole of His life from birth till death and resurrection. The justified and regenerated "are regarded as holy and righteous through faith and for the sake of Christ's obedience, which Christ rendered to His Father from His birth until His ignominious death on the cross . . . ." (22)

The Formula's answer to Osiander's teaching concerning the righteousness of Christ is simply this: the righteousness of

145

Christ is His obedience, obedience understood in the complete way just described and as summed up in paragraph 58:

> For this reason neither the divine nor the human nature of Christ by itself is reckoned to us as righteousness, but only the obedience of the person who is God and man at the same time. Faith thus looks at the person of Christ, how this person was placed under the law for us, bore our sin, and in His path to the Father rendered to His Father entire, perfect obedience from His holy birth to His death in the stead of us poor sinners, and thus covered up our disobedience, which inheres in our nature, in its thoughts, words, and deeds, so that our disobedience is not reckoned to us for our damnation but is forgiven and remitted by sheer grace for Christ's sake alone.

3.

The Formula's counter to Osiander was the most appropriate one thinkable when looked at in light of the Reformation's two all-important concerns: the comfort of poor sinners and the honor due to the merit of Christ.

True comfort for sinners and conscience or, to put it another way, the certainty of salvation and of possessing the favor of God, was preserved by the objectivity of the teaching on righteousness developed in the Formula. It was mentioned earlier that Osiander's teaching led the believing sinner to look within himself, even if his teaching could not be described as subjectivism. This must be examined more closely. The material brought together by Seeberg is particularly helpful at this point.

In *Concerning the One Mediator* (Q 3 r), Osiander says: "When He dwells in us through faith, He brings His righteousness, which is His divine nature, with Him into our hearts; this is then also imputed to us, as though it were our own." Seeberg continues:

> So Christ begins in man a suppression, a mortification, a sweeping away of sin. But this activity never comes to an end in this earthly life, so that no one can leave the state of faith behind and trust himself

146

to his own obedience. The situation is rather that *the righteousness of Christ active in us is imputed to us* [Seeberg's emphasis], "as though it were your own and came from you, although of course it does not come from you, it is My Son's who brought it with Him from heaven" *(Rebuttal,* J 2 v). But it is expressly asserted that the works produced in us through Christ are not our righteousness—only Christ's righteousness is that. "For His righteousness is not imputed to you by Me because it produces this or that big or small work in you, but only for the reason that it is in you through faith (J 3 r; N 4 r).[12]

The conclusion that Seeberg draws from this material and the whole presentation of Osiander's teaching is that he had no other concern than Luther: the certainty of being in the state of grace because of the ongoing working of the righteousness of Christ in spite of the continuance of sin. However, Seeberg does admit that we do not find in Osiander what we find frequently in Luther: the direct basing of the consciousness of forgiveness on the historical act of redemption. He admits, further, that the "exclusive description of righteousness as an effective power, which we find in Osiander, shows in him a predominating interest in moral renewal which threatens to circumscribe the basic religious spirit *(Grundtendenz*—basic tendency) of the Reformation."

Even if we grant the claim of Seeberg that Osiander was, like Luther, really concerned that the sinner be assured of being in the state of grace in spite of the continuance of sin within him, it is still necessary to point out that Osiander's way of meeting this problem of the sinner was incapable of achieving the end in view. So, the sinner sees that he continues to sin in spite of his earnest desire and intention to avoid sin and live in accordance with the will of God. This continuing sin makes him wonder whether he is really a believer at all. The advice of Osiander?

If you want to be righteous and inherit the kingdom of God, then, truly, He must dwell within you who ascends to heaven and goes to His Father, that is, God's Son, God Himself, who came from heaven—

otherwise you will never go to heaven or come to the Father. What would it help you, if you had all possible righteousness that men or angels could dream up, and if you did not have this eternal righteousness which the Son of God is according to His divine nature together with the Father and the Holy Ghost? No other righteousness can lift you to heaven and bring you to the Father. But when you seize this righteousness by faith and if Christ is in you, what can you lack, when you have richly, superabundantly, infinitely enough in His godhead?[13]

How does one believe in a righteousness within oneself? A righteousness within, even if it is not self-produced but comes from outside, from God, must somehow be experienced. If it is actually within, in the heart, in the soul, in oneself, then, there must be some signs of its presence for the human spirit to get hold of, to recognize, to be aware of. Suppose that the righteousness of Christ that dwells within renews the soul, producing fruits of righteousness, the good works and the love which please God—and this is repeatedly stated by Osiander— then these would be indications of the indwelling Christ. But then we are back with all the uncertainties of Christian spiritual experience. What are really good works? Can I be sure that what looks good really is so? Is not self-deception the easiest and most fatal of human proclivities? The sensitive Christian conscience suspects the "goodness" of every so-called good work, like St. Paul in Romans 7:14—25 and like Luther, who spoke in his own exaggerated fashion of our righteousnesses as mortal sins. So the witness or indications or hints of the indwelling righteousness of Christ are no support for the anxious, doubting sinner, and we are back with faith in the indwelling righteousness itself, of which there is no indication. How this can make for certainty of salvation or comfort the heart of the doubting sinner is beyond comprehension. Faith needs some certain thing to clutch and hang on to, something removed completely from the uncertainties and ambiguities of human experiences, especially those of the inner life. Osiander by his

148

teaching compels the inward look. His teaching may not be subjectivism in its essential structure, but it inevitably leads to subjectivism in its practical application.

In contrast with the teaching of Osiander, the teaching of the Formula on the righteousness of Christ is as objective a thing as can possibly be imagined. For it is identical with the obedience of Christ, with the holy and sinless life of Christ, lived in obedience to the Law and under the Law of God, an obedience involving the whole of His life, right up to the bitter end on the cross. He was "obedient unto death, even the death of the cross" (Phil. 2:8 KJV). This obedience in one way is something quite apart from every man. It was carried out long before the majority of all mankind existed. In that way it is as objective an action and matter as anything can be. The work of Christ, of course, in another way affects every man, for it was, as far as the Formula is concerned, vicarious. It was a work, an obedience, in the place and stead of all men, so that the obedience of Christ is in God's eyes the obedience of all men. When men are directed to the obedience of Christ through the preaching of the Gospel, they are being directed to something that took place quite apart from them, outside of them. When faith believes this word, this promise, this Gospel, it is dealing with something that human uncertainties and ambiguities cannot reach. You either believe in it or you don't.

So, by its insistence on the objective facts of the whole obedience of Christ as His righteousness, the Formula was directing the troubled and doubting sinner to a haven where his heart and conscience could find the certainty of faith. Osiander's teaching of the indwelling of the divine Christ could never accomplish this.

The Formula's doctrine of the obedience of Christ meets the needs of the distressed sinner seeking for certainty in another way as well. The obedience of Christ is complete and perfect, absolutely and wholly fit to be the object of a certain, undoubting trust. We recall that what was said earlier about the active and passive obedience, the involvement of the whole person of Christ in that obedience, and of the whole of His life from His birth to His death and resurrection, the last event marking both the end of the period of obedience and the Father's acceptance of that obedience as wholly sufficient.

The sinner confronted by the law of God, with his conscience aroused by the demands and condemnations of the Law, needs to be assured that the Law's demands have been completely satisfied, or else his conscience will never find peace. No relaxation of the Law's demands, no "cheap grace," no sentimental reference to the love of God will satisfy. He knows that God's righteousness and His demands of His creatures are eternal and unchangeable. A real righteousness, corresponding fully with the demands of the God who is forever righteous and holy, alone can bring the distressed conscience to rest. It is just this purpose that lies behind the Formula's thoroughgoing description of the obedience of Christ.

Not all of that description is of the same importance in this connection. For instance, the insistence on the person of Christ as being involved in this whole transaction, with the corresponding refusal to tie down the effect of that transaction to one or the other nature, is not particularly related to the concern we are discussing. But it has its importance. It is linked with the whole christological doctrine developed in Article VIII on "The Person of Christ." Here as there, it is maintained that all that Christ did for our salvation He did according to both His human and His divine nature, as the one indivisible person. That emphasis has its own particular importance against the splitting of the person through the opposite emphases of Osiander and Stancarus. However, once it has been made clear that what Christ did He did as a person, the emphasis of the Formula is on the actual obedience itself, and, more particularly, on the passive and active obedience of Christ.

Why the development of the idea that the obedience of Christ is both active and passive: "therefore His obedience consists not only in His suffering and dying, but also in His spontaneous subjection to the Law in our stead" (SD III 15)? It is clear that the Formula is not teaching a double obedience or an obedience with two parts, for there is no parallel listing of what belongs to the one and the other part of obedience. There is also no chronological separation, as though the active obedience

150

marked Christ's life for a certain period, when the passive obedience took up its role, as in the last days of Jerusalem. The obedience of Christ is quite plainly thought of as an integral matter. His one obedience is both passive and active at one and the same time, from the beginning of His life to the end point of His obedience for us, His resurrection. Looked at from one point of view, Christ's obedience was active; from another point of view it was passive. But the question still remains after this clarification: Why the emphasis on the double aspect of active and passive obedience?

The Formula does not furnish a specific answer to this question, but it is clear that it has to do with the assurance the sinner is to have that Christ has done for him all that the law of God demands. We may suggest that something like the following was in the minds of the compilers of the Formula. The Law requires fulfilment of its demands. It is to be obeyed and to be obeyed wholly, both as to its spirit and its letter. On the other hand, if it has been broken, then its demand is satisfaction in the way of punishment. Now, the Law has as a matter of fact been broken by the sin of man, and every man lies under its condemnation. The aroused conscience knows this and is full of the fear the Law inspires. How is his conscience to be brought to rest? Such a person needs that kind of fulfilment of the divine will that he is both set free from the damnation the law requires for sin and that he becomes qualified for salvation. The two are not the same. An unwilling and resentful suffering of punishment is, in effect, nonconformity with the divine will, which demands the punishment; it is renewed rebellion against God and provokes new satisfaction of the outraged Law through punishment. So suffering in itself is not sufficient. There is needed such a suffering of the punishment the Law demands that it is at the same time a recognition of the righteousness of God and wholehearted acquiescence in the holiness of the God who punishes. As Luther said on one occasion, if the damned could stand the judgment of God and say yes to it, they would be saved in that moment. In saying this we have, in effect, stated that the obedience of Christ was both active and passive. There was from beginning to the end of His life wholehearted submission to the law of God (Gal. 4:4), an obedience to the will of the Father that did not shrink from the awful and shameful death of the cross. This is the active obedience. But the whole life of Christ may be seen from the point of view of suffering. The voluntary acceptance of a life under the Law, to which He was not subject, this was the beginning of the passive obedience, which was continued to its end by patient acceptance of the total suffering to which His obedience to the will of His Father subjected Him.[14]

We turn now to the second purpose the Formula serves in its identification of the righteousness of Christ with His obedience: to preserve the riches of the grace of Christ.

Osiander, as has been pointed out, distinguished sharply between the redemption of Christ and the righteousness of Christ. In the eight sentences of his quoted earlier, Osiander asserts that God gave His only Son for us in love; that the Son became man and redeemed us from the curse of the Law; that He took all the world's sin on Himself and through His suffering, death, and resurrection overcame sin, death, and hell, and gained forgiveness of sins, reconcilliation with God, the grace and gift of justification, and eternal life: that whoever believes this as proclaimed in the Gospel and is baptized is justified and saved (sentences 1—5). One wonders what more any person, any poor sinner might possibly want or need beyond this. But Osiander goes on to state in three sentences that Christ dwells in the heart by faith; that Christ dwelling in us is our righteousness, and that according to His divine nature. The separation between the gifts of sentences 1—5 and the declarations of 6—8 have serious consequences for a proper view of the work of Christ. We can ask, what is the actual value of the redemption from wrath, sin, death, and hell through the work of Christ, when we who believe all this need something else as well in order not to fall to the same enemies in the end? If the divine nature of the indwelling Christ is our righteousness and without it the rest is of really no avail, why the rest in the first place? And even if the redemption by Christ is a necessary basis for the further act of indwelling, in point of fact the insistence on the latter effectively sets the former in eclipse. Now, the

152

Formula, by identifying Christ's righteousness with His obedience, concentrates all attention on the great act of redemption, gives total importance to what Jesus Christ, God and man in one person, did for all men, and allows nothing to detract from the glory of the one who is worthy "to receive power, and riches, and wisdom (and strength) and honor, and glory, and blessing" (Rev. 5:12 KJV). The believer who looks within, to his faith that Christ dwells within him, to the extent that he is concerned with what happens within, is led away from attributing all glory to Christ; but he who looks only to the act of obedience for him in life and death gives all glory to Christ the Lord.

Certain other prominent ideas of the Formula are in keeping with the thoughts we have developed. First of all, we turn to the role ascribed to faith. The righteousness of Christ may also be called the righteousness of faith, as the Formula does in the phrase "the righteousness of Christ or of faith" (SD III 1). When we look at the positive statements made concerning faith, as well as the negative ones, the reason for the equation "righteousness of Christ = righteousness of faith" becomes abundantly clear. "Faith is the only means whereby we can apprehend, accept, apply them [the treasures of the Gospel, i.e., the obedience of Christ] to ourselves, and make them our own" (10). "Faith trusts . . . solely in Christ and (in Him) in His perfect obedience" (30). "Only the righteousness of the obedience, passion, and death of Christ which is reckoned to faith can stand before God's tribunal" (32). "Faith's sole office and property is to serve as the only exclusive means and instrument with and through which we receive, grasp, accept, apply to ourselves, and appropriate the grace and the merit of Christ in the promise of the Gospel" (38). Compare with these the negative statements. "Faith does not justify because it is so good a work and so God-pleasing a virtue" (13). It is erroneous and to be rejected to say "that faith justifies only because righteousness is begun in us by faith, or that faith has priority in justification but that renewal and love likewise belong to our righteousness before God" (49); or to say "that the promise is made our own through faith in the heart, through the confession which we make with our mouth, and through other virtues" (51); or to teach "that faith does not look solely to the obedience of Christ, but also to His divine nature in so far as it dwells and works within us" (63); or to teach "that faith does not justify without good works, in such a way that good works are necessary for righteousness" (Ep III 23).

There is, according to these statements, an exact correspondence between the obedience, the righteousness, of Christ and faith. The whole gift of righteousness is in the obedience of Christ, and faith is nothing but reception of this righteousness, and the only means of reception. The whole of Christianity may with some simplification be described as Christ or as faith, Christ the gift, faith its reception.

It is part of this whole view of faith, next, when the confessors make some ado about the "exclusive terms" (SD III 36—39), the definition of the verb "to justify" (17 and 62), and the basic oneness of justification and salvation (52—53). The exclusive terms, e.g., "without works," "without the law," "freely," "not of works" are to set forth faith *only* as the means whereby the righteousness of Christ is made the possession of men. The insistence that "to justify" means "to declare righteous and free from sins and eternal punishment" coupled with the condemnation of the view that when the prophets and apostles speak of the righteousness of faith, the words "to justify" and "to be justified" do not mean "to absolve from sins" and "to receive forgiveness of sins," but to be made really and truly righteous on account of the love and virtues which are poured into them by the Holy Spirit and the consequent good works, has precisely the same end in view as the use of the exclusive terms: the definition insisted on is to preserve the objectivity of the righeousness of Christ, so that faith may remain pure receptivity and nothing else. The same can be said about the confessors' concern that nothing be taught concerning salvation that is in any way different from the teaching concerning justification. The two are at bottom the same, and the confessors saw that to insinuate something special in the way of a human contribution or in the way of human experience as necessary to salvation was to jeopardize the treasures they sought so hard to retain in the article of justification.

The proper understanding of faith, too, like the identification of righteousness and obedience, is meant to serve the glory of Christ's merit. If faith is nothing but reception and trust in the merits, obedience, righteousness of Christ, and if there is no human work of any kind which is to be rightly set alongside of faith as a means of gaining or acquiring the righteousness of Christ and justification, then Christ remains untouched in his preeminence as sole and total Savior. Nothing of man interferes with or detracts from the glory that is due Him. And the comfort of poor sinners, their certainty of salvation, is served at the same time. They are led to put all trust in a perfect act of obedience, a total fulfilling of the Law for them and in their stead. Nothing else is demanded of them as precondition for justification or salvation; no contrition, no renewal, no good works, nothing. All is of Christ, all is of faith. Every vestige of a reason for doubt and uncertainty, for fear and distress, is removed. A perfect salvation is provided, free and gratis. It needs only to be taken, accepted, appropriated.

It is the claim of the writers of the Formula, at the end of Article III, that their intention is to "remain steadfastly and constantly with the doctrine of justification by faith before God as it is set forth, explained, and demonstrated from God's Word in the Augsburg Confession and its subsequent Apology" (66). A careful study of the article shows that their treatment of the Osiandrian heresy indeed preserves intact the insights of the earlier confessions and the fundamental principles of the Lutheran Reformation. What is new will be seen to be only a more precise formulation of what was confessed half a century earlier, but one also that is wholly consistent with it.

4.

The theological position of Osiander concerning the indwelling righteousness of Christ was not completely met by what the Formula has to say on the obedience of Christ and faith. The heretical aspect of Osiander's teaching, indeed, was fully met by the confessors. But not everything that Osiander had to say about the indwelling of Christ was heretical. The

155

Formula grants that there was such a thing as the indwelling of Christ:

> On the one hand, it is true indeed that God the Father, Son, and Holy Spirit, who is the eternal and essential righteousness, dwells by faith in the elect who have been justified through Christ and reconciled with God, since all Christians are temples of God the Father, Son, and Holy Spirit, who impels them to do rightly (54).

But the Formula goes on to assert that this indwelling is not the righteousness of faith, it is rather something that follows the preceding righteousness of faith (54). There is a large and complicated problem involved in this simple statement of the situation, which needs to be examined now in some detail.

Many persons would feel that there was something very formal, legal, and arid about the picture of righteousness unfolded in the previous section: obedience to the Law, with active and passive aspects, offering of this to men through the Gospel, imputation of this righteousness of Christ to men through faith—it is all too lifeless in its objectivity; there is all too little personal involvement on the part of man. Such a judgment arises from ignorance of the whole situation or from superficiality. When it is understood what faith really is, and when faith is seen in the light of the whole gamut of experiences that precede, accompany, and follow it. complaints of formal abstraction and aridity of teaching will be seen to have no foundation. At the same time the nature of the problem referred to just now will become clear also.

One who becomes a believer does not become so by some sudden transformation arbitrarily imposed upon him by divine action, an action that somehow leaves his own personality untouched. Faith is indeed a gift, a creation of God. As the Formula says, the faith "whereby we rightly learn to know Christ as our redeemer in the Word of the Gospel and to trust in him" is "a gift of God" (11). And it must be.

> If faith . . . stretches out for a redemption and salvation quite different from that which has ever

156

entered into the heart of natural man, if the righteousness created by Christ and salvation is the object of its attention, then no one who has read the first two articles of the Formula needs further proof for the fact that . . . such faith must be the result of the power of the Holy Spirit[15]

But faith is what goes on in the heart of man, not in the heart of God. It involves the committal of the whole being to the Gospel of righteousness and salvation in Jesus Christ. It is knowledge and trust, an exclusive surrender to Christ as the one Savior in time and in eternity. Where this happens in a person there exists something that was never there before, but something also that involves a thoroughgoing reorientation of his whole being. Apart from the new thing that is faith itself, the Formula mentions preceding and subsequent inner experiences and happenings.

The preceding experience is that of contrition. "Nor, on the other hand, does this [i.e. continuing sin in the believer] mean that we may or should follow in the ways of sin, abide and continue therein without repentance, conversion, and improvement. For genuine contrition must precede" (22). Contrition involves the knowledge that one has not measured up to the demands of the living holy God and His will and that this failure makes one guilty and subject to condemnation. This knowledge leads to a feeling of guilt and pain for the failure and sin. The subsequent experiences accompanying faith and produced by it are variously described as renewal, or sanctification, or regeneration, or love, or good works.

To those who by sheer grace . . . are justified before God (that is, accepted into grace) there is given the Holy Spirit, who renews and sanctifies them and creates within them love toward God and their fellowman (23).

The confessors insist on the presence of these experiences with very great earnestness. Where these are not to be found there is no faith at all.

There cannot be genuine saving faith in those who
live without contrition and sorrow and have a wicked
intention to remain and abide in sin, for true contrition
precedes and genuine faith exists only in or with true
repentance (26).

The view is expressly condemned "that faith is a kind of trust in
the obedience of Christ that can exist and remain in a person
though he does not truly repent and gives no evidence of
resulting love, but continues to sin against his conscience" (Ep
III 17). And, positively, these experiences are always found
together with faith.

After a person has been justified by faith, a true
living faith becomes "active through love" (Gal. 5:6).
Thus good works always follow justifying faith and are
certainly to be found with it, since such faith is never
alone but is always accompanied by love and hope (Ep
III 11)

Or again: "Love is a fruit which certainly and necessarily follows
true faith" (SD III 27). And most distinctly of all:

After the person is justified, the Holy Spirit next
renews and sanctifies him, and from this renewal and
sanctification the fruits of good works will follow. This
is not to be understood, however, as though justification and sanctification are separated from each other
in such a way as though on occasion true faith could
coexist and survive for a while side by side with a
wicked intention. (41).

As strongly, then, as the Formula asserts that faith, and
faith alone, is the means by which the righteousness of Christ is
received and men are justified and saved, just so strongly it
insists that there is no such thing as faith without regeneration,
or without contrition, renewal, love, and good works, or without
the indwelling of God. And so the problem arises how the strict
teaching of the righteousness of Christ as developed in the
second and third sections of this article is to be maintained with
the equally strict insistences just mentioned. How are actions

158

and experiences coincidental with faith, without which faith would not be there at all, to be completely asserted as necessary without becoming part of the righteousness of faith?

The Formula, first of all, insists on a strict separation of faith in the doctrine of justification from whatever accompanies, precedes, or follows faith.

> It is indeed correct to say that believers who through faith in Christ have been justified possess in this life, first, the reckoned righteousness of faith, and second, also the inchoate righteousness of the new obedience or of good works. But these two dare not be confused with one another or introduced simultaneously into the article of justification by faith before God (32).

> Here, too, if the article of justification is to remain pure, we must give especially diligent heed that we do not mingle or insert that which precedes or follows faith into the article of justification, as if it were a necessary or component part of this article, since we cannot talk in one and the same way about conversion and about justification (24).

The regular way the Formula proceeds in such separation is to talk of contrition as "preceding" faith, and sanctification or the new obedience or love or good works as "following" faith, as in the sentences just quoted. "Love is a fruit which certainly and necessarily follows true faith" (27). "Similarly, although renewal and sanctification are a blessing of Christ, the mediator, and a work of the Holy Spirit, it does not belong in the article or matter of justification before God; it rather follows justification" (28). The idea of following faith must, of course, be properly understood, too. If "faith is never alone but is always accompanied by love and hope" (Ep. III 11), or, more strongly still, if justification and sanctification are not to be so understood, "as though on occasion true faith could coexist and survive for a while side by side with a wicked intention" (SD III 41), then, obviously, there can be no question of a *chronological* following of the new obedience upon faith. Once faith is there, the new obedience is there, at the same point of time. The following, then, is a logical following: faith is the source of the new obedience, and not the other way around. A similar argument cannot, by the way, be advanced in connection with contrition, as though the relation between faith and contrition as that which must precede faith were also logical and not chronological. There is a contrition which is not followed by faith, but by despair. In the relation between faith and contrition chronology has a place as well as logic.

So, in thinking and teaching rightly in the matter of justification, we must separate logically between that which does and that which does not belong to justification, though the various elements involved are always existing in the same heart at the same time. "The only essential and necessary elements of justification are the grace of God, the merit of Christ, and faith which accepts these in the promise of the Gospel" (25). Contrition must be there, regeneration must be there, the new obedience, love, good works, indwelling of Christ—all these, too; but justification does not depend on these accompanying elements, not in the largest or smallest part. Faith is never alone, but it justifies alone.

Though it may seem difficult to make the separation on which the Formula insists, it is not really so when one bears steadfastly in mind what the *object of faith is*. Christian faith is directed, always and only, to what Christ the Savior has accomplished. This probably becomes most evident when the Christian is faced with death or deliberately contemplates death and what follows. In such existential moments the Christian has or will have nothing in his heart but the grace of God and the complete obedience of the Son of God and the righteousness or the forgiveness of sins He has won for him and offers freely in the Gospel. The whole puzzling question how faith saves by itself when it is never by itself won't cause him a moment's worry, for his faith will be fixed immovably on the Lord Jesus and the salvation He has won. What causes endless debate among the learned theologians will be clearer than daylight in the moment of the great dissolution. As a specific example, we may think of the great medieval hymn of judgment, *Dies irae,*

160

dies illa. Much of the theology of the time must rightly be rejected as untrue to the Gospel, and completely out of harmony with the Reformation teaching of justification by faith. But the *Dies irae* teaches it, and much more convincingly and powerfully than Toplady's *Rock of Ages.*

> King of majesty tremendous,
> Who dost free salvation send us,
> Fount of pity, then befriend us.
>
> From that sinful woman shriven,
> From the dying thief forgiven,
> Thou to me a hope hast given.
>
> Worthless are my prayers and singing,
> Yet, good Lord, in grace complying,
> Rescue me from fires undying.
>
> To the rest Thou didst prepare me
> On Thy cross; O Christ, upbear me!
> Spare, O God, in mercy spare me!

The nice distinctions made by the Formula to safeguard the doctrine of justification by faith, which we have just analyzed, will probably be rejected by some as theological hairsplitting. But, far from being an exercise in logical abstractions, the careful labor of the confessors actually limps far behind the practical needs of the believing Christian heart. It is concern that the believing sinner be given complete comfort and certainty that called forth the labor of theological thinking in the first place, as well as concern for the honor of Christ. A few excellent sentences of Frank deserve to be quoted here as the end of this essay.

> It is really the case, as we have said, that theological thought is hardly able to carry out, with the clarity appropriate to the practical need, its task of separating and combining the elements which belong together but which still dare not be confused. The heart which has won through to life and peace solely by the grace of God is like the eye irritated by a speck of dust so small that the eye can hardly descry it. Nowhere more than here is

the experience shown to be true that the heart can be sure of its faith, quite apart from the labor of the meditating and inquiring mind. Nowhere can it be better demonstrated how little purely dialectical activity, divorced from experience, is in the position to become master of the spiritual problem.[16]

Article IV
The Formula of Concord

GOOD WORKS

David P. Scaer

1.

The Reformation contribution with the most startling effect was Luther's recovery of the Pauline doctrine of justification by grace through faith, *without the works of the Law.* Earlier church teachers, including the fathers, never contested that God's grace was the cause of salvation, but they saw the good works as Christians' instruments reaching up and taking hold of this divine grace. Luther's proclamation that faith was the means of obtaining this grace also meant the exclusion of works from God's justification of the sinner. Good works did not belong to the act of salvation itself (AC IV 1). Following the Reformer, Lutherans have seen this as the chief article of Christian doctrine. This teaching distinguished Lutheranism from other expressions of Christianity. The centrality and prominence of this concept of justification and salvation have falsely suggested that Lutheranism is opposed to good works. Historically, Lutherans have never been antinomians and they were very sensitive to any charge suggesting that they were opposed to good works (AC XX 1). They have stressed that the church does have the obligation to teach the necessity of good works. This sensitivity is reflected in Augsburg Confession XX, "Good Works", the longest of that document's 21 doctrinal articles. The Lutherans with their refusal to place works in the article on justification were never able to satisfy their Roman Catholic opponents who insisted that a man was justified by both faith and works (AC XX 5—7). Lutherans also experienced difficulties among themselves about the necessity of good works. One group claimed their necessity for salvation and another found them to be detrimental to salvation. Article IV of the Formula states that the debate among the Lutheran theologians was at first merely semantic, but such statements put forth in isolation without any explanation could lead to grievous errors. What originally was a problem in the meaning of words did give the Lutherans an opportunity to state more exhaustively how they stood on the entire issue on good works (Ep IV 4). Melanchton in Article XX of both the Augsburg Confession and the Apology had stated the Reformation position adequately, but the restatement of the Lutheran position in the Formula of Concord in an even more systematic way was not without benefit.

2.

Lutherans take a positive view of the good works of both Christians and non-Christians alike, as these works are performed in and viewed by the world. Every person is seen as creature who is morally responsible before God for fulfilling the Law. This responsibility of the rational creature to the Creator God includes performing acts contributing to the world and to society's well-being in general (AC SVIII 4—5). Acts harming others are to be avoided. Good actions earn God's favor in the world and they are rewarded. As Lutherans spoke favorably on good works, they immediately added that all these works make no contribution to the salvation of the one who performs them. Though these works benefit others as well as the one who performs them, they come from the flesh, man's sinful nature. These who do such works have their own best interests at heart and not God's (FC SD IV 8). Such positive and negative concepts towards good works, depending on one's perspective, have permitted Lutherans to participate in society and government and to appreciate contributions made by others here. At the same time, Lutherans recognize that all these works have no validity before God in the question of the sinner's salvation. A diametrically opposed position is offered by the Roman Catholic Church, which has regarded all works including those of unbelievers as having at least an ultimate benefit to the salvation of the one performing them (Ap IV 19—20).

3.

The Lutherans' prime concern in Article IV was not the obligations of all creatures to serve their Creator God, but a correct understanding of the Christians' obligation to perform good works. Lutherans say quite bluntly that good works are necessary for Christians. Faith never exists without works. In every instance faith by its inner nature produces good works. The Biblical image of the tree producing fruit is used in the Formula to illustrate faith's natural expression in good works. Just as it is impossible for a healthy tree not to produce good fruit, so it is equally impossible for a Christian not to please God through good works (cf. SD IV 8). The word *necessary* was applied to good works to emphasize the natural connection between faith and good works. Intolerable was the view that the Christian, who knew of his justification by faith without works, would entertain the thought of leading an immoral life without paying proper attention to the Law and to good works. The preacher of the Gospel has the obligation of urging his flock in the performance of good works (SD IV 15 and 40).

The term *necessary* as applied to good works was open to misunderstandings that the Lutherans wanted carefully to avoid. The Augsburg Confession and the Apology had said that Christians *ought to* or *should* perform good works (AC VI 1). The Latin word *debet* might wrongfully suggest that the Christian is indebted to God for salvation and must repay this debt by the performance of good works. This concept is forthrightly rejected. Repulsive is the concept that good works are performed from a sense of repayment to God for services performed. Works done from an unwilling heart might benefit the sinner in this world but were hardly pleasing to God. God loves the cheerful giver. He does not engage in extortion (SD IV 17—18).

The Christian belongs to God and has both Christ and the Holy Spirit within Him. He not only performs good works naturally from faith, but he enjoys doing them. He shows no respect to persons whether they are Christians or not, friends or enemies. Sufferings for the sake of Christ are considered an opportunity for joy and not a form of divine punishment. True faith is not introverted. Instead of engaging in self-reflection, faith is too busy doing good works. Faith does not have to be instructed to perform good works. The Christian's will has been freed from sin and expresses its confidence in God by performing good works to others. Before the Christian is asked, he is doing good works (SD IV 10—12).

The Christian's will, freed from sin, gladly and happily performs good works, but the Christian's will is never entirely freed from sin. His new self accepts Christ, but the flesh, the part of him that does not belong to God, resists Christ and enjoys sin. When the flesh, the sinful part of man, hears that good works are performed freely, it misinterprets this freedom to mean that good works are optional for the Christian. Freedom in the sense of option is rejected as false. When the Lutherans say that the Christian performs good works freely, they mean that good works flow naturally from faith. They do not mean that the Christian sits back, muses, and then decides whether he will perform them. In Lutheran theology moral neutrality in the matter of good works is impossible. The Christian from faith performs good works. The unbeliever and the unregenerate part of the Christian perform evil works. There is no neutral ground between good and evil works (SD IV 19—20).

4.

In the discussion of the justification of the sinner before God, works and the role they play have no part whatsoever.

166

There are many reasons for excluding works from justification. Lutherans regard works offered to God in order to justify the sinner as detracting from the glory of Christ's work in earning salvation. To Christ alone belongs all glory. A correct understanding of works is even more fundamental in excluding them from the article on justification (SD IV 21—24). Each man lives within two dimensions at the same time. He lives under God and is responsible to Him as the creature is responsible to the Creator. At the same time he lives with other human beings on a horizontal plane. As each lives under God, he is the recipient and God the Giver. The roles between God and man can never be reversed. God as Creator provides for man the creature. With the introduction of sin, God has also assumed for Himself the role of Redeemer and man is now the redeemed. Should man in this relationship between himself and God offer to God a gift, man would be assuming the role of Creator and Redeemer. From the Lutheran perspective man cannot and dare not offer a good work up to God. In the relationship between God and man, God and not man does good works. Good works have their place in the relationship of one person to another but not in the relationship of God to man. Luther saw this in the Ten Commandments and set it forth in his explanation of them. The First Table of the Law sets forth faith as the correct attitude to God and the Second Table sets forth good works as the proper posture of the Christian to others. Melanchthon, in the Latin text of the Augsburg Confession (XVI, 1), did not hesitate to identify civil ordinances as "the good works of God" because they were necessary for and contributed to the maintenance of society and government. Thus Christians did not have to withdraw from the world, as the Anabaptists were demanding, but participation in civil requirements could demonstrate their love through good works (AC XVI, 3 and 5). Unbelievers are also capable of external or civil righteousness, but since their works do not flow from faith, they are considered as sin before God (Apol IV, 24 and 34). Acceptable and favorable in God's sight are works performed by Christians as they indicate that in such a person faith is alive, vibrant, and productive. But these works can never be offered to God to earn His favor or to repay

Him for a debt. They can never be presented to God out of any sense of forced obligation. Within this context, Lutherans lodged their protest against any suggestion that good works are necessary for salvation. Works have their place as the proper behavior between human beings but not between the believer and God (SD IV 28).

Works set within the context of the sinner's justification before God were regarded as personally damaging to the sinner. The Christian, believing that his justification depends on the works he performs, directs his faith away from Christ and toward his own works. He thus deprives himself of the comfort of Christ's work and is driven to despair, or he begins trusting in his own righteousness. In either case he eventually loses the hope of his salvation. Even with a mitigating explanation, the phrase "good works are necessary for salvation" should never be used. No explanations can really remove the damage inflicted by misunderstandings.

5.

The Lutherans also discussed whether good works were beneficial in maintaining faith in a person who had become a Christian (SD IV 30). Quite definite was their view that faith and the intention to perform evil could never exist side by side. Wherever the intention to perform evil existed within the heart, no claim for faith's existence could be made. As the Lutherans said that good works played no part in the sinner's justification before God, they also affirmed that evil works destroyed faith. Evil works indicated that faith was absent. Threats of divine punishments are to be preached to Christians to warn them that persistence in evil can uproot faith. The concept of once saved always saved was simply unacceptable (SD IV 31—32). Some reasoned that if evil works destroyed personal salvation, then good works benefited it. Such a conclusion was rejected by the Formula. Justification is begun, maintained, and ended by faith and not works. Future hope does not rest on good works or our continuance in them but in faith in Christ alone. Flatly rejected is anything even faintly suggesting that good works maintain, preserve, or sustain salvation (SD IV 34).

168

6.

The negative view of Lutherans to good works as they pertain to the article on justification was developed one step further by one of their prominent theologians, Nikolaus von Amsdorf (SD IV 37). He held that good works were detrimental to salvation. He was virtually alone in making this assertion, but it was the kind of statement that opponents of Lutheranism saw as a natural result of the Lutheran position on justification (AC XXI). Like many of the other statements forming the center of this controversy, this also could be understood in a right and a wrong sense. Yes, good works are detrimental to salvation if the one performing them relies on them for salvation. Works have no place in the understanding of justification (SD IV 37). Quickly pointed out is that the fault lies not with the good works themselves, which are acceptable to God, but the real fault lies with the person who trusts in them for salvation. Quite defensible is the opposing opinion that good works are beneficial. They contribute to the well-being of the neighbor especially if he is in distress. They are rewarded, not in the sense that God gives salvation in exchange for good works, but in the sense that both the doer and the receiver benefit from them here in this world. Regardless of how carefully hedged is the phrase "good works are detrimental to salvation," it should be entirely avoided. Understood in an improper sense it could become an invitation to all forms of libertinism and antinomianism (SD IV 40).

7.

Some controversies are more imaginary than real. The controversy over good works and their necessity was this kind of controversy. The Lutherans themselves who were involved all held that justification was by faith alone and that Christians were to perform good works. The Roman Catholics and the Anabaptists and not the Lutherans saw good works as necessary for salvation (SD IV 26—27). Some had mistakenly understood Luther's doctrine of justification by faith alone without works as an invitation to libertinism, but this was never a serious possibility for any responsible Lutherans. Quite to the contrary, the law-abiding attitude of the Lutherans was recognized by most.

The controversy among the warring Lutherans might have been averted if each party had tried to determine with more care and precision what was really involved in the other's position. Each party had overstated its position and each overstatement in an isolated sense without further clarification proved to be wrong. The theologians of each party debated the merits and demerits of other's positions without considering the context in which they were offered. They might have been able to resolve these difficulties among themselves without hardening their views into irreconcilable positions. But as stated, their diametrically opposed views that good works on one hand were necessary for salvation and on the other hand detrimental for salvation had to be condemned because in an isolated sense both were equally wrong and both were confusing.

The chief and most valuable result was that the Lutherans said once and for all that works have no part in the article on justification and still they are a necessary part of the Christian's life. The negative but nevertheless important result emerging from the controversy was the necessity of avoiding possibly misleading statements. Setting forth isolated abstract theological phrases without clarifying explanations always opens the doors to misunderstanding. A statement of Christian truth possesses its truthfulness in connection with the totality of Christian doctrine and never in isolation. Customary in debating societies is arguing the pros and cons of a given statement. Such a procedure has no place in the Christian doctrine so that confusion and misunderstanding can be avoided. Had this principle been followed, this controversy over good works and their necessity might have been avoided.

LAW AND GOSPEL

Henry P. Hamann

*T*he importance of Article V of the Formula of Concord is to be seen more in the position it takes in relation to the harmony and distinction between Law and Gospel than in the way it tries to answer Antinomian views that made the article necessary in the first place. This importance of the article is indicated already in the opening sentence:

> The distinction between Law and Gospel is an especially brilliant light which serves the purpose that the Word of God may be rightly divided and the writings of the holy prophets and apostles may be explained and understood correctly (SD V 1; this quotation and those that follow in this chapter are from the Tappert ed.).

The proper distinction between Law and Gospel, together with a proper view of their union in God's purpose, is intimately bound up with the articles that precede it in the Formula. No one can present a clear and adequate teaching on "Free Will or Human Powers," on "The Righteousness of Faith before God," or on "Good Works" without a continual and proper application of Law and Gospel. Most of the weighty controversies and splits in the church have had their basis in differing or opposing views on the difference between Law and Gospel. At the present time, the big debate concerning the mission of the church in the world is at bottom a debate concerning Law and Gospel. There is more than ample reason why "we must . . . observe this distinction [i.e., between Law and Gospel] with particular diligence" (1). And not least for the reason that confusion of the two doctrines would change the Gospel into Law and "would darken the merit of Christ and rob disturbed consciences of the comfort which they would otherwise have in the holy Gospel when it is preached purely and without admixture" (1). We see here how the central Reformation concerns: the merit of Christ and the comfort of anxious consciences, again show their influence.

1.

The Antinomian ideas that lie behind Article V are many and various, and the reasons for them likewise. The prominent Antinomian among the early Lutherans was Agricola. His views had as their starting-point what every Lutheran would have regarded as right and proper: that the Law by itself does not lead to life but to death, and that conversion can be brought about only by a teaching that brings judgment and salvation with equal power. However, his presentation of the way of salvation involved a dangerous and misleading upsetting of elements of the Christian faith. In theses that he published in Wittenberg in 1537 he advanced the following statements: (1) Repentance should not be taught from the Ten Commandments or the law of Moses but from the suffering and death of the Son of God through the Gospel; and (2) The Law should not be taught at all, neither at the beginning nor at the middle nor at the end of the justification of men. Christ's command had only the preaching of the Gospel to all the world in view, but the Law stands in no sort of inner or necessary relation to justification; it does not transmit the Holy Spirit, does not produce a wholesome, saving repentance, but only punishes with condemnation. The Law

172

does not belong in the Christian church at all, its territory is limited to the outward works and business of human life. "The Decalog belongs in the city hall, not in the pulpit!" It is not necessary for salvation, for the Gospel of Christ teaches both together: the wrath of God and the righteousness that avails in His sight. Only the spirit of evangelical freedom is needed. Related to this view of Law and Gospel is Agricola's picture of the way a person is brought to repentance, i.e., to true sorrow for sin and faith in Christ. According to Agricola, salvation begins when a man sees in Christ how kindly God is disposed to men. Then "the heart is deeply moved, seizes on God's grace and kindness, and thanks Him from the heart." Then there follows pain and sorrow on account of sins previously committed. The believer is full of sorrow that he never before realized his crime and blasphemy of God. He forsakes his previous way of life. "That is repentance . . . the first stage of the new birth, the genuine breath and inspiration of the Holy Spirit." So the heart "gains a cordial trust in God, that He will not reproach him for his folly, since he did not know any better." The great benefaction that the sinner has experienced kindles within a childlike fear against rousing his good and gracious God and Father again to anger, lest he add new guilt to old.[1]

Agricola's ideas changed over the years more than once, partly as a result of criticisms of his position. Chief among the criticisms were the six *Disputations Against the Antinomians* by Luther. They appeared 1537—40. Agricola first modified his views, then retracted his early position altogether in his *Confession* of Dec. 9, 1540. Later, in 1565, he again changed his position to one approximating his modifications prior to the recantation of 1540. According to this last view of his, the teacher and preacher in the church is to preach the Gospel of Jesus Christ, the Gospel that teaches both repentance and the forgiveness of sins. However, this preaching of the Gospel does not imply that the preaching of the Law is to be eliminated. Rather the ministry of the New Testament is to maintain the ministry and office of the Old Testament, for the Law is to serve the preaching of the Gospel; but not the three letters *lex* only, but the eternal purpose of God that condemns all evil.[2]

Sentences of Melanchthon also figure prominently in the Antinomian debates. It was a very practical concern that led him to set forth the Gospel as a preaching of repentance and grace, in spite of his zealous emphasis of the difference between Law and Gospel. A church visitation had shown Melanchthon how many pastors at the time spoke only of the forgiveness of sins and said nothing or next to nothing about repentance, although forgiveness of sins can hardly be understood without a knowledge of sin. Melanchthon feared that the preaching of forgiveness without repentance would lead to fleshly security, and that the last state would be worse than the first. And so the pastors were admonished and instructed to preach the whole Gospel as was their duty, and not proclaim one part without the other. This sort of language, however, was hardly in the interest of a clear distinction between Law and Gospel and was actually inconsistent with Melanchthon's own teaching over the years. It is this Melanchthonian Antinomianism, if we can call it that, that is set forth in the Formula in opposition to the true teaching.

> The question has been, Is the preaching of the Holy Gospel strictly speaking only a preaching of grace which proclaims the forgiveness of sins, or is it also a preaching of repentance and reproof that condemns unbelief, since unbelief is condemned not in the Law but wholly through the Gospel? (Ep V 1).

Certain developments after Melanchthon will fill in the picture, and they are also of some importance for the understanding of the Formula. The view that good works are necessary for salvation (see Article IV), which arose among Melanchthon's followers, seemed to correspond with the unclear presentation of Law and Gospel and their respective effects that was regarded as a mark of the school of Melanchthon. In reaction against the error of Major, men on the other side were led to wild Antinomian statements, like those of Anton Otto of Nordhausen.

> The Christian's greatest art is to know nothing of the Law, for Moses knew nothing of our faith and our

religion, and the severe reprimands of the prophets don't concern us. A believing Christian is above all obedience, beyond all law. Laws, good works, new obedience don't belong in the kingdom of God, but in the world, like Moses and the rule of the Pope. Faith accomplishes everything by itself, without all good works; not merely without the merit of good works but also without the presence of good works. We should pray God that we may remain to our end steadfastly in the faith without all works. (Translated from Frank, 275—276; see footnote 2.)

There were reactions the other way as well, and just as wild and unguarded statements were formulated. Paul Crell, for example, said concerning the Gospel in its strictest and most proper sense that it was a preaching of repentance in the strictest meaning of the term, since not the Law alone but the Gospel directly showed up the greatness of the affront of man against God and the hatefulness of sin. He went so far as to insist that the Gospel alone was really a preaching of repentance and conversion because it [the Gospel] alone revealed and condemned the greatest and most terrible sin.[3]

All in all we have quite a kaleidoscopic picture in the Antinomianism that lies behind the fifth article of the Formula (and to a lesser degree behind the sixth article as well). Antinomianism can arise from quite different causes, even contradictory ones. However, the whole complicated picture certainly supports the observations of Luther that the person who can teach rightly concerning Law and Gospel deserves to be called a master in theology.

2.

As was stated above, the Formula directs its attention particularly to the Antinomian sentence of Melanchthon that "the Gospel is not only a proclamation of grace but also at the same time a proclamation of repentance, which rebukes the greatest sin, unbelief" (SD V 2). The contrary view is: "Strictly speaking, the Gospel is not a proclamation of repentance or reproof. This . . . is strictly a function of the law of God, . . . whereas the Gospel in its strict sense is a proclamation of the grace and mercy of God for Christ's sake" (2).

It is the view of the Formula that the controversy was chiefly occasioned by ambiguities in terminology and the failure of the contending parties to keep the various meanings in mind. Thus, "Gospel" may mean "the entire preaching of Christ" or simply and narrowly "the preaching of God's grace." In the first sense, the term includes both the proclamation of repentance and the preaching of the forgiveness of sins; in the latter sense only the forgiveness of sins is in view. Similarly, "repentance" has a wider meaning and a narrower. The wider meaning points to "the entire conversion of man," while the narrow meaning has reference only to a true recognition of sins, sorrow for them and the will to desist from them. These differences in terminology are seen as existing in the Holy Scripture as well as in the language of the theologians. The discussion of terminology fills sections 3—8.

Central and basic truths concerning conversion follow the discussion of the term "repentance" (9—15). It is pointed out that the knowledge of sin that comes from the Law is insufficient for true conversion; for conversion to happen, the Gospel in its narrow sense is needed. On the other hand, the Gospel promise of forgiveness presupposes oppressed and penitent sinners. The mere preaching of the Law "either produces presumptuous people, who believe that they can fulfill the Law by external works, or drives man utterly to despair." So the Spirit of God must perform an alien or strange work, i.e., that of convincing the sinner of his sin, before He can enter on His proper work of bringing to faith and conversion. Support for this material is found in a sermon of Luther's, quoted at some length (12—13), in the Smalcald Articles, and in the Apology (14—15). As a result of this exposition it is held that "we justly condemn the Antinomians or nomoclasts [destroyers of the Law] who cast the preaching of the Law out of the churches and would have us criticize sin and teach contrition and sorrow not from the Law but solely from the Gospel" (15). In the middle of this short section is found the most important sentence: "Thus both doctrines are always together, and both of them have to be urged side by side, but in proper order and with the correct distinction."

At this point the confessors move to wider and more comprehensive aspects of Law and Gospel, to a consideration of their specific nature, especially in their distinction from one another (17—23). The Law is defined, positively, as "a divine doctrine which reveals the righteousness and immutable will of God, shows how man ought to be disposed . . . in order to be pleasing and acceptable to God," and, negatively, as "everything that rebukes sin." The Gospel may illustrate and explain the law, but no more. On the other hand, rebuking of unbelief or rejection of the Gospel is part of the office of the Law, although "this Gospel alone, strictly speaking, teaches about saving faith in Christ." As for the Gospel, it is "that doctrine which teaches what a man should believe in order to obtain the forgiveness of sins from God"; its content is the redemption won by Jesus Christ; it is "everything which comforts and which offers the mercy and grace of God to transgressors of the Law." "There is a vast difference between the knowledge of God which comes from the Gospel and that which is taught by and learned from the Law"; even the heathen know something of the latter, but, it is implied, this is not the case with the Gospel. It is held as the concluding thought of this main section that "these two proclamations have continually [i.e., from the time of the patriarchs] been set forth side by side in the church of God with the proper distinction."

The article concludes with some repetition of material, but this is now presented from the viewpoint of the importance of the doctrines of Law and Gospel in their distinction from one another and their essential complementarity: "these two doctrines must be urged constantly and diligently in the church of God until the end of the world." Confusing the two doctrines "would easily darken the merits and benefits of Christ . . . rob Christians of the true comfort which they have in the Gospel . . . and reopen the door to the papacy in the church of God." The final words are a reiteration of the thought that the Gospel, in its strict sense, "is the promise of forgiveness of sins and justification through Christ, whereas the Law is a message that rebukes and condemns sin" (24—27).

It was a significant achievement of the compilers of the article on Law and Gospel to point out the necessity of distinguishing between different uses of both "Gospel" and "repentance." The article itself declares that the controversy was "chiefly occasioned" by inconsistent terminology. A study of the writings of the Reformation period from Luther on till the writing of the Formula demonstrates to the hilt that such inconsistent terminology was the order of the day. It was true of the theological giants of the Reformation period, Luther and Melanchthon. The double meaning of "Gospel" is found even in the early confessional writings. For instance, the wider meaning appears in the Apology IV:62: "The Gospel declares that all men are under sin and are worthy of eternal wrath and death. For Christ's sake it offers forgiveness of sins and justification." And there are other places also: Ap XII 29, XXVII 54; SA-III III 41. The narrow use of the term, of course, is more common and found everywhere. There seems no reason at all to dispute the judgment of Frank:

> I really don't know how the historical judgment concerning the actual double description of what the Gospel is and what it does could have been other than this: that the word "Gospel" was used now in its "real" meaning by the fathers of the church, now in a wider sense apart from the difference between Law and Gospel. In the former sense it embraces only the preaching of the grace of God, while in the latter it embraces at the same time also the preaching of repentance.

And again:

> We see already that a great step forward was taken to remove the controversy when people became aware of the double meaning of the word and so also of the lack of contradiction (i.e., in contexts where the word is used differently).

178

What was true of the word "Gospel" was even more important in respect to the word "repentance," since it was just here that the controversy began. It was important for the settlement of the controversy to realize that the question was not whether the Gospel in its wide sense worked repentance in the wide sense of that term. The question was whether the Gospel in its essential and strict sense produced repentance in the strict sense of that word, i.e., penitence. The discussion on the terminology of the controversy was a very important contribution to the understanding of the issues involved in the controversy and to their resolution.

However, when all this has been granted, the really important contribution of Article V of the Formula of Concord lies in a different direction, in the clarity it brought to bear on the relation of Law and Gospel. Its summary statement here is: "Thus both doctrines are always together, and both of them have to be urged side by side, but in proper order and with the correct distinction" (15). We turn now to an examination of this sentence with its various applications and implications.

3.

Some preliminaries must be attended to first. No one is likely to be impressed by the statements of the article: "The distinction between Law and Gospel is an especially brilliant light" (1) and that "these two doctrines must be urged constantly and diligently in the church of God until the end of the world" (24) who is not convinced that a man is justified by grace, without works, for the sake of Jesus Christ, through faith. There is a very intimate relation between the doctrine of justification by faith and the relation of Law and Gospel. The justified Christian is both sinner and righteous at the same time, *simul iustus et peccator*. He knows himself to be subject to the righteous wrath of God because of his sins, but also that he is removed from that judgment because of the merits and obedience of Christ, through whom grace and pardon are now his. "With the same right and for the same reason that we have the double thing just mentioned, the Law is distinct from the Gospel. To confuse them at any point is to confuse the

179

righteousness we have from God as His gift with a righteousness which we imagine we have through some achievement in relation to the righteous demand of God" (Frank).

A second preliminary may be mentioned merely in passing. How Law and Gospel affect the Christian is more particularly dealt with by the Formula in Article VI, "The Third Function of the Law." In Article V their function in relation to the conversion of the sinner is specially outlined.

The Formula puts the process leading to the saving of the sinner like this:

> Therefore the Spirit of Christ must not only comfort but, through the office of the Law, must also convince the world of sin. Thus, even in the New Testament, He must perform what the prophet calls "a strange deed" (that is, to rebuke) until He comes to His own work (that is, to comfort and to preach about grace). (11).

The quotation from Luther that follows contains the same scheme of bringing to a knowledge of sin by the Law preparatory to the preaching of the Gospel to create faith:

> At the same time it is true and right that the apostles and the preachers of the Gospel, just as Christ Himself did, confirm the proclamation of the Law and begin with the Law in the case of those who as yet neither know their sins nor are terrified by the wrath of God. (12)

Both passages look on the process just described as the normal thing, as the repeated "must" in the former more particularly declares.

If we were to ask, *why* this should be the invariable rule, the answer must run that it lies in the very nature of things. It is an impossible task, even unthinkable, to proclaim reconciliation without proclaiming who was reconciled and why reconciliation was necessary. Even if one were to ignore the way in which God freed men from the guilt incurred by transgression against the Law and were to be satisfied simply with saying that God freed men by His grace in Christ, this would remain incomprehensible

180

if one did not go on to show why grace was necessary, viz., because all men are debtors before the Law. To get rid of the Law completely, one would have to describe grace as love in a very general way and regard this love as a necessary act of God the Creator towards His creatures. But in doing that, one would simply give up the essence of the Christian teaching of redemption. The concern of Luther was well founded, when he declared that the devil through the teaching of Agricola did not want to do away with the Law so much as to do away with Christ Himself, who fulfilled the Law. The remonstrances of Agricola led Luther to declare further that the consequences he drew from Agricola's teaching were not his own but those of the Holy Spirit; for he who does not teach the Law can't teach anything about sin, and he who teaches nothing about sin, can't teach anything about grace and Christ.[4]

This is the way that the confessors would have argued. Agricola, it will be recalled, unfolded a different order of salvation: man sees how kindly disposed God is in Christ, his heart is touched by this goodness, there follow pain and contrition for past sin and blasphemy against God, he forsakes the past evil life and thus enters the first stage of the new birth, he then gains a hearty confidence that God will forgive him his sin and folly, and the great grace he has experienced produces in him a childlike fear against arousing the gracious God to anger anew. This is certainly not a less complicated picture of what happens when the sinner comes to faith and fellowship with God. However, it is not necessary to pursue Agricola's scheme of salvation any further, for the Formula does not do that either. But it is necessary to ask the question whether the final word has been said by the Formula itself on the matter.

At first blush the position of the Formula seems unassailable: first Law, then Gospel; first consciousness of sin and terror which the Law inspires because of sin, then the comfort of the forgiveness that the Gospel offers. A savior from sin implies the presence of sin, and no person will be interested in the savior from sin who does not see himself as a sinner needing salvation. If we take the comprehensive view, see the conversion of sinners as one, try to describe briefly what is true of all, then, I think, there is no doubt that the position of the Formula is logically, pedagogically, theologically sound. But it may be at least a matter for further investigation whether every conversion follows the one pattern, whether what the Formula sets down as the rule must invariably happen in every case.

Be that as it may, what the FC has to say about Law and Gospel in that process and what it has to say about the nature and effects of these two doctrines—this, I hold, needs no modification, it needs only study and attention by the church. The position here of the Formula is really a restatement of Luther's own exceptionally clear and illuminating definition:

> Everything that preaches about our sin and the wrath of God, no matter how or when it happens, is the proclamation of the Law. On the other hand, the Gospel is a proclamation that shows and gives nothing but grace and forgiveness in Christ. (12)

The merit of this definition is that Law and Gospel are determined by what is actually being said at any time and by the purpose actually being pursued. All purely formal distinctions are swept aside, like that between the Old Testament and the New. Sentences of the Scripture are no longer to be classified as either Law or Gospel. It is what is being actually, practically, existentially done with them that determines the difference. For example, what normally would be described as a statement of the Gospel, the presentation of the suffering and death of Christ for mankind, may in some situations be a real preaching of the Law because of the purpose being pursued by the speaker or writer at the time. As Luther himself says in the same connection as the words just cited:

> In fact, where is there a more earnest and terrible revelation and preaching of God's wrath over sin than the passion and death of Christ, his own Son? But as long as this proclaims the wrath of God and terrifies man, it is not yet the Gospel nor Christ's own proclamation, but it is Moses and the law pronounced upon the unconverted. (12)

With this clear distinction between Law and Gospel continually in his mind, the preacher and pastor knows how to

182

use the Word of God in every situation that confronts him; in fact, every Christian can apply that Word aright to himself from time to time as well. At bottom the question is: Am I as preacher to warn this man or comfort him, comfort or warn myself? Is this person or group of persons self-satisfied, secure in their Christianity, turned inward to how good they are, priding themselves on their achievements and spiritual accomplishments? Evidently they need the Law, to be taught afresh what God's perfect and holy will is, so that their complacency and self-righteousness may be dissipated and that they may see afresh how salvation is by faith and faith in Christ alone. Or have I before me a person in distress over his sin and failures and shortcomings, or worried about his unwillingness or inability to put forward a wholehearted effort in living the Christian life? Here is a person, it is plain, who needs comfort from the Gospel and its promise of full and free forgiveness; he needs the encouragement that assurance of peace with God will give him to lead the life in Christ. This thought could be pursued in further detail with the aid of more examples; that would show the practical value of the Formula's and Luther's definition of Law and Gospel. But, so it seems to me, the definition itself is self-illuminating, the definition itself demonstrates the judgments of the Formula: that "the distinction between law and Gospel is an especially brilliant light which serves the purpose that the Word of God may be rightly divided" (1); "that there is a vast difference between the knowledge of God which comes from the Gospel and that which is taught by and learned from the Law" (22); and that "it is necessary to urge and to maintain with all diligence the true and proper distinction between Law and Gospel" (27).

In two other instances—it is granted that they are of only minor importance—one may wonder whether the article on Law and Gospel has found the best theological statement.

The first of these makes a distinction between two kinds of Law preaching.

The mere preaching of the Law without Christ either produces presumptuous people, who believe that they can fulfill the Law by external works, or drives man utterly to despair. Therefore Christ takes the Law into His hands and explains it spiritually (Matt. 5:21 ff.; Rom. 7:6, 14); thus he reveals His wrath from heaven over all sinners and shows how great this wrath is. This directs the sinner to the Law, and there he really learns to know his sin, an insight that Moses could never have wrung out of him. (10)

In his careful investigation of this passage, Frank distinguishes no less than three forms of penitence ("*Reue*"): (1) the sort of penitence or knowledge of sin that the Law produces by itself; (2) the penitence that results when 'Christ takes the Law into His hands and explains it spiritually," so that a person "really learns to know his sin"; and (3) that same sort of penitence linked with faith, for Frank holds that "even full and complete penitence can exist as the fruit of the evangelical preaching of the Law without faith necessarily coming into being" (303). The dominant thought here is that there is no true knowledge of sin (or of the Law) without a knowledge of the Gospel—this is the only way in which the Gospel can be regarded as "a proclamation of repentance." Frank describes the whole process as follows:

> The fact remains: faith is impossible without true, antecedent penitence, and to that extent the order must be that the preaching of the Gospel must follow that of the Law. Christ takes the Law into His hands, not in order to remove the sting, but in order to sharpen it; not in order to begin with the preaching of comfort, but in order to make it possible. Even if the *knowledge* of the evangelical work of Christ in the way described must precede penitence in the believer: that knowledge will never become faith unless it (faith) is preceded by penitence, that is, unless knowledge takes from the work of Christ first the understanding of the preaching of the Law and afterward the understanding of the preaching of grace. (309)

The commentary of Frank probably quite rightly interprets the meaning of the writers of the Formula.[5]

We turn to the way our article treats the thought that the

184

Gospel is a proclamation of repentance, *because "it rebukes the greatest sin, unbelief."* The Formula insists that the Law rebukes unbelief. The Gospel is seen as part of the wider concept "Word of God." The argument in detail is as follows:

> This is the way in which the Law rebukes unbelief, when a person does not believe the Word of God. Since the Gospel (which alone, strictly speaking, teaches and commands faith in Christ) is the Word of God, the Holy Spirit through the office of the Law rebukes the unbelief involved in man's failure to believe in Christ. Nevertheless, the Gospel alone, strictly speaking, teaches about saving faith in Christ. (19)

It is obvious that the Formula had to insist that unbelief was condemned by the Law; its definition demands that condemning is an office of the Law. The Formula is consistent enough in its judgment as to what condemns unbelief. But in describing a function of the Gospel the Formula uses terminology usually reserved for the Law. The Gospel offers men the gift of gracious pardon, forgiveness of sins, life, and salvation. Those who accept this offer in faith, who take the gift and appropriate it by an Amen to the Word of God (this is faith, of course), have all that is offered. Those who reject it have nothing. But they are not strictly condemned either by the Gospel or by the Law. If anything, they have condemned themselves to their fate by their rejection of the proffered salvation. Some words in John's Gospel are a clue as to the fitting way in which to determine what condemns unbelief. Jesus says there (John 3:17-18 RSV): "God sent the Son into the world, not to condemn the world, but that the world might be saved through Him. . . . He who does not believe is condemned already, because he has not believed in the name of the only Son of God." Unbelief is its own condemnation. It is that because of its very nature.

"Thus both doctrines are always together, and both have to be urged side by side, but in proper order and with the correct distinction" (15). This is the real concern of the article on Law and Gospel. To present both in their real distinction and their necessary togetherness is the task of the church in all ages. It is a challenge, too, for the task is particularly difficult as some words of Luther make abundantly clear.

> Here we see again that the Law and the Gospel, which in themselves are so widely separated from each other and which are more than contradictory, like fire and water, can exist together in the same heart. . . . For, although these in their nature are very far from each other, yet they are very closely associated in one and the same heart. For nothing is more closely associated than fear and trust, Law and Gospel, sin and grace. For their association is such that the one devours the other. So no mathematical conjunction can be found that is like this one. (Luther's *Commentary on Galatians* of 1535; translated by the writer from the St. Louis Edition, IX, columns 447 and 454, paragraphs 551 and 570.)

The reason, finally, for this task is easy to state. Any confusion of Law and Gospel means a loss of the *Gospel*. The Law never seems to be the loser, as the situation with Agricola illustrates. When the Law is thrown out of one window it comes back through another—by a wrong definition of the Gospel. The Law is not eliminated; finally, the Gospel is. The tenacity of the Law in men's minds has been well characterized by the Apology (IV 265):

> In human eyes, works are very impressive. Human reason naturally admires them; because it sees only works and neither looks at nor understands faith, it dreams that the merit of these works brings forgiveness of sins and justification. This legalistic opinion clings by nature to the minds of men, and it cannot be driven out unless we are divinely taught.

As much then as we treasure the Gospel of Jesus Christ, so greatly we must be concerned about the proper distinction between Law and Gospel. Confusion here "would easily darken the merits and benefits of Christ, once more make the Gospel a teaching of Law . . . and thus rob Christians of the true comfort which they have in the Gospel against the terrors of the Law" (FC SD V 27).

186

Article VI
The Formula of Concord

THE THIRD USE
OF THE LAW

Eugene F. Klug

1.

*A*rticle IV (Good Works), Article V (Law and Gospel), and Article VI (The Third Use of the Law) of the Formula of Concord form a trilogy, properly relating the Christian's renewal of life, his sanctification, to his justification, the righteousness by which he stands forgiven before God (Article III).

Renewal of life, or sanctification, inevitably and necessarily flow out of justifying faith. Love must be there, because faith is. In no way, however, can such holiness of life, or striving after it, be counted as necessary to salvation. The faulty notion of Georg Major and of his sympathizers was dealt with by the Formula's emphasis on good works as a fruit of faith that will always follow, like good fruit on a good tree (Art. IV). The issue was to distinguish clearly between justification and sanctification.

Law and Gospel have a close working relationship. Luther

could not have put their existential tie in the sinner's life more graphically than when he compared the Law to the upper grindstone and the Gospel to the lower grindstone. The Law crushes the pretension of self-achieved righteousness out of the human breast; the Gospel breathes life and forgiveness into the smitten sinner. Even the regenerate man, because of the continuing presence of the sinful flesh, stands in daily need of such mollifying, hammering, smashing clout of the Law, if repentance and contrition are to be part of his life day for day. The Law's accusatory function, therefore, never ceases, even for the Christian man; moreover, it is very necessary as the context within which the Gospel successfully wins the sinner with its sweet balm of grace and forgiveness.

Johann Agricola's antinomianism, which drew many misguided supporters, needed to be sharply repudiated (Art. V). To try to make the Gospel responsible for working repentance and contrition, was to confuse Law and Gospel terribly. Neither can do the work of the other; they stand in sharpest disjunction and antithesis. To say that there are elements within the Gospel that work contrition or recognition of sin, is to try to make the Gospel into Law and to do what only the Law can effect. Luther's rule simply stands: between the two, Law and Gospel, there is no mean, or middle ground, or commonplace; they differ from each other as a demand laid upon us differs from a gift given to us.

The framers of the Formula of Concord rightly saw that the dangers of antinomianism were very great and equally as lethal to the Gospel as synergism. The latter posits man's cooperation alongside God's enabling grace as a factor in his conversion, thus destroying *sola gratia*; the former turns the Gospel into Law and thus in effect becomes blatant antigospelism, for the Christian's so-called "freedom in the Gospel" then amounts to his being his *own* man, apart from the Law's accusing finger in repentance or its guiding hand in sanctification of life.

Synergism and antinomianism thus stand closer together than most people realize. The Formula of Concord recognized the peril. Article V, which dealt with the prior antinomian notion that regeneration is worked by the Gospel, not by the

Law, is followed immediately by Article VI, which dispelled the notion that the Christian man is no longer guided by the Law in seeking after godly, righteous living. Antinomianism needed to be quashed on both counts. The justified man continues to live in constant need of the Law's rebuke, because of his sinful flesh. Likewise he requires constant guidance in bringing forth fruits of faith that accord with God's norm and not his own self-chosen standard. Article V of the Formula summed this up very nicely: "It remains the peculiar office of the Law to reprove sins and teach concerning good works" (SD V 18; this quotation and those that follow in this chapter are from the Triglot).

It was really, therefore, a second stage in the antinomian disturbance that led to the writing of Article VI in the Formula. Some of the followers of Agricola, steeped in the notion that the Law ceases to have further relevance for the regenerate man, argued that a Christian does not have to be taught or guided by the Law in his quest for holiness. Their deemphasis of the Law can probably be traced in part to a reaction against the views of Georg Major, who had stated that good works are necessary for salvation. While Agricola may be named as chief catalyst, others were also involved, chiefly Pastors Poach, Otto, Musculus, Neander. To their credit it may be said that, when confronted with this disparagement of the Law as useful and needed by the regenerate man for guidance in Christian living, they eventually yielded. The aggregate testimony of the Scriptures mustered against them was overwhelming. So was the testimony from the earlier Lutheran Confessions.

With explicit clarity and directness the Formula of Concord asserts the threefold significance and continuing relevance of the Law on three counts: (1) for maintaining outward discipline, (2) to press home the knowledge of sins, and (3) to provide a fixed rule according to which to regulate life (Ep VI 1; cf. SD VI 1—3). The argument could not be *whether* the regenerate were moved in this pursuit of godliness "by God's Spirit," or *whether* they were thus acting "according to the inner man" and spontaneously seeking to "do God's will from a free spirit." Rather it was the question whether the Law was for them "a sure rule and standard of a godly life and walk;" and to this question the Formula answered categorically, yes, on the basis of clear Scriptural witness: "It is just the Holy Ghost who uses the written Law for instruction" (SD VI 3). They that "have been born anew by the Spirit of God" and who have "the veil of Moses . . . lifted from them" through justification by faith now "live and walk in the Law." (SD VI 1)

The liberated child of God delights in the Law of God because he is a child of God, a justified man (by faith in Christ). Such a man is in full sympathy with the psalmist whose "delight is in the Law of the Lord" and who meditates day and night in that Law (Ps. 1:2; cf. 119:1; quotations in this chapter are from the KJV) states the Formula (SD VI 4). Though the Law no longer is a burden to him, the justified man does not live without the Law (SD VI 5). It is true, of course, that if the regenerate man were completely renewed in this life, he would have no further use for the Law, for he would be completely free from the motions of sin and the flesh (SD VI 6). Their sin is covered, but believers never attain perfection in this life, though they earnestly strive after it. Mortification of the Old Adam is begun but never completely attained, as the apostle Paul points out in Rom. 7:15, 18, 23 and Gal. 5:17. (SD VI 7—8) Therefore even the regenerate continue to require the Law's admonitions, strictures, penalties, the Formula states on the basis of Psalm 119:71; 1 Cor. 9:27; Heb. 12:8; and then it adds an affirming, supportive word from one of Luther's postils or sermons (SD VI 9).

There can be no question that there is a basic, profound difference and "distinction between the works of the Law" as done by the unregenerate, where faith is lacking and where, as a result, conformity is by constraint and under threat or pressure; and the "fruits of the Spirit" which proceed "without constraint and with a willing spirit" out of a believing heart (Ep VI 5—7). "In this manner the children of God live in the Law and walk according to the Law," is the Epitome's plain, ingenuous way of putting it, on the basis of Rom. 7:25; 8:2, 7; Gal. 6:2 (Ep VI 6).

Thus on the basis of Scripture the framers of the Formula sought to establish irrefutably, both with thesis and antithesis, the continuing relevance and place of the Law in the believer's life. At the same time they demonstrated their complete accord with the Lutheran Church's *magna charta*, the Augsburg Confession. The Confessors at Augsburg were at pains to state very plainly their wholehearted support for good works in the life of the Christian, as fruits of faith, "commanded by God" (AC VI 1). They were pointing to the Ten Commandments (AC XX 2). Melanchthon emphasized that believers, who seek after God's will, live after or out of the content of the Ten Commandments (Apol. III); but he reminds the reader that "the Law is not observed without Christ" (148), a thought in perfect harmony with the architects of the Formula, who stressed good works as the fruits of the Spirit. The believer forever and a day lives out of the power of the Gospel, according to the inner man, the man of faith, as he conforms himself gladly to the holy will of God in the Law.

New obedience in the life of the regenerate has its source in the quickening power of the Gospel. (FC VI 10) On this point there could be no doubt. The base from which good works flow remains God's unmerited love and mercy in Christ. It was the "kindness and love of God our Savior," not "works of righteousness which we have done," by which God in "His mercy . . . saved us," through the water of Holy baptism, "the washing of regeneration and renewing of the Holy Ghost" (Titus 3:4-5). In this way alone (*sola gratia*), we were "justified by His grace" and "made heirs . . . of eternal life" (Titus 3:7). Then the apostle proceeds to exhort Titus, and all to whom he ministers, to "be careful to maintain good works" (Titus 3:8). The standard by which such works were to be gauged is certainly not the natural, carnal conscience of man (Rom. 8:7-8), nor the law of Moses, which contained many precepts—ceremonial, sacrificial, political—that were abrogated by Christ's coming (Col. 2:16-17), nor commandments devised by men or churches (Matt. 15:9; Col. 2:22). God's abiding standard of holiness in His moral code, the two tables of the Law, on which "two commandments hang all the Law and the prophets" (Matt. 22:40).

But, while the law of God is able to inform the regenerate man *what* God's will is, it is unable to prompt or effect godliness and new obedience. This only "the Holy Ghost" can accomplish, "who is given and received, not through the Law, but through the preaching of the Gospel, Gal. 3:14" (SD VI 11). "To reprove is the peculiar office of the Law," a function that the Holy Ghost continues to press, for the sake of true contrition in the believer; but now, in addition, for the justified man, who has and knows God's mercy in Christ, the Holy Spirit exhorts him to be zealous for "good works which are in accordance with God's Law" (SD VI 14—15). "The driver" for the believing sinner, who now "is born anew by the Spirit of God," is no longer Satan but the Spirit of Christ. Though the godliness which characterizes his life is precisely "according to the immutable will of God comprised in the Law," his works of love and charity are now "not properly works of the Law, but works and fruits of the Spirit," Rom. 7:23; 8:2; 1 Cor. 9:21 (SD VI 17). So while the old man (or old Adam) continues to need to be driven by the Law's threats and judgments, the Christian delights "according to the inner man," the man of faith, "in God's law." (SD VI 18) Self-evidently, and on the basis of Holy Scripture, the Formula stressed the continuing need that the regenerate man has, because of the presence of the flesh, for the Law as an instrument of condemnation, lest he ever "imagine that his work and life are entirely pure and perfect" (SD VI 21), and as an instrument of spiritual radar and guidance for the inner man, lest he "hit upon a holiness and devotion of [his] own ... [and] set up a self-chosen worship" (SD VI 20).

2.

Who had the mind of Luther and of the confessors at Augsburg, 1530? In the years between Luther's death (1546) and the writing of the Formula (1577) dissension raged like a storm over the question whether the regenerate "have a fixed rule according to which they are to regulate and direct their whole life," and "whether," therefore, the Law "is to be urged or not upon regenerate Christians. The one side has said, Yea; the other, Nay" (Ep VI 1). The signers of the Epitome said yes and for support drew entirely on clear Scriptural teaching. Not incidentally, however, Luther's position was also shown to be totally in support of this continuing function of the Law as a

192

teaching, informatory instrument in the life of the justified man, contrary to what the antinomians held.

When Luther at the outset of the Reformation smashed the icon of good works, he did so because, as he explained at Heidelberg, "the works of the righteous would be mortal sins if they would not be feared as mortal sins by the righteous themselves out of pious fear of God" (Thesis 7). It was one thing to do good works; quite another "to trust in works," because that would be "equivalent to giving oneself the honor and taking it from God," really "to adore oneself as an idol."[1] "To say that works without Christ are dead, but not mortal, appears to constitute a perilous surrender of the fear of God" (Thesis 9). In commenting on that point the Reformer himself explains that "in such a way God is constantly deprived of the glory which is due Him." "Whoever is not in Christ or who withdraws from Him," like the work-saint who seeks to be righteous before God by his own striving, "withdraws glory from Him [God]."[2]

It was the historic clash between *theologia gloriae*, theology of glory, and *theologia crucis*, theology of the cross, which Luther was the first really to set forth clearly in the church since the time of the apostle Paul. On this hinge everything turned: the proper relationship between faith and good works, between justification and sanctification, between Law and Gospel. None had so clearly distinguished these concepts, so important in the Christian theology, as had Luther. At the same time he reinforced the important *nexus indivulsus* between faith and works. For while the twain, in a sense, never meet—for the one can never become the other—there is nonetheless an inevitable bond or link between the two. But first of all, Luther saw the need of getting down to the bedrock of the Christian faith, that "not by works of righteousness which we have done, but according to His mercy He saved us" (Tit. 3:5), "by faith in Jesus Christ." (Gal. 2:16)

This necessitated cutting down every last one of the self-conceived and self-constructed ladders of human pretension of righteousness and good works as the way to God. Luther rightly assessed the situation. The task of Christian theology was to unmask "theology of glory" and label it for what it was, "ascent theology," human scrambling up ladders of man's own creation. Even the 20th-century agnostic and existentialistic novelist, Albert Camus, saw the lethal fault in this. He characterized French Catholicism as so much scrambling up the cross by one's own pious, spiritual gymnastics, as it were to get a better view, only to end up displacing Him who has hung there so long. Theology of glory is egocentric to the core; theology of the cross has but one object, Jesus, Jesus only. In theology of glory man is really saying: I am Christ. It was against this intolerable affront to the gracious and merciful God, this insufferable idolatry, that Luther agitated throughout his life, beginning even a few years before the nailing of the theses on Wittenberg's Castle Church door. He saw it as the dire heresy not only within the Romish system, but also wherever synergism raised its ugly head, his own Lutheran church not excepted.

But no one could ever mistake Luther's great and constant concern for godly, pious living. At the same time that he drove home the article on justification *sola gratia/fide*, he prodded his fellowmen, as well as himself, with exhortations to love and charity. The years from the Reformation's dawning in 1517 to the end of Luther's life in 1546 are filled with writings and sermons calling forth fruits of the Spirit. The rise of antinomian "spirits" within the Lutheran camp disturbed and incensed Luther just as much as the ever-present synergistic "termites." None knew better than the Reformer himself how subtly Satan could work as he infiltrated the ranks of the Reformation's own theologians; to be specific, Agricola with his antinomianism, Melanchthon with synergism.

Agricola plied his antinomianism cleverly. Luther had stated that the believer's greatest knowledge was not to know the Law, not to have anything more to do with it. Justification is solely by faith in the Gospel's promises. By no means should the believer return under the Law. His hope lay alone in God's forgiveness proclaimed by the Gospel. This was the "righteousness of faith or Christian righteousness," as Luther termed it, or "passive righteousness," thus an "alien" righteousness, because it comes from outside of us and "is the righteousness of Christ and of the Holy Spirit, which we do not perform but receive."[3] His lectures on Galatians are especially rich in explication of this righteousness, by which "God accepts you or accounts you righteous only on account of Christ, in whom you believe."[4] Never must this perfect righteousness be diluted or adulterated with the admixture of our righteousness, or, to use Luther's terms, "active righteousness," "domestic righteousness" (*LW* 26, 356), "righteousness of the Law."

But there is a place and time for the latter, and we teach it too, said Luther, "*after* the doctrine of faith."[5] This was the point that Agricola missed, deliberately, as it appears. There is a sharp dialectic here, not a wooden time-clock, stilted sort of thing, but one that stands in sharpest cause and effect relation. When a man has Christ's righteousness reigning in his heart, then he will gladly work in his calling, be he "minister of the Word," "father," "magistrate," "servant," or whatever.[6] "Christ is our . . . perfect righteousness"; and because He is, now "we should take pains to be righteous outwardly as well" and not "yield to our flesh" but "resist it through the Spirit." Such outward, active righteousness, of course, does not "make us acceptable in the sight of God,"[7] that is, for salvation and justification, but "genuine saints" are those who confess "that Christ is their wisdom, righteousness, sanctification, and redemption," *and* who then "do their duty in their callings on the basis of the command of the Word of God [*ex praescripto verbi Dei,* according to the prescription of God's Word]"[8]

From the earliest days of the Reformation Luther had clearly distinguished between the righteousness that is ours through imputation from Christ by faith and the righteousness of life, or active righteousness, that godly children pursue with all zeal because they are God's children. Nor did he ever fail to emphasize "active righteousness" in his own great zeal to keep "passive righteousness" pure and uncluttered! His sermons and writings are replete with exhortations to godly living by God's saints. His treatise *On Good Works* appeared early in 1520 and stands as harbinger of writings to come, a veritable flood, including his two catechisms (1529), sermons, hymns, letters, and table talk, All bear record to Luther's great concern that

Christian faith blossom forth in works of love. At the end of the commandments in his Large Catechism, he counseled:

> Thus we have the Ten Commandments, a compend of divine doctrine, as to what we are to do in order that our whole life may be pleasing to God, and the true fountain and channel from and in which everything must arise and flow that is to be a good work, so that outside of the Ten Commandments no work or thing can be good or pleasing to God, however, great or precious it be in the eyes of the world.[9]

Luther's famous preface to the Epistle of Paul to the Romans is a veritable "Manifesto of Faith," the Protestant panegyric for justification by faith! Yet it is in this very famous brief in behalf of salvation *sola gratia/fide* that Luther, ever true to the text, points out how the apostle Paul exhorts believers to fruits of the spirit, or good works. "Faith," he writes, "is a living, daring confidence in God's grace, so sure and certain that the believer would stake his life on it a thousand times," and "because of it, without compulsion, a person is ready and glad to do good to everyone, to serve everyone, to suffer everything, out of love and praise to God, who has shown him this grace."[10] Faith's intimate tie with good works was never stated better. Little wonder that the Formula of Concord quotes him. (SD IV 10)

Luther had pretty well anticipated the faulty thinking and theologizing of antinomian spirits like Agricola, and he confronted their errors squarely. Luther credits them with being fine preachers of the Second Article of the Creed and of the Gospel, but poor preachers of sanctification, the Third Article; that is, "fine Easter preachers, but . . . very poor Pentecost preachers, for they do not preach *de sanctificatione et vivificatione Spiritus Sancti.*"[11] In fact they really are neither, because by failing to do the one, they also fail to do the other. This pungent comment appears in the middle of his redoubtable *On the Councils and the Church* (1539). The trouble with these people, Luther avers, is that they grant the premise and deny the conclusion. "Christ did not earn only *gratia,* 'grace,' for us, but also *donum,* 'the gift of the Holy Spirit,' so that we might have not only forgiveness of, but also cessation of, sin."[12] No man, says Luther, can boast of being Christian, and then boast that he can "at the same time remain an adulterer, a whoremonger, a drunken swine, arrogant, covetous, a usurer, envious, vindictive, malicious, etc!" "Our Antinomians fail to see that they are preaching Christ without and against the Holy Spirit because they propose to let the people continue in their old ways and still pronounce them saved."[13] To Luther, inculcating saving faith and godly living are integral parts of the same Christian sermon; not as equal parts that add up to salvation, but in cause and effect relationship. Disciples of the Master will *want* to pursue discipleship; this cannot be otherwise, though such discipleship in no way determines, effects, prompts or sustains faith. Faith sustains discipleship. Where Dietrich Bonhoeffer went wrong in emphasizing the cost of discipleship was not in stressing discipleship as necessary fruit of the faith relationship with the Master, but in repeating the error of Melanchthon and Major, making discipleship necessary for salvation, thus turning the effect into cause, or at least partial cause.

Between 1537 and 1540 Luther prepared a series of six disputations trying to settle the dust raised by Agricola's antinomian meandering. There are reasons to believe that "the Eislebener" (Luther's pejorative label for Agricola, who was born at Eisleben and later became preacher and director of the Latin school there; incidentally, Eisleben was also Luther's birthplace) was motivated more by petty reasons than purely theological reasons when he brewed the storm of opposition to Luther's teaching. He seemed never to forget nor forgive Luther for the role he played in having Melanchthon appointed to the faculty in Wittenberg when he himself coveted it so dearly. But Luther extended him every courtesy, even calling on him to substitute for him while he was away at Smalcald. Daring to be different seemed to be one of the tactics by which he hoped to lay claim to fame. Since Melanchthon had earlier, at the time of the parish and school visitations in 1528, made very clear the importance of the Law as a teaching instrument for sanctification of life, it seems that Agricola tried the opposite tack, stressing that the Gospel alone continued to have relevance in the life of the regenerate man, both in working contrition and in shaping his life.

Luther's repudiation of Agricola's antinomian notions is sharp and to the point. In fact, his *Second Disputation Against the Antinomians* minces no words in ranking Agricola in the company of other "Schwaermer" or "new spirits," like Münzer, Karlstadt, and the Anabaptists.[14] Luther, in his customary way of not keeping his thoughts hidden up his sleeve, simply states that "Master John Agricola . . . is the instigator and the master of this game," the dastardly trick of claiming that Luther taught that the Law was no longer to be preached in the church. "It is most surprising to me that anyone can claim that I reject the Law or the Ten Commandments," Luther exclaims, totally disagreeing with the argument of "the new spirits who have dared to expel the law of God or the Ten Commandments from the church and to assign them to city hall."[15] He grieves over the fact that these "new spirits" do not understand that the story of Christ's Passion contains not only sweetest Gospel but also graphic portrayal of the Law's sting and God's wrath and judgment against all unrighteousness. "The Law terrifies me more," confides Luther, "when I hear that Christ, the Son of God, had to fulfill it for me than it would were it preached to me without the mention of Christ and of such great torment suffered by God's Son."[16]

So the Law has to be preached, Luther explains, for the Gospel's sake, "for Christ's sake;" for "how will we learn what Christ is, what He did for us, if we do not know what the Law is that He fulfilled for us and what sin is, for which He made satisfaction?"[17] Christ's Passion vividly portrays God's wrath against sin too. "I did teach, and still teach, that sinners shall be stirred to repentance through the preaching or the contemplation of the Passion of Christ."[18] But to those who are "dejected and downcast" and "who feel their sin" under God's threatening judgments of the Law, Luther counsels, "to such, the dear Jesus can never be portrayed sweetly enough."[19] But Agricola was for halting the preaching of the Law at all to sinners, or for turning

198

the process around, "a new method whereby one is to preach grace first and then the revelation of wrath"—shades of Karl Barth who came off with the same kind of formula! Luther's judgment on such distortion of the proper sphere and function of the Law and the Gospel is very severe: "It is apparent from this that the devil's purpose in this fanaticism is not to remove the Law but to remove Christ, the fulfiller of the Law."[20] Thus "antinomianism" is always the cocoon that bursts into "antigospelism!"

It is apparent that at this stage in Agricola's assault on the Law Luther's concern was primarily for the continuing pertinence and impact that it had in its condemnatory, accusatory function for working contrition and repentance. Unless such preaching preceded, the secure sinner would not be ready for the sweet Gospel. In fact it will be distasteful to him. But Luther at this early date is not insensible to what became the second stage of antinomianism, the denial that the Law had teaching value for the Christian in daily living and new obedience. He mentions in this same document, the *Second Disputation Against the Antinomians*, that his writing on the Ten Commandments is available in many sources, in his "exposition of the Ten Commandments" in the catechisms, in his sermons, and in some of his hymns. The "Confession (Augsburg) and the Apology" also stand as a witness against the antinomians, he adds. Undoubtedly he has hymns like his "These Are the Holy Ten Commands" of 1524 and "Man, Wouldst Thou Live All Blissfully" of 1524,[21] in mind when he states: "Furthermore, the commandments are sung in two versions," and they are, as a matter of fact, "painted, printed, carved, and recited by the children morning, noon, and night."[22] With penetrating, pungent insight he adds: "I know of no manner in which we do not use them, unless it be that we unfortunately do not practice and paint them with our deeds and our life as we should."[23]

Self-evidently from what has been cited, the concept of the Law, not only in its political and theological functions as curb and mirror, but also as the norm for schooling the righteous man or believer in works that are godly, in active righteousness, was very much an integral part of Luther's theology. Well and clearly did he point out that thereby no man is justified; but well and clearly he affirmed that thereby a man lives if indeed Christ lives in him.

The Usus triplex legis and Contemporary Theology

In spite of Luther's clear support of the concept of the third use of the Law there is a strange opposition on the part of many ranking Luther scholars to the idea that he taught it or supported it. Werner Elert argued that not only is the term "third use of the Law" foreign to Luther, but the concept itself. His argument is largely built on the contention that the words, "Thirdly, the law is to be retained so that the saints may know which works God requires," appended at the end of Luther's Second Disputation Against the Antinomians, are a forgery and that they were interpolated from Melanchthon's *Loci Communes*.[24] It is possible that such an interpolation may have occurred. But to dismiss out of hand the fact that Luther nonetheless used the *concept* of the third use of the Law, if not the exact term, is without substantiation.

Elert grossly oversimplifies the whole matter, simply ignoring the countless references in Luther's writings and sermons and letters that plainly uphold the Law's use in the Christian's life as a guide for godly living. Elert mistakenly conceives the Christian's freedom from the Law—its curse, punishment, coercion—to include freedom "to live without the law," as though the Law no longer needed to inform regenerate Christians what to do.[25] This leads him to insist that for Christians the Law has but a twofold function: (1) to expose sin—the theological, paedogogical, elenchtical function; and (2) to hold evildoers in check—the political or civil function. Luther would not quibble that these are the two *principal* functions of the Law; but he would insist that, for the Christian in whom Christ lives, the Ten Commandments, or Law, are the informing norm according to whose prescription believers seek to conform their lives.

The believer finds this table of duties not a burdensome,

200

irksome, unpleasant sort of thing, according to the inner man, but a delight in his service to his God. Elert, therefore, is quite wrong when he criticizes the Formula of Concord for following Melanchthonian thinking in adding an article on the third use of the Law. But Elert does not stop there. He juggles its meaning until the teaching of Article VI on the informatory function of the Law is telescoped, absorbed, and submerged into the accusatory. His problem seems to be the notion that some Lutherans, specifically the orthodox theologians of the 17th century and others like them, may somehow have failed to emphasize the Law's chief (and only, according to Elert) function of accusing the sinner and driving him to Christ. He apparently is unaware, or prefers to have it that way, that no Lutheran theologian worth his salt ever denied that *lex semper accusat* is a principle basic to Scriptural theology.

The only remaining conclusion, therefore, is that Elert himself, like Agricola and the second wave of antinomians (Otto, Poach, Neander, et al.), holds that a regenerate man needs no teacher of what is right or godly, since the Gospel itself teaches him. Precisely this form of antinomianism is what Luther feared would sweep the church, falsely parading its so-called love for and freedom in the Gospel. The Reformer saw that this "piety" was a "fanaticism" whose purpose finally was "not to remove the Law but to remove Christ, the fulfiller of the Law."[26]

Paul Althaus, likewise generally a respected Luther scholar, represents no improvement over Elert on the question of whether the third use of the Law is a concept congenial to and inherent in Lutheran theology. He tries to soften Elert's attack on the third use by emphasizing the distinction between Law and command, *Gesetz* and *Gebot*. He reasons that, through the Gospel, Law becomes command. He is quite right in stating that Law and Gospel "stand in strict disjunction and antithesis."[27] But when he asserts that "the relationship of Gospel and command is quite different" and that the latter "is in fact an element in the gospel itself," he clearly contradicts a position that Luther nailed down tight, namely, that there can be no middle ground between demand laid upon us (Law *or*

201

command) the gift (Gospel) given to us. Althaus acknowledges, however, that Luther used the concept, and thus is fully in tune with the Augsburg Confession, Apology, and Formula of Concord.[28] In fact, at that point, by stating that command is an element in the Gospel, Althaus has surrendered to the Barthian (and Romanist!) position, that the Law is the necessary form of the Gospel whose content is grace! Precisely this is the conclusion to which antinomianism inevitably leads.

Ultimately Althaus avers regarding the third use of the Law: "We find it impossible to retain this concept."[29] Like Elert he wants to admit only the Law's accusatory function and demurs at the slightest suggestion that the Law might also have a regulatory or informatory function for the believer, claiming that this immediately implies legalism. "The Spirit of God wants to teach us," he counters. True, but how, Luther would have asked? And the Reformer would immediately have bunched Althaus with the rest of the "new spirits" who want to pitch out the Law of God in favor of their own so-called "Gospel-prompted" pieties. In place of the third use of the Law Althaus makes a nebulous gesture towards "the voice of Scripture" and, of all things, to "Christendom" and "Christian tradition," as though these indeed could rescue him from a terrible dilemma.[30]

Gerhard Ebeling, in *Word and Faith*, a scholarly work on Luther's theology, insists, too, that the Law in its twofold function, *duplex usus legis*, is as far as Luther goes in his treatment of the Law's meaning and application to the Christian life. Many other contemporary Luther scholars[31] have apparently taken it as their mission in life somehow to drive a wedge between Luther and the Confessions, particularly the Formula of Concord. The strategy in each case is to demonstrate that either Melanchthon or the architects of the Formula, or both, presented a caricature somehow of the Reformer's true views. Luther himself was all too familiar with this technique, the distorting of another man's view, in order to justify one's own. He labeled them "Schwaermer," or "heretics," because such "new spirits" are really fighting against God's Word of truth itself, Holy Scripture. They find their "own explanation convenient."[32] Equally as pertinent is this insight by Luther:

I have noticed that all heresies and errors in
handling the Scriptures have come, not from the
simplicity of the words (as almost all the world tells
us), but from not regarding the simplicity of the words,
and from hankering after figures and implications that
come out of men's own heads."[33]

With right, therefore, the writers of the Formula of
Concord stood in judgment of the faulty theologizing that ruled
out the pertinence of the Law as a teaching and guiding
instrument for the regenerate man:

Accordingly, we reject and condemn as an error
pernicious and detrimental to Christian discipline, as
also to true godliness, the teaching that the Law, in the
above-mentioned way and degree, should not be urged
upon Christians and the true believers, but only upon
the unbelieving, unchristians, and impenitent. (SD VI,
26)

Conclusion

Article VI of the Formula of Concord, "The Third Use of
the Law," accurately reflects Luther's teaching on the subject.
Most importantly, it affirmed exactly—intent and meaning—
what the Augsburg Confession (Articles VI and XX) and the
Apology (Articles IV and XX) taught on the relation of good
works to faith as fruits of the Spirit. In no way can it be shown
that a man like Martin Chemnitz, himself one of the greatest
Luther scholars that ever lived, expanded on the master's
theology on this point. Above all, of course, Chemnitz, like his
co-workers on the Formula, was concerned to present a solid
Scriptural base for each article. Their work stands for all to
judge. Holy Scripture was their advocate, and it pleads a strong
case in their favor. Not incidentally, however, they were also
dedicated to the proposition that Luther had laid out the articles
of faith in Christian doctrine so clearly, that it was impossible
for anyone to mistake his meaning. History records the accuracy
of their position.

Luther, of course, would have been the last one to think

himself indispensable, or his theological writing beyond criticism. But on the articles of faith, because they were taught of God, he knew he was right because God's Word taught so clearly. No man could be in doubt as to the Lord's meaning. What was required was not a clever interpreter, he contended, but an attentive listener and obedient believer.

God would take care of the rest. The church need never fear for its life, or its doctrine. God would see to that. He and His Word alone are indispensable. At the conclusion of his *Second Disputation Against the Antinomians* Luther painted this truth very vividly:

> A thousand years ago you and I were nothing, and yet the church was preserved at that time without us. He who is called "who was" [Rev. 1:8] and "yesterday" [Heb. 13:8] had to accomplish this. Even during our lifetime we are not the church's guardians. . . . For it is another Man who obviously preserves both the church and us. . . . It is a tragic thing that there are so many examples before us of those who thought they had to preserve the church, as though it were built on them. In the end they perished miserably.[34]

Luther's concern was for what the self-styled "heroes," the "sheer spirits," would do to the church, who believe that all their "thoughts and ideas are surely and certainly inspired by the Holy Spirit."[35] That story, says Luther, always "has such a nice ending—namely, that both steed and rider break their necks."[36] Therefore, do the Holy Spirit the honor of doffing your hat before His Word, Holy Scripture, and bend low before its footprint. They that are taught of God will not cavil at His Word, neither on this article of faith, on the third use of the Law, nor on any other.

THE HOLY SUPPER

Lowell C. Green

Much new knowledge and corrected information regarding the Lord's Supper in the Confessional Age has been uncovered during the past 25 years. We shall try to share some of these fresh insights as we also present an interpretation of Article VII in its historical setting.

It is generally agreed that Article II (Free Will, or Human Powers) and Article VII presented the most sensitive issues to the writers of the Formula of Concord, and consequently represented their most important achievements. It is noteworthy that both of these articles were prepared in their semifinal form (Torgau Book) by a faithful pupil of Melanchthon, David Chytraeus, and then revised by Jacob Andreä, who tried to counteract Melanchthon's influence. Article VII preserved a delicate balance between Luther's position on the right, with its emphasis that the bread *is* the body of Christ from the consecration onward, and Melanchthon's position on the left, holding that the body of Christ exists in, with, and under the bread during its "use" (consecration, distribution, consumption). It only remained for recent Lutherans to depart from Luther, Melanchthon, and the Formula of Concord in teaching that the pastor or even lay-assistant distributes only bread (see liturgical rubrics), which imparts at the moment of eating the body of Christ also.[1] Our Study of Article VII and its age will show that Lutherans in America, conservative as well as liberal, have espoused teachings and practices that represent a substantial departure from those of Luther, Melanchthon (!), and the Formula of Concord.[2] It is hoped that these lines will lead the church today to a better understanding of the confessional position and to a reevaluation of its own stance.

Part One: The Place of the Lord's Supper in the Formula of Concord

The Lord's Supper takes its place in the distinctively Lutheran doctrine of the means of grace. The preaching of the Word is not merely the impartation of religious information; where Law and Gospel are rightly divided, the preached Word is an exhortation and consolation from God Himself, actually creating faith and conferring salvation through the words of the minister. Baptism is not merely a sign of regeneration acquired previously or elsewhere, but it is a rebirth, through which one retroactively participates in the crucifixion and resurrection of Christ, is transformed into a child of God, and becomes an heir of heaven. The Holy Supper of Christ is no mere repristination of a Jewish *chaburah,* nor is it only a memorial of the Last Supper, nor is it just a symbol of redemption, but rather it is a participation in the very body and blood of Christ, once offered and sacrificed for sins, in an act of communion with the crucified, glorified, and omnipresent Savior.[3]

The Formula of Concord, like the earlier Lutheran Confessions, avoided the pitfalls of developing the Lord's Supper out of some general concept of sacraments or doctrine of the Word. But the close relationship with the doctrine of the person and work of Christ was carefully maintained, especially in the parts contributed by Andreä. This means that in studying

206

the Formula, Article VIII must often be consulted when reading Article VII.

We note that the word "Eucharist" had begun to pass from Lutheran usage during the framing of the Confessions, and that this word was avoided in the Formula of Concord. Was this a deliberate suppression of the term? This would be hard to prove. Nevertheless, one almost senses the earnest concern to avoid the Roman concept of sacrifice of the mass; though Luther and Melanchthon had redefined the "sacrifice" in evangelical terms, the dangers of mingling Law and Gospel perhaps seemed too real to permit the use of the word "Eucharist." However, scattered usage appears among various Lutheran writers in the history leading up to the Formula of Concord.[4]

Article VII did not repeat many of the statements of the earlier symbols regarding the practical use of the Sacrament, but expressly endorsed these documents and their contents (SD VII 9—34). The Augsburg Confession and its Apology had spoken about the frequency of communion, noting that in some places the Sacrament might be offered as often as once a week (Art. XXIV). But such frequent attendance was to be accorded only those who had been thoroughly instructed, examined, and heard in private confession. Where frequent attendance today is insisted on without such reference to the care of souls, the spirit, if not the letter, of these confessions is violated.[5] In one of two places in the Confessions where the word "Eucharist" appears (Ap XXIV 19), Melanchthon emphasized the sacrament as a joyful gift, to be received with thanksgiving; since the Reformed tendency to regard the Lord's Supper as a penitential event is appearing in some Lutheran congregations today, as can be observed even in the selection of hymns for the service, this emphasis of joy by Melanchthon might help to bring the church today to a more adequate concept of the presence of Christ, as it is eloquently proclaimed in the Formula of Concord.

Part Two: The Problem of the Place of Melanchthon in the Formula of Concord

The Lutheran Church has been seriously hindered from coming to an authentic self-understanding because of her inability to recognize the role that Melanchthon's teachings have played.[6] Writers such as Friedrich Bente have unconsciously rejected Luther's own teaching in favor of Melanchthon's actual teaching, which they imagined to be that of genuine Lutheranism. If Melanchthon had really taught what Bente felt he had, any genuine Lutheran would have to reject such a position; Bente was partly correct from the viewpoint of systematics, but his historical judgments can no longer be accepted.[7] Since both Chemnitz and Chytraeus defended Melanchthon's teachings throughout their lives, not to speak of Selnecker's former close relationship with the "Preceptor of Germany," we must expect to find a position mediating between Luther and Melanchthon (rather than between the Gnesio-Lutherans and the Philippists). Our investigation will justify this expectation.

The Formula of Concord was irenic in character: it avoided mentioning names and tried to condemn only positions, not men. Although many of the Gnesio-Lutherans wanted to have Melanchthon expressly condemned, this was avoided by the writers. In fact, it is uncertain whether any of his teachings were really those included among the condemned positions. But when his pupils, such as Chytraeus, wished to have the name of Melanchthon included among the orthodox teachers, they did

Table 1—A Comparison of the Swabian-Saxon Concord and the Formula of Concord

SSC: Chytraeus	FC VII: Andreä
Therefore our revered fathers and preceptors, such as Luther in many passages and also Philipp [Melanchthon] in the book of the Saxon Visitation,	Therefore our revered fathers and forebears, like Luther and other pure teachers of the Augsburg Confession,
explained this passage of Paul . . . (Heppe III/B, p. 262)	explained this passage of Paul . . . (SD VII 58; Tappert, p. 579—580)

not succeed. Only Luther was accorded this distinction. The preceding example will illustrate this point (Table 1). In the left-hand column is the statement of the Swabian-Saxon Concord, ascribed to Chytraeus, and in the right-hand column is the revision in the Formula, which was essentially the work of Andreae. Not only was the name of Melanchthon excised from this sentence, but it was taken completely out of Article VII, whereas Luther was mentioned more than 20 times, in 5 instances of which his was called the authentic Lutheran teaching (SD VII 33, 34, 41, 58, 91).

The role of Melanchthon in the events that led up to the drafting of Article VII were intricately interwoven with the controversies between Lutheran and Reformed spokesmen after 1525. Zwingli had abandoned the doctrine of the real presence by 1524 and had attacked Luther's position shortly thereafter. The followers of Luther and those of Zwingli had separated at the Marburg Colloquy of 1529. But some of the Upper Germans had been reconciled with Luther in the Wittenberg Concord of 1536, a document quoted in SD VII 12—16. During Luther's last years, it seemed as though a revival of the controversy were imminent, but aside from several polemics by him, a major confrontation was avoided. The second sacramental controversy was triggered by the *Consensus Tigurinus* (1549).[8] The Lutherans had not realized how far Calvin diverged from their position until he and his followers reached this compromise with the Swiss Reformed disciples of Zwingli. This Reformed consensus threw into question the friendly relationship that had existed between Calvin and Melanchthon, permanently separated the Calvinists from the Lutherans, and brought on the controversy between Calvin and Westphal, an erstwhile follower of Melanchthon. The second sacramental controversy was to produce three fateful consequences for Melanchthon and his place in subsequent Lutheranism. (1) Through guilt by association he was suspected of being a Crypto-Calvinist, a false impression that was heightened when some of his pupils (Philippists) proved to be undercover agents of Calvinism. (2) This diverted the attention of his contemporaries and of subsequent scholars from the position that Melanchthon actually held, which, in turn, became incorrectly identified with the teaching of Luther, so that the latter fell into the category of the forgotten. (3) Although it can hardly be proved that Melanchthon ever rejected the position of the Lutheran Confessions, [9] it seems clear that he became discouraged by the attacks of the Gnesio-Lutherans, so that he became more and more ambiguous in his formulations. The worst example of the attempts of the aged reformer to avoid confronting the issues is his opinion regarding the Reformation of the Palatinate, which helped Elector Frederick III to decide to expel the Lutherans and introduce a form of Calvinism (CR 9, 960—964). This was late in 1559, a few months before Melanchthon's death. It did irreparable damage to the image of Melanchthon in the immediate and distant future.

An adequate study of the doctrine of the Lord's Supper as taught by Melanchthon does not exist, nor has a suitable comparison of Melanchthon and Luther on this point ever been produced. Luther did not feel that Melanchthon's position differed greatly from his own. Yet there were important differences in emphasis. The following list of differences (Table 2) is only tentative and must therefore be used with great caution. In some instances either reformer may be found on either side. But it might prove helpful to the reader of FC VII to look for divergencies between Luther and Melanchthon and their followers at the points listed in Table 2.

Luther regarded the Roman Catholic position as improper as to action, but valid (body and blood are received), and the Reformed sacrament as both improper and invalid (body and blood not received); Melanchthon tried to compromise with the position of Calvin while maintaining a relationship with the Erasmian group among the Roman Catholics. Neither reformer regarded the Altered Augsburg Confession of 1540 as a substantive departure from the original form of 1530. In the *Loci theologici* of 1559 Melanchthon insisted that Christ was present "not merely in efficacy, but also in substance" (CR 21, 863), a formulation that seems to place him plainly within the Lutheran camp.

Luther	Melanchthon	FC SD VII
The body and blood of Christ are present.	Christ as a person is present.	The body and blood of Christ are present.
The bread *is* the body of Christ.	The body is given *in*, *with*, and *under* the bread.	The bread *is* the body (20-21); the body exists *in, with*, and *under* the bread (35).
The doctrine of the sacrament should be based on Christology (later called "ubiquity").	The doctrine of the sacrament should not be complicated by Christology; the Word as point of departure. [WA 48, 236; CR 9, 1087 f.]	Lord's Supper developed out of Words of Institution, and then defended with Christology (93—106; 93—103 quote Luther). (Multivolipresence.)
Adoration of the sacrament defended (WA 11, 448; WA 18, 191, etc.).	Adoration excoriated as "bread worship" (CR 8, 660 f., etc.)	Not the bread and wine are to be adored, but Christ Himself, who is truly present, is adored, unless we are Arians (126).
An accident with the consecrated host/chalice is a serious matter (WA Br 10, 337).	An accident with the consecrated host/chalice affects only bread/wine, not the body/blood of Christ, and is not sacrilegious (CR 9, 470).	(Not discussed.)
Reconsecration important (WA Br 10, 86). Leftover consecrated host/chalice treated after the service as body/blood (WA Br 10, 339 f.)	Reconsecration no issue (CR 8, 598). Remaining elements are only bread/wine and are treated as such (CR 7, 877).	Reconsecration implied (80—82, 86). Disposal of leftover species not discussed.

Part Three: An Analysis and Interpretation of Article VII

In our study of Article VII we shall adapt the outline provided by one of its chief writers, Chytraeus [Heppe III/B, p. 252 f.]. We shall indicate the corresponding paragraph numbers of the Solid Declaration as supplied in the Tappert edition and add the enumeration of the parallel paragraphs in the Epitome.

Outline

	S.D.	Ep.
I. The Status of the Controversy		
A. The deceptive position of their Reformed opponents	1—8	1—5
B. The position of the earlier Lutheran Confessions against the Reformed opponents	9—34	
II. The presentation of the Lutheran Doctrine of the Real Presence of Christ		
A. As sacramental union	34—41	6—7
1. Based on the Words of Institution	42—53	8—9
2. Lutheran Christology	(Cf. 91—106)	10—14
B. As oral manducation	54—59	15
C. As the certainty that not only the pious but also the impious receive the body and blood of Christ	60	16—18
III. The Consequence of the Real Presence: Sacramental Eating and Drinking		
A. The difference between spiritual and sacramental eating and drinking	61—72	(15)
B. The importance of the act of consecration.	73—90	(8—9)
C. This all follows from the doctrine of the person and work of Christ	91—106	(10—14)
IV. The Refutation of the Arguments of the Opponents		
A. The propriety of such condemnations	107	21
B. Rejection of some aspects of the Roman Catholic position	108—110	22—24, 40
C. Rejection of teachings of the Reformed "sacramentarians"	111—123	25—39, 41—42
D. A false view of preparation for communion	124—125	18—19
E. Impertinent speculations to be rejected	127	
Conclusion	128	

212

Interpretation

I. The Status of the Controversy

At the Religious Peace of Augsburg in 1555 adherents of the Augsburg Confession had been granted toleration. Unfortunately, the Reformed had separated from the Lutherans in 1529, and the wedge that separated both groups had become even greater when the Calvinists had accepted the Consensus Tigurinus of 1549. Some of the Reformed now sought political advantages by claiming that they too accepted the Augsburg Confession, even though they rejected Lutheran doctrine. Not only did this claim place the followers of Zwingli and Calvin in an awkward, dual position, but it also led to much confusion among the Lutherans.

This is the historical background for the opening of Article VII, which distinguishes two kinds of "Sacramentarians": the crass ones, who clearly teach that nothing but bread and wine is received, and the subtle ones, who pretend to believe a real presence, but actually teach that the presence of Christ takes place only spiritually through faith, since they say that Christ's body is confined to heaven (Ep 3—6). Especially the latter dissimulation had misled many, including prominent people (SD 6); noteworthy had been the case of Albertine Saxony, where Crypto-Calvinism had almost succeeded in driving out genuine Lutheranism. Fortunately, the deception had been exposed, and Lutheranism had been restored in Saxony. In fact, this unlovely incident had been a major factor in Elector August's energetic promotion of the emerging Formula of Concord.[10]

The Problem of Christology and the Sacrament. In his "Great Confession on the Supper of Christ" (1528) Luther had developed his doctrine of the Sacrament in a close relationship to Christology, and he held this line for the rest of his life. Although this work of Luther was copiously quoted in SD VII (28—31, 32, 78, 93—97, 98—103), his Christological emphasis was neglected in favor of an exegesis of the Words of Institution, except for the long excerpt in 93—102. Had they based their argument more fully on Luther's foundation in the person and work of Christ, their case would have been much more easily established. Why did they not follow Luther more closely? Theodor Mahlmann gives the answer to this question in a recent book in which he shows how a statement by Melanchthon, wrongly ascribed to Luther in the Jena edition of Luther's works as published by the Gnesio-Lutherans, had misled the strict Lutherans into following Melanchthon instead of Luther.[11] The statement of March 16, 1546, is given in its entirety in WA 48, p. 236, from which we provide the following excerpt:

> The true body and true blood is given in the bread and chalice. Now the question is raised: How can Christ be bodily present in the Sacrament, if the body is not able to be in many places at the same time? I reply: Christ has said that he would be present; therefore he is truly present, bodily, in the Sacrament. . . . Concerning ubiquity there must be no disputation; the problem in this controversy is a completely different matter. Nor did any of the schoolmen speak concerning ubiquity, but they retained the simple understanding of the corporal presence of Christ.

Although Luther had made the doctrine of the ubiquity an important mainstay of his teaching regarding the Lord's Supper, his followers obeyed instead the above injunction to base the doctrine of the sacrament on the Words of Institution, aside from Christology. Mahlmann has shown (p. 41) how Johannes Bötker of Hamburg, followed by Johann Brenz and Jacob Andreä of Württemberg, led the way back to Luther's Christological foundation for the Sacrament.

The way back to Luther had been prompted by the polemics of the Reformed, who had insisted that since Christ had ascended to heaven in the body, and since it was the property of a body to be circumscribed to only one place, the body of Christ could not be received in the sacramental bread but only in a spiritual manner (SD 91). Beginning with Bötker's book in 1557, an unconscious but dramatic struggle went on, with the Gnesio-Lutherans and the Philippists representing the axiom of Melanchthon that had been mistakenly ascribed to

Luther, and the Swabish with a few others espousing Luther's real position, dubbed by their opponents the "ubiquity." When the Formula of Concord was assembled, Chytraeus, the principal writer of SD VII, seems to have been led by the axiom, "Concerning ubiquity there must be no disputation" in the doctrine of the Lord's Supper. However, a strong Christological statement from Luther was provided by Andreä, 93—97 (the same by Andreä in Ep 11—14), and even extended by Chytraeus, 99—103.

It might surprise the reader that Article VII mentions only once the doctrine of the exchange of the properties between the human and divine natures (*communicatio idiomatum*), and that in this single occurrence it is treated very coldly (SD 4) and as a trick of the Crypto-Calvinists. We should remember, however, that Melanchthon had been charged with teaching a doctrine of the communication of the properties as a verbal but not a real (*verbalis sed non realis*) phenomenon[12], that Crypto-Calvinistic followers of Melanchthon had actually misused that doctrine in this manner, and that Andreä himself had strongly opposed the idea of the *communicatio idiomatum* in his Six Sermons.[13] In Article VIII, the Formula would take a more positive view of this doctrine, firmly stating that it must be taught as a real and not merely verbal phenomenon (18—19), and giving it a prominent place in Lutheran Christology.

The Earlier Lutheran Confessions and Luther (SD 9—41). Now the writers of the Formula recalled earlier statements given in the Augsburg Confession, Luther's Small Catechism, and the Apology (SD 9—11), the compromise effected with the Upper Germans in the Wittenberg Concord (12—16), and the position taken in the Smalcald Articles and the Large Catechism (17—27) as well as citations from theologians of the ancient church and from other writings of Luther (28—41).

Prominent among these citations was the argument of Melanchthon in the Apology, Article X, where, after affirming that the "body and blood of Christ are present in truth and in substance, and are truly given" with the bread and wine, he went on to flay the notion of a merely spiritual presence, or that concept that the Holy Ghost rather than Christ is the principal

215

actor. Referring to 1 Cor. 10:16-17, he insisted that Paul did not say that the consecrated bread and wine were the communion of the *spirit* of Christ, but rather of the *body* of Christ (SD 11). The reference to the Wittenberg Concord of 1536 must have been reassuring to the Philippists who accommodated themselves to the Formula of Concord; it underscored the fact that this new confession was to be irenic and inclusive. In this connection, the much-debated quotation of the statement of Irenaeus that there are two things in the sacrament, a heavenly and an earthly, *coelesti et terrena* (14), should not be excessively criticized. It wanted to exclude the Neoplatonism of the Reformed and the Roman Catholics alike. For the Reformed denied that an earthly substance could convey a heavenly gift, and the Roman doctrine of transubstantiation denied that the earthly substance even existed after the consecration. The Lutheran view, based on the theology of the incarnation, stressed the divine condescension in which spiritual gifts were conveyed through earthly means of grace.

As we observed in Part Two, the final draft of the Formula of Concord (technically, the Bergen Book) brushed Melanchthon aside and named only Luther as its principal teacher. In today's situation it may be helpful to consult Luther's position regarding how far a Lutheran should go in the attempt to reach communion fellowship with the Reformed. Shortly after Luther's death, certain Crypto-Calvinists had circulated the rumor that Luther had stated privately before he died: "We have gone too far in the matter of the Supper," and had asked his followers to moderate his teachings. The writers countered this false report by quoting Luther's prediction that exactly this would happen after he was gone, and his sturdy denial that such a change was possible (29—31).[14] Next they cited Luther's statement (WA 26, 506) according to which the body and blood of Christ are truly given in the Sacrament because this promise rests on the Word and command of God; but if that Word and command be altered or explained away, as the sacramentarians do, then only bread and wine are received (32). This position of 1528 was strengthened in his open letter to the Lutherans at Frankfurt am Main in 1533, warning that when a Reformed teacher publicly claimed to teach the real presence, but actually taught that Christ was present in the Sacrament only spiritually and not bodily, the congregation would actually receive only bread and wine (WA 30 III, 559). Likewise in the Table Talk of 1544, Luther maintained that a Lutheran should not receive the Sacrament from a minister who said that Christ was present but only spiritually; in such a case, there was no real sacrament (WA-T V, No. 5661, p. 303 f.). In his "Short Confession" of 1544 (WA 54, 155 f.), Luther said that any who denied "that the Lord's bread in the Supper is His true, natural body" could not have communion fellowship with him; the Formula adopted this statement as its position (SD 33). Accordingly, it must be admitted that the Formula of Concord has taken a clear stand in the question of communion fellowship that ought to advise us in our ecumenical conversations today.[15]

II. The presentation of the Lutheran doctrine of the real presence of Christ

The three distinctive aspects of the confessional Lutheran doctrine of the Lord's Supper are the sacramental union, the oral manducation, and the communication of the unworthy. These aspects, which are treated SD 34—60, will now occupy our attention.

A. The Sacramental Union (unio sacramentalis)

Luther taught, the bread *is* the body of Christ (33); Melanchthon preferred the formula, the body of Christ is given *in, with,* and *under* the consecrated bread (SD 35—36). Both views were inherent in the doctrine of the sacramental union, which was developed in an analogy to the doctrine of the two natures of Christ as taught by the ancient teachers of the church (37).

For as in Christ two distinct and untransformed natures are indivisibly united, so in the Holy Supper the two essences, the natural bread and the true, natural body of Christ, are present together here on earth in the ordered action of the sacrament, though the union of the body and blood of Christ with the bread and wine is not a personal union, like that of the two natures in Christ, but a sacramental union . . . .

This position is next backed with Scripture, stating that the Words of Institution are the basis on which the sacramental union must be established. Human reason must bow to humble faith (45), just as Abraham believed what seemed impossible (46—47). The kind of statement popular among ecumenical dissimulators, such as "that the body of Christ is a spiritual bread or a spiritual food for souls," is explicitly rejected in favor of terminology that is unambivalent and faithful to the Holy Scriptures (48). The Words of Institution show clearly enough that the bread *is* the body, and the wine *is* the blood (52—53).

Especially in his later years Luther showed less and less displeasure with the concept of transubstantiation. At least the Roman Catholics accepted the real presence, though they used a defective theory to explain it; this was far preferable to the teaching of the sacramentarians. In 1529 and 1533 Luther suggested that the bread and wine were changed into the body and blood of Christ (WA 30 I, 122; WA 38, 201, 242). Melanchthon could make similar statements. Ap X 2 uses the words of Vulgarius to assert that "the bread is not merely a figure but is truly changed into flesh" (Tappert, p. 179). In the Regensburg Colloquy of 1541, at which Calvin was also present, Melanchthon's inclinations toward transubstantiation were positive enough that in a brief on that doctrine he wrote: "We certainly affirm that the true body is present, and the bread is converted or changed by a mystic mutation, by which after the consecration it becomes the presentation [*exhibitio*] of the body which is present" (CR 4, 263). These statements of Luther and Melanchthon were hardly typical, but they do underscore the earnestness with which both men approached the sacramental union.

B. *The Oral Manducation (manducatio oralis)*

If the body and blood of Christ are indeed united with the consecrated bread and wine, then it follows that he who takes the bread and wine eats the body and blood of the Lord. The confessors added to the Words of Institution the reference to 1 Cor. 10:16-17 (54—59), a passage that had been a favorite text of Melanchthon. It had not been used in the Swabian Concord of Andreä, but was introduced into the Swabian-Saxon Concord by Chytraeus, the pupil of Melanchthon (Heppe III/B, p. 261 f.), and then made its way into the Solid Declaration. The writers of the Formula keenly distinguished between a "spiritual eating" that could take place aside from the Sacrament through faith, on the one hand, and sacramental eating and drinking, on the other. (See also 61—72.) The Reformed view of an uncorporeal, spiritualized communion (104) fell short of Biblical teaching, whereas the Lutheran doctrine, which held that the body and blood of Christ were actually received, spiritually, to be true, but through the mouth (105), faithfully reproduced the teaching of the Holy Scriptures. Chytraeus states (56):

> If Paul were speaking only of a spiritual participation in the body of Christ through faith, as the Sacramentarians pervert this passage, he would not say that the bread but that the spirit or faith is participation in the body of Christ. But he says that the bread is participation in the body of Christ, and that means that all who receive the blessed bread also partake of the body of Christ. Therefore he certainly cannot be speaking of a spiritual eating but of a sacramental or oral eating of the body of Christ in which both the godly and the godless participate (Tappert, p. 579).

This brings us to the third emphasis, that unbelievers as well as believers receive the body and blood of Christ.

C. Manducation of the Unworthy (manducatio indignorum)

This principle has always demarcated the line between Lutheran and Reformed teaching. Since Lutherans trace the real presence not to the faith of the individual but to Christ and His Word, the unworthiness of the communicant cannot cancel out the reality of Christ's presence. Also the unbeliever who chances to find admittance at the Lord's table receives the body and blood of Christ, but he eats and drinks divine judgment upon himself, according to 1 Cor. 11:27. Those who followed the teaching of Zwingli or Calvin have never been willing to admit this, and the doctrine of the communication of the unworthy has therefore served as a sort of shibboleth for Lutheran churchmen. It was only when Bucer accepted this principle that fellowship was established between the followers of Luther and of Bucer in the Wittenberg Concord (1536), for, in Lutheran thinking, if Christ is not received by all who receive the consecrated species, then He is not received by anyone at all. This doctrine has provoked hostility and even obscenities from Reformed opponents. Although Chytraeus [Heppe III/B, p. 268 and SD VII 67] gave the remarks of Theodore Beza and Peter Martyr in Latin, saying they were too shameful to put into the vernacular, Arthur Piepkorn with wry humor has Englished their words (Tappert, p. 582). Beza ridiculed this "oral eating and drinking on the part of the unworthy [as] 'two hairs of a horse's tail and an invention of which even Satan himself would be ashamed,'" while Martyr dubbed the Lutheran doctrine of the majesty of Christ with the obscenity, "Satan's dung" (*excrementum Satanae*).[16]

Why then did the Lutherans insist on keeping this hated doctrine? There appear to have been three reasons. (1) As we have previously noted, the doctrine was clearly taught in Scripture, and helped to show whether one were teaching the real presence or not. (2) This doctrine brought comfort for those of weak faith, for it told the struggling sinner that Christ came to him in the Sacrament in spite of his weakness. It underscored the gracious condescension of God, in contrast to the Reformed teaching that only he who had a strong faith could commune with Christ by ascending to heaven.[17] (3) It kept awake the concern for the church for individuals who had not been properly instructed, or who for some other reason should be warned against possibly eating and drinking judgment to themselves. In each case, therefore, it was the concern for the Biblical teaching and for the spiritual welfare of the individual that prompted the Lutheran Church to keep this doctrine alive.

Who are the "worthy" and the "unworthy" attenders at the Lord's table? The "worthy" are essentially those who see nothing good in themselves. (1) They are humble, they feel that their faith is too weak, and they complain that they are not so obedient to God's commands as they would like to be (69). But actually they in their humility are well prepared to attend (70). (2) "Worthiness" consists not in any quality within the believer, not even in the comparative weakness or strength of his faith, but in the merits of Christ, received through justification (71). (3) True faith makes one ready, even when one has lacked time for "fasting and bodily preparation" (124—125; cf. SC VI 10).— And who, then, are the "unworthy"? Andreä, who had a marked interest in church discipline, developed this more fully in the Swabian Concord than it was to appear in the Bergen Book. He identified them as impenitent hypocrites, as unbelievers, as those who think that only bread and wine are given in the sacrament and not the body and blood of Christ (Hachfeld pp. 62—66; Fritschel pp. 44—46). Andreä's rather comprehensive statement was reduced by Chytraeus in the Swabian-Saxon Concord (Heppe III/B, p. 268 f.) to the form in which it was taken into the Formula of Concord (68):

> It is essential to explain with great diligence who the unworthy guests at this Supper are, namely, those who go to this sacrament without true contrition and sorrow for their sins, without true faith, and without a good intention to improve their life and who by their unworthy oral eating of the body of Christ burden themselves with judgment (that is, temporal and eternal punishments) and profane the body and blood of Christ (Tappert, p. 582).

Although Andreä's contention—that those who deny the doctrine of the real presence thereby (1 Cor. 11:29) eat and drink judgment to themselves—seems the logical conclusion of the Lutheran position, it is noteworthy that the Formula of Concord chose not to retain that assertion. The irenic spirit of Melanchthon's pupil prevailed.

III. The Consequence of the Real Presence:
Sacramental Eating and Drinking

Of "Spiritual" and "Sacramental" Eating. Hermann Sasse has noted that although neither Luther nor Zwingli regarded John 6 as a text that discussed the Lord's Supper,[18] Zwingli made it normative for his interpretation of the Words of Institution. Going out from John 6:63, "It is the Spirit that quickeneth; the flesh profiteth nothing," Zwingli interpreted this according to the Neoplatonic opposites of the flesh and the spirit. This led him to assert that a material thing, such as bread or wine, could not convey a spiritual blessing, such as the body and blood of Christ. Moreover, he held that a spiritual gift, such as faith, could not apprehend a material thing, the body and blood of Christ. Out of this grew the controversies over the interpretation of John 6.

The Formula of Concord rejected this intrusion of Neoplatonism into revealed truth, declared that the spiritual eating of John 6 must be distinguished from sacramental eating, and identified the former with faith in God and his Word (61—62). It affirmed, however, that the other kind of eating, the Holy Supper, in which the true body and blood of Christ are received orally, can also be called a "spiritual" eating (63). Sacramental eating and drinking must not be understood "in a coarse, carnal, Capernaitic [cannibalistic] manner," but "in a supernatural, incomprehensible manner" (64). This is paralleled by a statement drawn from the Maulbronn Evaluation of the Torgau Book (Heppe III/B, 367 f.), in which the writers explained the Lutheran understanding of a spiritual eating and drinking. "We use the word 'spiritual' [in the sense of] the spiritual, supernatural, heavenly mode according to which Christ is present in the Holy Supper" (105). They go on to reject "a gross, carnal presence" that their adversaries have knowingly and falsely ascribed to them, and they conclude:

> In this sense, too, we use the word "spiritual" when we say that the body and blood of Christ in the Holy Supper are received, eaten, and drunk spiritually, for although such eating occurs with the mouth, the mode is spiritual (105).

Reformed writers have often alleged that Lutherans teach a "physical presence" of Christ in the sacrament.[19] This rests on a misunderstanding, perhaps prompted by Neoplatonic notions in the minds of such writers. Neither Luther nor the Confessions ever spoke of a "physical presence" of Christ. However, Calvin taught that one must distinguish between the physical signs (bread and wine) and the spiritual things (body and blood), whereby the physical is the *symbol* of the spiritual things (Institutes IV xvii 3, 11, 21). He thought of the body of Christ as finite, and "contained" in heaven to the last day (IV xvii 26), with the Holy Ghost serving as the connecting link between this "spiritual" heaven with its finite Christ and the "physical" earth. Thus, Reformed Christology has tended to land in a sort of modalism, with the Holy Ghost mediating between an absent Christ and the communicants (IV xvii 10). Therefore, the Roman Catholics must destroy the physical elements of bread and wine through transubstantiation, and the Reformed must deny the possibility that the "physical" body and blood of Christ could be present. In both cases, a prayer that the Holy Ghost will assist (the *epiklesis*) seems to fill the need for bridging the gulf between the physical and the spiritual, and between the finite and the infinite. In Lutheran liturgics, there is no place for such a prayer to the Holy Ghost, since the glorified Christ himself who is omnipresent is both Giver and Gift.

Doctrine Must Determine Liturgy. The 16th-century followers of Luther emphasized the act of consecration (73—90). The receptionist concept of some modern Lutherans, according to which the body and blood of Christ are present only at the moment of the oral manducation, does not seem to have been held by Lutherans in the confessional age. They taught that the body and blood of Christ were present (at least) in the *use*, which included the words of consecration, the distribution, and the eating and drinking (86). All of them rejected the canon of the mass, the eucharistic prayer, and the offertory. The actual words of Jesus (*verba institutionis*) replaced the eucharistic prayer. It was held to be necessary to chant or speak these words, loudly and clearly. Reciting the Words of Institution served three purposes: (1) thereby, the words of Christ, "This do in remembrance of me," were obeyed; (2) on hearing these words proclaiming the grace of God, the faith of the believers would be strengthened; and (3) by this action the elements of bread and wine were consecrated and the sacramental union took place (79—82).

The "Use" or "Action" in the Sacrament. We have just noted that the Formula of Concord established a threefold action constitutive of the Lord's Supper: the consecration, the distribution, and the reception. An overwhelming mass of material—the writings of Luther and Melanchthon and many of their contemporaries on liturgical matters, the 16th-century church orders, the great chorales, and superb church music culminating in Bach—all bear witness to the validity of this shape of the liturgy as it was determined by a theology of Law and Gospel. However, much of this ecclesiastical and cultural history is unfamiliar to American liturgical innovators, who have lately sought to make a new liturgical tradition for the Lutheran churches. Under the feeling that they are making it more "contemporary" and "ecumenical," they have tried to abandon the threefold action of the Confessions and replace it with the fourfold action of other denominations. The troubled fourth century, the time when Christianity accommodated itself to the demands of becoming a state religion, is selected as a golden age. It is felt that at this time, a fourfold action of the Eucharist emerged, consisting of these steps: the offering, the eucharistic prayer, the fraction of the bread, and the distribution.[20]

This is not the place for an extended criticism of the fourfold action, but several things should be said from the viewpoint of the Formula of Concord. (1) The offering and the eucharistic prayer turn acts of God into human actions; this is a confounding of Law and Gospel, FC III—VI. (2) The insistence that the consecrated bread (the body of Christ) must be broken is legalistic. Christ did not command the fraction. Calvinists insisted upon the fraction to "prove" that the "human body" of Jesus was not present. Does this not place Lutherans *in statu confessionis,* depriving the fraction of any adiaphorous character? (3) Followers

224

of this historistic repristination seem indifferent to the theology of the sacramental union. Even the Anglo-Catholics and Lutherans refer to the consecrated elements as bread and wine, a terminology unacceptable to our Lutheran fathers of the 16th century. Nevertheless, those who follow this tendency seem almost obsessed about "the rite thing" where external liturgical practices are concerned. It ought to be the other way around: first, a concern for revealed truth, and only, second, the search for an appropriate liturgical expression of one's faith. Here tradition might help more than innovation.

We turn to an axiom that developed out of the theology of the Reformation and was quoted or alluded to six times in the SD (15, 73, 83, 85, 88, 108). It asserts: "Nothing has the character of a sacrament outside the divinely instituted use or action." Peters has carried out a scholarly investigation of this statement, connecting it with Melanchthon, and, before him, with Bucer and Zwingli.[21] The axiom must be understood in the context of SD VII 86, which defines the use or action as "the entire external and visible action of the Supper as ordained by Christ," that is, the consecration, distribution, and reception. The citation of the axiom was invariably directed against Roman Catholic practices: the reservation of the sacrament in a pyx for adoration *after* the Mass, or the carrying of the sacrament in procession on occasions such as Corpus Christi day (15, 83, 108).—It is clear that SD VII 83—86 should be related to the "Beatinian Controversy" of 1568—69.[22] Johann Saliger ("Beatus"), who filled short-lived pastorates in Lübeck and in Rostock at that time, had asserted that the body of Christ is present "before the action"; he had probably meant that the body was present before the reception, that is, beginning with the consecration; in that case, he was arguing against receptionism, the notion that Christ was only present when the bread passed the lips of the communicant. At any rate, Saliger was thought to be teaching that the sacramental union could exist before or after the threefold use or action. Saliger also criticized the custom of mingling unconsecrated wine with that

225

which had been consecrated without an additional blessing. He seems to have represented the stricter position of Luther, in conflict with Calvinistic influences. At any rate, the opinion of David Chytraeus, later embodied in the Formula (SD VII 83—86), took a moderating position; an additional opinion refrained from accusing Saliger of false doctrine, but called for greater care in making formulations and asked that extreme statements be avoided (Peters, p. 355 f.).[23]

Sixteenth-century Lutherans often referred to the statement of Augustine: "Add the Word to the element and it becomes a sacrament." They held that it is the word of Christ, and not the office of the ministry or the faith of the communicants, that caused the Real Presence. Accordingly it quoted these words of Luther (WA 38, 240):

> Thus it is not our work or speaking but the command and ordinance of Christ that, from the beginning of the first Communion until the end of the world, make the bread the body and the wine the blood that are daily distributed through our ministry and office (77).

FC SD VII 91—106 consists principally of statements by Luther on Christology as they are related to the Lord's Supper. We have already treated this important material earlier in the chapter.

IV. The Condemnations of the Arguments of the Opponents

The last portion of Article VII consists almost entirely of condemnations of the teachings of the Roman Catholic and the Reformed teachers. The whole aspect of condemning the beliefs of others presents many difficult problems. In our own time with its emphasis on ecumenical goodwill, there is a strong distaste for polemics. In Germany, the Leuenberg Agreement (1973) stated that it could not repeat the antitheses of the Reformation period, and in the United States, Lutherans have tended simply to ignore the condemnations of the Confessions. A recent monograph by Hans Werner Gensichen however should make us more tolerant toward the 16th-century confessors. He points out the presence of the concept of the condemnation of false doctrine in the Bible, in the early church, in the middle ages, and in the Reformation era.[24] Various Scripture passages call upon the follower of Christ to uphold the distinction between doctrinal integrity and false teaching. In every age where someone has cared, this has taken place. This was especially true of the Protestant reformers. The Formula of Concord reflected the same concern for pure teaching.

In Article VII of the Solid Declaration, the position of the post-Tridentine Roman Church was condemned (107—110). The remainder of the article was devoted almost entirely to a repudiation of the teachings of the "sacramentarians," that is, of the Zwinglians and Calvinists (111—127). A polemic against the adoration of the Sacrament, which might have come from Calvinists or Philippists, was brushed aside with the statement that one should not adore the consecrated bread and wine, but that to reject the adoration of Christ, who is truly present in the sacrament, would be to propound Arian heresy (126).[25] Finally, a blanket condemnation is issued against "all presumptuous, scoffing, and blasphemous questions and expressions which are advanced in a coarse, fleshly, Capernaitic way about the supernatural and heavenly mysteries of this Supper" (127).

Conclusion

The Formula of Concord was born of controversies that threatened to destroy Luther's church in its infancy. The most vital question was the controversy over the Lord's Supper. Article VII helped end the strife, and established itself as the greatest confession of the Lutheran understanding of the sacrament. We have seen how several strands came together: the heritage of Luther, which was embodied especially in the thinking of Jacob Andreä and the church of Württemberg, the approach of Melanchthon, which was represented in David Chytraeus and the churches of Saxony, and the mediating position of Martin Chemnitz, superintendent of the churches of Braunschweig. Working together, these men successfully eliminated the extreme positions to the right and to the left, and avoided unnecessary polemics. The result was not a perfect statement. Nevertheless, it represents one of the highest achievements in regard to this doctrine. It was written with an inexorable fidelity to the Holy Scriptures and a deep sensitivity toward the feelings of Lutherans representing various tendencies. We would do well to study this Article thoroughly and to heed the teachings of our Lutheran fathers today.

Bibliography: Sources

Johann Georg Bertram, *Das Evangelische Lüneburg: Oder Reformations- Und Kirchen-Historie/Der Alt-berühmten Stadt Lüneburg,* "Beylagen zum II. Theile," after p. 760. Braunschweig: Ludolph Schröders Buchladen, 1719.

Die Bekenntnisschriften der evangelisch-lutherischen Kirche. Herausgegeben im Gedenkjahr der Augsburgischen Konfession 1930. Göttingen: Vandenhoeck & Ruprecht, 1952.

The Book of Concord: The Confessions of the Evangelical Lutheran Church, ed. Theodore G. Tappert (Formula of Concord translated by Arthur C. Piepkorn). Philadelphia: Fortress, 1959.

Concordia, or Book of Concord. The Symbols of the Ev. Lutheran Church. With Indexes and Historical Introductions. St. Louis: Concordia, 1922.

Martin Chemnitz, *Examen Concilii Tridentini,* ed. Eduard Preuss. Berlin: Schlawitz, 1861.

Martin Chemnitz, *Examination of the Council of Trent,* tr. Fred Kramer. St. Louis: Concordia, 1971.

Martin Chemnitz, *Loci theologici . . . Quibus et Loci Communes D. Philippi Melanchthonis Perspicve Explicantur, & quasi integrum Christianae doctrinae corpus, Ecclesiae Dei sincere proponitur,* ed. Polycarp Leyser. *Fvndamenta Sanae Doctrinae de Vera et svbstantiali Praesentia, Exhibitione, & sumptione corporis & sanguinis Domini in Caena. Libellvm de Dvabvs Natvris in Christo, earundem hypostatica unione, &c. De Communicatione Idiomatum.* Frankfurt and Wittenberg, Tobias Mevius and Elerd Schumacher, 1653.

Martin Chemnitz, *Two Natures in Christ,* tr. Jacob A. O. Preus. St. Louis: Concordia, 1970.

David Chytraeus, *On Sacrifice,* tr. John Warwick Montgomery. St. Louis: Concordia, 1962.

Confutatio & Condemnatio praecipuarum Corruptelarum, Sectarum & errorum, hoc tempore ad instaurationem et propagationem Regni Antichristi Rom. Pontificii aliarumque fanaticarum opinionium, ingruentium & grassantium, contra ueram sacrae Scripturae, Confeßionis Augustanae & Schmalkaldicorum Articulorum Religionem . . . Jena: Thomas Rebart, 1559. This is the "Weimar Confutation" of 1559.

Corpus Reformatorum. Philippi Melanthonis Opera Quae Supersunt Omnia, ed. Karl Gottlieb Bretschneider and Heinrich Ernst Bindseil, 28 vols. Halle: Schwetschke, 1834ff. Abbreviated: CR.

George J. Fritschel, ed., *Die Maulbronner Formel,* No. 2 in "Quellen aus der Zeit der C.F." Dubuque; mimeograph, 1910. This is a reprint of the text published by Pressel, below. Abbreviated: Fritschel.

George J. Fritschel, *Die Schwaebische Concordie, "Schwaebischer Kirchenbegriff zu einer heilsamen Union in Kirchensachen,* No. 1 in "Quellen aus der Zeit der C.F." Dubuque: mimeograph, n.d. Reprint of Hachfeld, below. Abbreviated: Fritschel.

H. Hachfeld, "Die schwäbische Confession nach einer wolfenbütteler Handschrift." *Zeitschrift fur historische Theologie,* NF, Vol. XXX (1866), 234 ff. Abbreviated: Hachfeld.

Heinrich Heppe, *Geschichte des deutschen Protestantismus in den Jahren 1555-1581,* Vol. III, Part B: Beilagen. Marburg: N. G. Elwert, 1857. Includes texts of the Six Sermons of Andreä, pp. 1—75, the Swabian-Saxon Concord, largely by Chytraeus, pp. 166—352, and other important documents.

B. J. Kidd, *Documents Illustrative of the Continental Reformation.* Oxford: Clarendon Press, 1911; reprint 1967.

Robert Kolb, tr. and ed., *Andreae and the Formula of Concord: Six Sermons on the Way to Lutheran Unity.* St. Louis: Concordia, 1977.

Theodor Pressel, "Zwei Aktenstücke zur Genesis der Concordienformel." *Jahrbuch für deutsche Theologie,* XI, 1 (1866), 640—711. Includes the Maulbronn Formula.

Philipp Julius Rehtmeyer, *Antiqvitates Ecclesiasticae Inclytae Urbis Brunsvigae, Oder: Der berühmten Stadt Braunschweig Kirchen-Historie,* III, B: Beilagen. Braunschweig: Christoph-Friedrich Zilligers Wittib und Erben, 1707. Includes important documents, especially relating to Chemnitz.

Johann Michael Reu, *Quellen zur Geschichte des kirchlichen Unterrichts in der evangelischen Kirche Deutschlands zwischen 1530 und 1600,* 11 vols. Gütersloh: Bertelsmann, 1906—35. Abbreviation: Reu, *Quellen.*

Aemilius Ludwig Richter, *Die evangelischen Kirchenordnungen des sechszehnten Jahrhunderts.* Urkunden und Regesten zur Geschichte des Rechts und der Verfassung der evangelischen Kirche in Deutschland, 2 vols. Nieuwkoop: De Graff, 1967; reprint of 1st ed., 1846. Abbreviation: Richter.

Robert Stupperich, ed., *Melanchthons Werke in Auswahl,* Studienausgabe, 8 vols. plus supplements. Gütersloh: Bertelsmann, 1951—. Abbreviation: SA.

Emil Sehling, *Die evangelischen Kirchenordnungen des 16. Jahrhunderts,* 7 vols., 1902—61. Abbreviated: Sehling, KO or KOO.

Von Gottes gnaden vnser Christoffs Hertzogen zu Würtemberg vnd zu Teckh/ Grauen zu Mümpelgart/ etc. Summarischer vnd einfältiger Begriff/ wie es mit der Lehre vnd Ceremonien in den Kirchen vnsers Fürstenthumbs/ auch daneben Kirchen anhangenden Sachen vnd Verrichtungen/ bißher geübt vnnd gebraucht/ auch fürohin mit verleihung Göttlicher gnaden gehalten vnd volzogen werden solle. Getruckt zu Tüwingen/ Im jar 1559. This is the Württembergische Große Kirchenordnung, 1559.

D. Martin Luthers Werke. Kritische Gesamtausgabe. Weimar: Böhlau, 1883ff. Abbreviated: WA. Tischreden abbreviated: WA-T. Briefe abbreviated: WA-Br.

Bibliography: Secondary Literature

Gerhard Friedrich Bente, "Historical Introductions to the Lutheran Symbols." *Concordia, or Book of Concord.* St. Louis: Concordia, 1922. pp. 1—266.

Ernst Benz, *Studien zur Geschichte des Abendmahlsstreits im 16. Jahrhundert,* Vol. 46 in "Beiträge zur Förderung christlicher Theologie," Series 2. Gütersloh: C. Bertelsmann, 1940.

Friedrich Brunstäd, *Theologie der lutherischen Bekenntnisschriften.* Gütersloh: C. Bertelsmann, 1951.

Werner Elert, *Eucharist and Church Fellowship in the First Four Centuries,* tr. Norman E. Nagel. St. Louis: Concordia, 1966.

Werner Elert, *Der christliche Glaube. Grundlinien der lutherischen Dogmatik.* Hamburg: Furche-Verlag, 1956.

Werner Elert, *Structure of Lutheranism,* tr. Walter A. Hansen. St. Louis: Concordia, 1962.

Werner Elert, "Über die Herkunft des Satzes *Finitum infiniti non capax."* *Zeitschrift für systematische Theologie,* XVI (1939—40), 500—504.

Franz Hermann Reinhold Frank, *Die Theologie der Concordienformel* historisch-dogmatisch entwickelt und beleuchtet. Erlangen: Theodor Blaesing, 1863.

George J. Fritschel, *The Formula of Concord: Its Origin and Contents.* Philadelphia: Lutheran Publication Society, 1916.

Hans-Werner Gensichen, *We Condemn: How Luther and 16th-Century Lutheranism Condemned False Doctrine,* tr. Herbert J. A. Bouman. St. Louis: Concordia, 1967.

Hans Grass, *Die Abendmahlslehre bei Luther und Calvin.* Eine kritische Untersuchung, Vol. 47 in "Beiträge zur Förderung christlicher Theologie," Series 2. Gütersloh: C. Bertelsmann, 1954.

Tom G. A. Hardt, *Venerabilis & Adorabilis Eucharistia.* En Studie i den Lutherska Nattvardsläran under 1500-Talet, Vol. 9 in "Acta Universitatis Upsaliensis: Studia Doctrinae Christianae Upsaliensia." Upsala: Ljungberg, 1971.

Leonhard Hutter, *Concordia Concors. De Origine et Progressu Formulae Concordiae Ecclesiarum Confessionis Augustanae.* Wittenberg: Clement Berger, 1614.

Theodor Mahlmann, *Das neue Dogma der lutherischen Christologie. Problem und Geschichte seiner Begründung.* Gütersloh: Gerd Mohn, 1969.

Marburg Revisited: A Reexamination of Lutheran and Reformed Traditions, ed. Paul C. Empie and James I. McCord. Minneapolis: Augsburg, 1966.

Wilhelm Maurer, "Formula of Concord." *The Encyclopedia of the Lutheran Church,* ed. Julius H. Bodensieck, II, 868—875.

Wilhelm H. Neuser, *Die Abendmahlslehre Melanchthons in ihrer geschichtlichen Entwicklung (1519—1530),* Vol. 26, Part 2 in "Beiträge zur Geschichte und Lehre der Reformierten Kirche." Neukirchen: Verlag des Erziehungsvereins, 1968.

Oliver K. Olson, "Luther's 'Catholic' Minimum." *Response,* (XI (1970), 17—31.

Oliver K. Olson, "Contemporary Trends in Liturgy Viewed From the Perspective of Classical Lutheran Theology," *The Lutheran Quarterly,* (XXVI (1974), 110—157.

Edward Frederick Peters, "Luther and the Principle: Outside of the Use There Is No Sacrament." *Concordia Theological Monthly,* XLII, 10 (Nov. 1971), 643—652.

Gottlieb Jakob Planck, *Geschichte der protestantischen Theologie von Luthers*

Tode bis zu der Einführung der Konkordienformel, III. Leipzig: Siegfried Lebrecht Crusius, 1800.

Johann Michael Reu, "Can We Still Hold to the Lutheran Doctrine of the Lord's Supper?" in *Two Treatises on the Means of Grace*, ed. Emil W. Matzner, pp. 39—120. Minneapolis: Augsburg, 1952.

Michael Rogness, *Melanchthon, Reformer without Honor*. Minneapolis: Augsburg, 1969.

Hermann Sasse, *Here We Stand. Nature and Character of the Lutheran Faith*, tr. Theodore G. Tappert. Minneapolis: Augsburg, 1946.

Hermann Sasse, *This Is My Body. Luther's Contention for the Real Presence in the Sacrament of the Altar*. Minneapolis: Augsburg, 1959.

Edmund Schlink, *The Theologie of the Lutheran Confessions*, tr. Herbert J. A. Bouman. Philadelphia: Fortress, 1961.

Ernst Sommerlath, "Lord's Supper." *The Encyclopedia of the Lutheran Church*, ed. Julius H. Bodensieck, II, 1336—42.

Bjarne W. Teigen, "The Real Presence in the Book of Concord." *Concordia Theological Quarterly*, XLI, 2 (April 1977), 41—57.

THE PERSON OF CHRIST

Bjarne W. Teigen

$\mathcal{L}$utherans are determined to draw their doctrine of the Lord's Supper directly from the Scriptures themselves; for the words of institution are "simple, clear, certain, and truthful" (SD VII 52; quotations in this chapter are from the Tappert ed.). Hence Article VII of the Formula lays out in explicit language this doctrine as understood by the Lutherans.

But in the course of the controversy over the real presence there came a constant objection from the opponents to the Lutheran doctrine that went this way: If Christ's body were at one and the same time in heaven and on earth in the Holy Supper, then it really could not be a true human body. The denial of the real presence was predicated on a false Christology. Calvin and Zwingli taught that the body of the exalted Christ was locally confined to a place at the right hand of God. This false Nestorian view of the person of Christ, however, had gone far beyond that of the Reformed circles, having been accepted by the Melanchthonians also within the external Lutheran church, chiefly in Wittenberg and Leipzig.

Article VII of the Formula dealt with this objection by taking over Luther's statement of the Biblical meaning of Christ's session at the right hand of God and the modes of Christ's presence (SD VII 91—106). But it was quite evident that a more in-depth presentation and confession would have to be made if the Formula was to give the necessary answer to the Crypto-Calvinism that had infiltrated the Lutheran church. The only way to do this was to tackle anew on the basis of the revealed Scripture the entire problem of the person of Christ.

Although Luther probably for the first time treats in some detail the omnipresence of Christ in his sermon "The Sacrament of the Body and Blood of Christ—Against the Fanatics" (*LW* 36, 335—361), it is clear from this sermon that Luther does not depend on the doctrine of the omnipresence of the body of Christ for the real presence of Christ in the Sacrament but rather that he clearly teaches that when in accordance with Christ's command the words of institution are spoken over the elements, then Christ is truly present (*LW* 36, 341.)[1]

Article VIII takes as its fundamental point of departure the two-nature doctrine of the Council of Chalcedon (451 A.D.). But since there are different viewpoints regarding what Chalcedon actually taught, it is more precise to say that Luther and his faithful followers presented the christological doctrine along Alexandrian lines against the Antiochian interpretation. They were convinced that the early church, particularly the eastern branch represented by theologians such as Cyril of Alexandria and John of Damascus, expressed most fully the Scriptural doctrine confessed at Chalcedon. On that occasion the church confessed "that one and the same Jesus Christ, the Son, the Lord, the Only-begotten, is known in two natures, without being commingled, without being changed, without being taken apart [or divided], without being segregated, the difference of the natures being in no wise abolished on account of the [personal] union, but the peculiarity of each nature being rather preserved, and running together into one person and subsistence." (*Trig.* 1109).

When references are made to Luther's writings (SD VIII 2, 17, 38—44, 80, etc.), the authors of the Formula have in mind chiefly these three major works, "The Sacrament—Against the Fanatics" (*LW* 36, 335—361), "That These Words of Christ 'This Is My Body' Still Stand Firm Against the Fanatics" (*LW* 37, 13—150), and his "Confession Concerning Christ's Supper" (*LW* 37, 161—372). These and similar works from Luther's pen are intended to serve as commentaries or "clear expositions" (SD VIII 86) of the doctrine of the person of Christ and hence they have normative value above any of the other Reformers for a correct understanding of Article VIII.

This Article is grounded on careful exegesis of the pertinent Scripture passages, but not many passages are quoted or explained in the Article itself. Two observations need to be made with regard to this, since the Confessions stake their position on the principle that "the word of God shall establish articles of faith and no one else, not even an angel" (SA-II II 15). First, many of the Scripture references that have to do with the Trinity and the person of Christ had been under the most careful scrutiny from the days of the early church, and their precise meaning had been determined and acknowledged by the church fathers in their writings. This was the apostolic, orthodox proclamation that the Lutherans had accepted, and they felt no need endlessly to repeat these accepted expositions.[2] Second, a "Catalog of Testimonies," compiled by Chemnitz and Andreä shortly after the completion of the Formula, was added to the *Book of Concord* as an "Appendix." Though it does not form a part of the *Book of Concord,* it carries considerable weight as a commentary on Article VIII, since the authors were asked to compile this list of Scripture passages and quotations from the fathers to demonstrate that the Lutheran doctrine of the person of Christ is not something newly devised but rather that this doctrine is clearly taught in the Scriptures as well as by the orthodox fathers of the early church.

After establishing the points of controversy that have become evident among the "theologians of the Augsburg Confession" (SD VIII 1—4), the article summarizes in nine theses what the confessors believe on the basis of the "Word of God" regarding the person of Christ (SD VIII 5—14). The fundamental purpose is to confess the unity of the person Jesus

234

Christ. In harmony with the Ecumenical Creeds, the Augsburg Confession (AC I and III) and the Smalcald Articles (SA I), the article reiterates the truth that although God is but one, there are three distinct persons in the Godhead, identical in substance and identical in attributes, and yet they differ as persons so that the Son of God in time took the human nature into the unity of His person (SD VIII 6). This is the "Assumption Theology." In the incarnation the human nature is so united with the divine that the two natures form one person, the God-Man, the theanthropic person, Jesus Christ. In this personal union each nature retains its identity through all eternity and the essential qualities of the one nature do not become the qualities of the other (SD VIII 7 and 8).

The natures are defined more specifically. Back of the language regarding the "person" and the two "natures" is the acceptance of the Augsburg Confession that the word "person" is to be understood as the fathers employed the term in this connection to "signify not a part or a quality in another but that which subsists of itself" (AC I 4). But, of course, the three persons in God are in one another (John 10:38; 14:10). The term "nature" is used in a quite general sense as the two sources or elements that constitute the person of Christ. The "divine nature" includes the attributes of infinity, eternity, omnipotence, omnipresence, and omniscience. Conversely, the "human nature" involves the characteristics of being corporal, finite in movement, subject to hunger, thirst, heat, cold, and even death. The "attributes" refer to everything the natures do or suffer according to their respective essence (SD VIII 9 and 10). The attributes of these two natures, however, never become the essential attributes of the other (SD VIII 8—10, 18—19, 62).

The "Assumption Theology" is clearly confessed: "We believe, teach, and confess that the Son of man according to his human nature is really . . . exalted to the right hand of the omnipotent majesty and power of God, because he was assumed into God when he was conceived by the Holy Spirit in his mother's womb" (Ep VIII 15; cf. SD VIII 6 and 11). The incarnation is the assumption of a human nature by the preexistent eternal Son of God. It is the addition by the Son of

God of a human nature to the divine nature. The human nature of Christ at no time subsisted of itself, and no time had a personality of its own, but it subsisted in the personality of the Son of God (*Enhypostasia*).[3] Although Christ's human nature is a genuine personality in the sense of a human soul with all its characteristics, it does not have, and never had, independent existence. The eternal Logos is the sole factor that creates the personality of Jesus Christ. And, as Luther explained, this took place through the power of the Word of God, "one cannot deny the fact that she [the Virgin Mary] thus becomes pregnant through the Word" (*LW* 36, 341).

When the Son of God in the incarnation assumed the human nature into the unity of His person, the human nature was so united with the divine that they form the one person, the God-man Christ Jesus. This is the personal union, which is most carefully defined in the Article: "We also believe, teach, and confess that after the incarnation neither nature in Christ henceforth subsists for itself so as to be or constitute a distinct person, but that the two natures are united in such a way that they constitute a single person in which there are and subsist at the same time both the divine and the assumed human nature, so that after the incarnation not only His divine nature but also His assumed human nature belong to the total person of Christ" (SD VIII 11). The term "personal union" is meant to express the truth that in Christ, God and man do not form *any* kind of union, but rather constitute a personal unity which is totally unlike every other union and which must be carefully perceived from the Scriptures as to what it is and what it is not. Hence the Confession considers the doctrine of the personal union in considerable detail (SD VIII 13—30).

Lutheranism retains the integrity of the two natures but nevertheless admits the communication of the divine attributes to the created human nature (SD VIII 17 and 18). By doing this it rejects out of hand any and all kinds of Nestorianism that would separate the two natures from each other and thus make two Christs, so that Christ is one person, and God the Word who dwells in Christ is another (SD VIII 15). Thus the Formula with its many rejections of Nestorian aberrations serves as a

236

bulwark against the perennial tendency within the church to substitute some kind of Nestorian theory that would divide the person of the God-man.[4]

At the same time the Lutheran doctrine rejects Eutychianism (Ep VIII 18, 21; SD VIII 17). The Reformed constantly charged the Lutherans with the error of Eutyches of confounding the two natures of Christ with the result that there was only one nature after the incarnation. The Calvinists also claim that Luther's christology "abolish[es] the human nature of Christ or change[s] the one nature into the other" (Ep. VIII 18). But the Lutherans stoutly deny the charge, affirming that they teach precisely what was confessed at the Council of Chalcedon and what is affirmed in the Athanasian Creed (SD VIII 18 and 62). Jesus Christ "is consubstantial with the Father as regards the deity, and that the same is consubstantial with us according to the humanity; that He is in all respects like us, excepting sin" (*Trig.* p. 1109). In the words of the Athanasian Creed, "He is God, begotten before the ages of the substance of the Father, and He is man, born in the world of the substance of His mother, perfect God and perfect man, with reasonable soul and human flesh." But "He is not two Christs but one Christ." And He is one "not by changing the Godhead into flesh but by taking on the humanity into God" (Athanasian Creed, 29—33). Then, as if to emphasize especially the rejection of any form of Eutychianism, the Athanasian Creed confesses, "one certainly not by confusion of substance but by oneness of person."[5] The personal union, if it means anything at all, means that the two natures were united in the closest union possible so that when the Word took part of flesh and blood (Heb. 2:14), the human nature became Christ's nature so truly and fully that all the fullness of the Godhead dwelt in it, Col. 2:9 (SD VIII 30).

The fullness of the Godhead dwells in the human nature as the soul in the body, but only in an ineffable manner does it penetrate and permeate it so that they who see and handle the flesh see and handle the divine glory (John 1:14). On account of this personal union the flesh is no longer apart from the Word nor the Word from the flesh: "Wherever this person is, it is the single, indivisible person, and if you can say, 'Here is God,' then you must also say, 'Christ the man is present too.'" (SD VIII 82). Not only does the terminology of the Lutherans agree with the ancient church (SD VIII 22; *Trig.* p. 1131) but the Lutherans accept the canon of the Council of Ephesus that in virtue of the personal union the Virgin Mary is truly "the mother of God" (SD VIII 24).

Since the two natures are united in a personal union, this personal union includes the communion of the divine and human natures in the person of our Lord. A real communication of attributes, or an exchange of properties, takes place (SD VIII 31). All the divine and all the human attributes belong to this person and yet the essential attributes of one nature never become essential attributes of the other. Nothing new is being added to the doctrine of "the two natures" by this treatment, but that which Scripture teaches is more clearly elucidated and false errors regarding the person of Christ are more readily exposed.

Since the Biblical statements regarding the person of Christ are "not all of the same kind and mode," it is necessary that one discuss them with "due discrimination" under three main points (SD VIII 35).[6] As a matter of fact, Scripture does not ascribe the divine and human attributes to the person of Jesus Christ in the same manner. Therefore it is of the utmost importance here to see whether one lets the Scriptural doctrine stand as it is clearly expressed or whether one will let human speculation enter, limiting the scope of the revealed doctrine so that it becomes palatable to the human reason. This is the error of Nestorius in refusing to grant the full personal union in all its implications, and it is the error of Zwingli with his theory of *alloeosis* (SD VIII 39—40).

Article VIII first gives a short, precise definition of the first genus or kind of exchange of attributes resulting from the personal union (*genus idiomaticum*): "In the first place, since in Christ two distinct natures are and remain unchanged and unblended in their natural essence and properties, and since both natures constitute only one person, therefore any property, though it belongs only to one of the natures, is ascribed not only to the respective nature as something separate but to the entire person who is simultaneously God and man (whether He is

238

called God or whether He is called man)" (SD VIII 36).

The authors of the Formula were at considerable pains to insist that they are not here inserting something new, but that they are merely reiterating what the ancient church has always taught concerning the unity of the person and the distinction of the two natures in Christ and their essential properties (*Trig.* p. 1107). The entire introduction of the "Catalog of Testimonies," addressed "To the Christian Reader," uses chiefly some of the canons of the Council of Ephesus (431) that represent the christology of Cyril of Alexandria. The Symbol of the Council of Chalcedon is also adduced as are the writings of Leo that were given official sanction by that Council (*Trig.* p. 1107—13).[7] These orthodox theologians of the Reformation wanted to testify to the reality of the personal union by stressing the general, mutual permeation of the specifically divine and the specifically human attributes to the divine-human Jesus Christ. By virtue of the personal union, this historical person is in possession of all human and divine attributes. But since the natures are united without being confused or mixed, the **attributes of the one nature** never become the *essential* attributes of the other (SD VIII 37). It should be noted, however, that since the pertinent Scripture passages speak of the entire person of Christ, it is not significant whether the person of Jesus Christ is designated according to the divine nature or the human nature or according to both natures.

The Formula then binds itself to Luther's exposition as found in his "Great Confession Concerning the Holy Supper" (*LW* 37, 209—213). Luther asserts that "if the works are divided and separated, the person will also have to be separated, since all the doing and suffering are not ascribed to the natures but to the person. It is the person who does and suffers everything, the one thing according to this nature and the other thing according to the other nature" (SD VIII 43). When Luther concludes this statement with the remark, "All of which scholars know right well," it is clear from the "Catalog of Testimonies" that he has reference to the words of the two Councils of Ephesus and Chalcedon (*Trig.* p. 1111). Since in his exposition Luther had used the terms "divinity and humanity" which are abstract terms, but he had also used concrete terms, such as "Savior," "God," "Man," and "Son of God," the "Catalog of Testimonies" is careful to explain that the meaning of all such terms must be retained in their true sense: "for concrete terms are words of such a kind as designate the entire person in Christ, such as *God* and *man*. But abstract terms are words by which the natures in the person of Christ are understood and expressed, as *divinity, humanity" (Trig.* p. 1111). This distinction is necessary in order to be thoroughly Scriptural. In the concrete we can say, "God is man and man is God." But we cannot say in the abstract, "divinity is humanity and humanity is divinity." Luther, therefore, acknowledges that the objection that the deity cannot suffer and die, is correct, but because of the personal union whereby the divinity and humanity are one person in Christ, we must say, pointing to Christ, "the person . . . suffers, dies" (SD VIII 41-43).

The refusal on the part of Zwingli to accept the personal union of the two natures in the one person was clearly evident from his inability to accept the concrete term that the Son of God died. He tried to evade the citations from Scripture that plainly declared this by resorting to a rhetorical figure which he called *alloeosis*. Zwingli had asserted that the Sacrament of the Altar could not have been instituted to provide a bodily eating of Christ's body, because such a notion would be absurd. In reality he held that when Christ says, "This is my body," Christ is using a figure of speech exactly as He does when He speaks of His human nature but He really has in mind the divine. The *alloeosis,* Zwingli had postulated, is an interchange (*Gegenwechsel*) of the two natures, which are in one person, so that in naming one nature the other is meant, or in naming both only one is meant.[8] Luther quickly saw that this type of exegesis led to Nestorianism with a vengeance, because it destroyed the personal union of the two natures of Christ and thus the basis of our salvation: "Beware, I say, of this *alloeosis,* for it is the devil's mask since it will finally construct a kind of Christ after whom I would not want to be called a Christian, that is, a Christ who is and does no more in his passion and death than any ordinary saint" (SD VIII 40).

240

The Formula never loses sight of the soteriological significance of the personal union and the communication of attributes. If the finite flesh was incapable of receiving the infinite God in the second person of the Trinity (*finitum non est capax infiniti*), then there was not a real union of the divine and human natures of the one person Jesus Christ, and in reality one could not say that the Virgin Mary was the mother of God. The divine and the human natures were then at best like two boards glued together without any real communion of these two natures so that there were really two Christs. The other alternative seems to be that when Jesus Christ became man, the two natures were blended into a new essence, which eliminated the Biblical teaching that Jesus Christ was a true man, such as we are, in all points except without sin (SD VIII 63).

Here the Formula, using words of Luther from his "On the Councils and the Church" (*LW* 41, 103f), shows in a most striking way what is at stake if we do not do full justice to what the Scriptures teach about the incarnation of the Son of God, "We Christians must know that unless God is in the balance and throws in weight as a counterbalance, we shall sink to the bottom with our scale. I mean that this way: If it is not true that God died for us, but only a man died, we are lost. But if God's death and God dead lie in the opposite scale, then His side goes down and we go upward like a light and empty pan. Of course, He can also go up again or jump out of His pan. But He could never have sat in the pan unless He had become a man like us, so that it could be said: God dead, God's passion, God's blood, God's death. According to His nature God cannot die, but since God and man are united in one person, it is correct to talk about God's death when that man dies who is one thing or one person with God" (SD VIII 44). Luther and the Confessions after him attached to the suffering of Christ the entire weight of His deity. In 14 theses Chemnitz, in *The Two Natures,* published almost simultaneously with the Formula, demonstrates how necessary it was for our Savior "to be not only God or only man and why the divine and human natures had to be united in the person of the Mediator." Thoughtfully considered, "the entire doctrine of the hypostatic union shines as a light." Christians could well emulate the ancients who "respected the wisdom of this mystery with reverence and reserve rather than trying to explain it."[9]

In proceeding with its examination of all the implications of the personal union, the Formula declares that Christ performed His Messianic work of salvation according to both natures, each nature performing therein that which is peculiar to it. Each nature, however, does not work independently but in the most intimate and unbroken communion with the other, so that every act of the God-man is one undivided and indivisible act. The work of Jesus Christ is never separated from His person, as the second kind of communication of attributes (*genus apotelesmaticum*) clearly shows. The concrete result of the incarnation and the personal union is the salvation of mankind (SD VIII 46—47).

The Article does not enter into great detail with regard to this aspect of the person and work of Christ, except to emphasize that the acts of Christ for man's salvation are saving acts because they are theanthropic acts. When, for example, Christ in His human nature suffers and dies, even this takes place in communion with the divine nature, but not with the result that the divine nature in itself also suffers and dies. Rather, the divine nature is present personally in the suffering of the human nature and wills it: "Had not (He) been true eternal God, the obedience and passion of the human nature could not be reckoned to us as righteousness" (SD III 56). "Thus Christ is our mediator, redeemer, king, high priest, shepherd, and so forth, not only according to one nature only, either the divine or the human, but according to both natures" (SD VIII 47).

The doctrine of the exchange of properties according to its third kind (*genus majestaticum*) is the most severely contested one. The Sacramentarians had directed their most violent polemics against the doctrine that Christ's divine attributes are communicated to His human nature. The words of Martin Chemnitz are quite mild: "Some people compress and confine this entire doctrine [i.e., the hypostatic union] within the bounds of the essential attributes or natural properties, and they will permit nothing more for themselves nor will they allow it to others. . . . Some men have understood this point in so

242

erroneous a manner and have urged their case in so wicked a way that they are willing to recognize only the essential and natural attributes in Christ's human nature" (*The Two Natures*, p. 242). As a result, the Lutheran Confessors treat this point in great detail (SD VIII 48—75). And the chief thrust of the "Catalog of Testimonies" is to support this truth from the Scriptures and to show that this was the teaching of the ancient church "on the basis of Scriptures" (SD VIII 54).

Since God is immutable (James 1:17), Article VIII acknowledges that nothing was added or detracted from the essence and properties of the divine nature in the incarnation (SD VIII 49). In a rather complicated sentence the Formula sets forth the doctrine that in the personal union the divine nature has communicated its full majesty and glory to the human nature: "The Holy Scriptures, and the ancient Fathers on the basis of the Scriptures, testify mightily that, because the human nature in Christ is personally united with the divine nature in Christ, the former (when it was glorified and exalted to the right hand of the majesty and power of God, after the form of the servant had been laid aside and after the humiliation) received, in addition to its natural, essential, and abiding properties, special, high, great, supernatural, unsearchable, ineffable, heavenly prerogatives and privileges in majesty, glory, power, and might above every name that is named, not only in this age but also in that which is to come" (SD VIII 51).[10]

The analysis of the pertinent Scriptural evidence pertaining to this third genus takes one more deeply into all the implications of the personal union than does the first genus. In the first genus the point was made that the divine and human attributes are to be ascribed to the entire person of Christ. The eternity and the age of eight days are predicated as equally real and true. But the divine attributes are attributed according to the divine nature and the human attributes according to the human nature. In this third genus, on the other hand, the divine attributes are ascribed to the person of Christ also according to His human nature. "The Catalog of Testimonies," by way of introduction to its 10 theses, which delineate in detail this third genus, asserts that "since we must not only know and firmly believe that the assumed nature in the person of Christ has and retains to all eternity its essence and the natural essential attributes of the same but it is a matter of especial importance, and the greatest consolation for Christians is comprised therein, that we also know from the revelation of the Holy Scriptures, and without doubt believe the majesty to which this His human nature has been elevated in deed and truth by the personal union, and of which it thus has become personally participant, as has been extensively explained in the Book of Concord" (*Trig.* pp. 1111—13).

To be sure, the Lutheran Confessions in no way wanted to deny that Christ in His human nature received created gifts, but these are to be clearly distinguished from the divine qualities. The problem, however, is that the Calvinists wanted to restrict all the qualities given to the human nature to created gifts (Ep VIII 35).[11] But the testimony of Scripture is so clear that to deny, in contrast to created gifts, that the assumed nature in Christ has received "divine and infinite qualities" (SD VIII 55), is to undermine the foundation for all Christian doctrine, the sacred Scriptures, and to substitute another epistemological basis for determining what is Christian doctrine, namely, human reason (SD VIII 40 and 41).

It is indeed true that Scripture wants us to recognize that divine attributes are ascribed to Christ according to His divine nature, as when it declares that the Son of man shall ascend up "where He was before" (John 6:62), and that He existed before Abraham (John 8:58). But at the same time Scripture ascribes divine attributes to Christ according to His human nature. The force of the incremental repetition of this truth in so many passages is overwhelming: John 5:21, 27; 6:39, 40; Matt. 28:18; Dan. 7:14; John 3:31, 35; 13:3; Matt. 11:27; Eph. 1:22; Heb. 2:8; 1 Cor. 15:27; John 1:3, 10. (SD VIII 55).

The Lutheran Confessors, however, have never understood the term "real exchange" (*realis communicatio*) as referring to an "essential, natural exchange or transfusion which would blend the natures in their essence and in their essential properties," as the Calvinists had constantly charged against them (SD VIII 63 and 89; Ep VIII 21).[12] The Lutherans clearly

244

recognized and condemned the erroneous doctrine of the Schwenkfelders that both natures in Christ possess only one divine essence and that the flesh of Christ belongs to the essence of the holy Trinity (SD XII 29). On the other hand, the orthodox Lutherans have used the term "real exchange" to ward off the *alloeosis* misrepresentation that in the personal union there is only a verbal exchange, a manner of speaking to indicate that the personal union causes only the names and the titles to be held in common. As a matter of fact, an exchange has taken place in deed and truth without any blending of the natures and of their essential properties. Once again, it must be emphatically stated that the Lutheran christology, as the Cyrillian christology, holds to the integrity of the natures but nevertheless admits the communication of the divine attributes to the human nature of Jesus. Cyril's guiding principle was that "he could admit of no division in the Incarnate. By 'flesh' he meant human nature in its fulness, including a rational soul; . . . This humanity was real and concrete. . . . The humanity was as real as the divinity and the modern allegation that he regarded it as a collection of purely abstract qualities conflicts with his express language."[13]

The point that this communication is not "merely a matter of words" (SD VIII 56) is so decisive that the article argues it persuasively for three reasons:

1. The Scriptures testify that whatever Christ received in time He received according to the assumed human nature (SD VIII 57). "The Catalog of Testimonies" adduces Scripture passages beyond those quoted in Article VIII to demonstrate the thesis "that Christ has received this majesty in time, moreover, not according to the divinity or the divine nature, but according to His assumed nature, or according to the flesh as man, or as the Son of Man" (*Trig.* p. 1115). In a catena of quotations from the early Fathers it is evident that this has always been the teaching of the orthodox church. Athanasius had said that "we must bear in mind everywhere [in the Holy Scriptures] that none of those things which He says that He received, namely, in time, He received in such a way as though He had not had them; for, being God and the

Word, naturally He had those things always" (*Trig.* p. 1117). Cyril on several occasions had made this point, "As man He sought His glory which He always had as God" (*Trig.* p. 1119). And Leo warns of the dire results that befall one who maintains that "Sublimity was exalted": "But a person holding such views Arius receives into his fellowship." If such were the case, the exalted one "was inferior to Him who exalted" (*Trig.* p. 1121).

2. Further, Scripture never lets us forget the soteriological reason for the *communicatio majestaticum:* Our Savior Jesus Christ in the discharge of His office as our Mediator, Redeemer, High Priest, King, etc., acts in, with, and through both natures, as the statement of Leo canonized by the Council of Chalcedon declares, "each form [nature] does what is peculiar to it in communion with the other" (*Trig.* p. 1109).

3. Finally, one must keep in mind the distinction the Scriptures make between the two natures in Christ, the divine and the assumed human nature. In the personal union the divine nature in its essence lost nothing nor did it receive anything new or greater than it possessed from eternity (Rev. 1:4). But this was not the case with the assumed human nature, which because of the personal union with the deity, is exalted above every name and given all power in heaven and earth (Eph. 1:21-22; Matt. 28:18).[14]

The particular attributes that the assumed nature received through the personal union are enumerated in detail: The power to make the dead alive, to execute judgment (SD VIII 58). Not only His divine nature but His blood actually cleanses us from all sins. And just as the Council of Ephesus had decreed, His flesh has power to give life (SD VIII 59). In short, the human nature of Christ has received majesty according to the manner of the personal union because the fullness of the deity dwells in Christ as in its own body (Col. 2:9). As a result, this fullness shines forth in the widest ways possible "with all its majesty, power, glory, and efficacy in the assumed nature" (SD VIII 64).[15]

246

As a result, Article VIII does not hesitate to take over the ancient analogies of the soul in the body and the fire in the glowing iron (SD VIII 66; Ep VIII 9). Cyril of Alexandria recognized the distinction of the divinity in the humanity by the use of the analogy of the union of body and soul, since it pointed towards an absolute unity, but the distinction of natures, which involved no separation, was there to be perceived.[16] The Athanasian Creed incorporated the analogy into its confession to ward off Nestorianism but certainly not to countenance Monophysitism.[17] Cyril of Alexandria, among the ancients, had also used the fire analogy, "In a coal, as an illustration, we can see how God the Word, united indeed to humanity, has transformed the assumed nature into its glory and efficacy. As fire adheres to wood, so has God been united to humanity in a manner that cannot be grasped, conferring upon it also the operation of His nature" (*Trig.* p. 1141).

But there is only one set of divine attributes, not two, because the communication did not involve their separation from the divine essence. Rather, there remains in Christ "only a single divine omnipotence, power, majesty, and glory, which is the property of the divine nature alone" (SD VIII 66). The divine attributes dwell in Christ's human nature not by way of a natural union or by way of a mystical union but solely by way of the personal union (SD VIII 67—70).

The communication of the divine attributes to the human nature of the God-man Jesus Christ has been described by the Solid Declaration in broad, unrestricted terms, as resulting from the personal union. This cannot but raise questions regarding the historical Jesus whom the Gospels describe as living in the most lowly circumstances and exhibiting the weaknesses of the human nature. And yet the identity of the Son of God with the man Christ is repeatedly expressed in the Gospels without any reservations. The objection has been raised that Christ's human nature cannot find room for development if it is embodied in one and the same person with the divine nature.[18]

This is indeed a puzzle to the human mind. But, as Article VIII states, "the best, safest, and most certain way in this controversy is to realize that no one can know better and more thoroughly than the Lord Christ Himself what Christ has received through the personal union." Here, too, it is necessary that we very carefully follow the Scriptures (SD VIII 53). It is true that in the Scriptures there are two groups of differing statements on the earthly life of Christ, but all these statements receive their just weight when we have accepted the fact that the finite is capable of receiving the infinite. The holy Scriptures plainly set forth the two states or stages of Christ. He lived in the state of humiliation from the time of His birth until His death and burial, whereupon He entered into the state of exaltation in which He lives and rules into all eternity.

On the basis of the clear Scripture the Formula defines these states with great precision, "According to the personal union He always possessed this majesty. But in the state of His humiliation He dispensed with it and could therefore truly increase in age, wisdom, and favor with God and men, for He did not always disclose this majesty, but only when it pleased Him" (Ep VIII 16). The Solid Declaration, in a more amplified form, insists that on the basis of the personal union, in the state of humiliation "Christ performed all His miracles and manifested His divine majesty according to His good pleasure, when and how He wanted to" (SD VIII 25). Lutherans today, in rejecting the modern views that Jesus of Nazareth was only a true human being locked in the Palestinian culture of 19 centuries ago, must indeed be careful that they do not slip into docetic ways of thinking. They must believe and confess the true and perfect humanity of Christ so clearly taught in the Scriptures, because a denial of it involves a denial of the personal union and consequently of the work of redemption. When the Epitome (VIII 16) declares that the Son of God in His humiliation dispensed with the use of His divine majesty, it is pointing to the fact that He is also a genuine human being. He assumed the true human nature at His conception and He never laid it aside (SD VIII 26).

It should be noted that the humiliation and exaltation affect only the human nature of Christ and in no sense His divine nature, which was not "intrinsically diminished or augmented" (SD VIII 49). It is a blasphemous interpretation to refer the humiliation and exaltation to the divine nature (Ep VIII 39).

The Formula's entire presentation is anchored in Phil. 2:6-11. Following the exegetical insights of Luther, Article VIII refers Phil. 2:6 to the incarnate Christ and not to the preexistent Logos. Because of the personal union the Savior appears in the "form of a servant" and in the "form of God." The brilliance of Christ did not always shine forth during the time of His humiliation when He became a lowly man by abstaining from the full and constant use of the divine majesty communicated to His human nature. This nonuse made the genuine human development of Christ possible. It should be just as carefully noted that because Christ refrained from using His divine power in the state of humiliation, one should not draw the conclusion that Christ's humanity had lost the fullness of the deity, for He did manifest and exercise it in performing His miracles (SD VIII 25).[19]

To summarize, the Formula's doctrine on Christ's state of humiliation, by means of its expressions, such as "the divine majesty was concealed and restrained" (SD VIII 65), and that in the form of a servant he abstained from using this divine majesty (Ep VIII 16), adequately express the statements of Scripture. Possession and nonuse simply reproduce what Christ said in John 10:18. These terms accept the solution of the Scripture itself in how to understand the two series of passages that on the one hand ascribe divine power and glory to Christ and on the other hand, limited power and knowledge.[20]

Though Jesus Christ did not exercise the properties of His person resulting from the personal union in uninterrupted splendor, there came a time when He entered into His full glory. His exalted state began with the quickening and His descent into hell as the triumphant Christ who had achieved the victory over sin, death, and the devil. "The entire person, God and man, descended into hell" (SD IX 2). The *genus majestaticum* is in full force in both the state of humiliation and exaltation. But now since the form of a slave has been laid aside, this exercise of the divine power also according to the human nature "takes place fully, mightily, and publicly, before all the saints in heaven and on earth, and in yonder life we shall behold His glory face to face" (SD VIII 65).

The implications of the Scriptural doctrine are breathtaking: "Thus He entered into His glory in such a way that now not only as God, but also as man, He knows all things, can do all things, is present to all creatures and has all things in heaven and on earth and under the earth beneath His feet and in His hands, as He Himself testifies" (Ep VIII 16). The chief references from the Scriptures used as proof for this doctrine are Phil. 2:9-11; Matt. 28:18-20; Eph. 1:20-23; 4:10 (Pieper, II, 284). Here, probably as nowhere else, the Sacramentarians reveal their fundamental presupposition that the finite was incapable of receiving the infinite. There was an out and out rejection of the postulate that Christ according to His human nature is omnipresent. At most, the Calvinists might invest the human nature of Christ with great finite powers, but not with communicated divine power, and hence, they asserted, He now as the risen Lord at the right hand of God must be in some circumscribed locality.

The "Catalog of Testimonies" reiterates the teaching of the Formula by presenting Thesis VII, "This communication of the divine majesty occurs also in glory, without mingling, annihilation, or denial of the human nature" (*Trig.* P. 1141). Article VIII wants it clearly understood that the testimonies of the Scriptures that speak of the majesty to which the human nature of Christ has been exalted do not merely mean that Christ "shares the bare titles and the names in words alone" (SD VIII 67). On the contrary, "through the personal union the entire fullness of the Spirit (as the ancient Fathers say) is communicated to Christ according to the flesh that is personally united with the Son of God" (SD VIII 73).[21] This point was so important to those who subscribed to the entire Book of Concord in 1580 that they single it out as one of the issues that needs to be particularly studied and confessed (Preface to the Book of Concord, Tappert ed., p. 11).

Because of the controversy regarding the bodily presence of Christ in the Lord's Supper, Article VIII, together with Luther (*LW* 36, 342), teaches the communicated omnipresence of the Son of God. First it confesses His general omnipresence with all

250

creatures: "Also as man, He knows all things, can do all things, is present to all creatures . . . . He exercises His power everywhere omnipresently, He can do everything, and He knows everything" (Ep VIII 16).[22] This is the "repletive" presence (Pieper, III, 348; cf. SD VII 101—102).

At the same time Article VIII clearly confesses that the exalted Christ has other modes of presence so that "with this same assumed nature of His, Christ can be and is present wherever He wills" (SD VIII 78; cf. 92).[23] The confession of this "multipresence" (or "multivolipresence") keeps Article VII! in harmony with Article VII of the Formula and the doctrine of Luther that the sacramental presence of Christ in the Lord's Supper does not coincide with the omnipresence of the body of Christ. It also safeguards the truth that Christ according to His human nature dwells in His church in a very *special* way: "This promise [Matt. 28:20] . . . is correctly understood of the whole Christ, God and man in both natures. For He who was present there before them promises His presence to the church always."[24] In other words, Article VIII also distinguishes the "repletive" presence from the "definitive", and both of these from the "circumscriptive" (cf. Pieper, III, 348; SD VII 94—103).

Despite the rather complex assertions expressing the Scriptural doctrine of Christ's two natures, the Confessors never lose sight of the significance of all this for our salvation. They do not separate the doctrine of Christ's person from the doctrine of His work. The salvation of the world depends on the personal union. The disruption of the person gives us two Christs, one "who is and does no more in his passion and death than any other ordinary saint" (SD VIII 40). At the same time we must have a Christ who is of our nature and can act for us: "He would remain a poor Christ for me if He were present only at one single place as a divine and human person and if at all other places He would have to be nothing more than a mere isolated God and a divine person without the humanity. No, comrade, wherever you put God down for me, you must also put the humanity down for me. They simply will not themselves be separated and divided from each other" (SD VIII 84).

But in the final analysis we face in the incarnation of the Son of God a mystery beyond reason and speculation (SD VIII 96). It defies any attempt at an explanation satisfactory to the human mind. To philosophy it is "simply impossible and absurd." [25] We dare not deprive Christ of His majesty according to His human nature because He has "tasted every tribulation in His assumed human nature and . . . can therefore sympathize with us as with men and His brethren and . . . wills to be with us in all our troubles" (SD VIII 87). At the same time, plucking out the eyes of our reason and taking the intellect captive in obedience to Christ, the simple believers "comfort themselves therewith, and rejoice constantly that our flesh and blood in Christ have been made to sit so high at the right hand of the majesty and almighty power of God" (SD VIII 96).

The example *par excellence* of how the Christian uses the doctrine of the two natures in the one person Jesus Christ for the very heart of his theology is Luther himself. A few weeks before his death, physically ill, plagued by the petty bickering of state officials, greatly concerned about the theological integrity of his Wittenberg faculty, he in a letter comforts his loving and concerned wife, Katherine, "I have a caretaker who is better than you and all the angels; He lies in the cradle and rests on a virgin's bosom, and yet, nevertheless, He sits at the right hand of God, the almighty Father. Therefore be at peace. Amen." [26] (*LW* 50, 302)

Article IX
The Formula of Concord

CHRIST'S DESCENT INTO HELL

C. George Fry

*I*n contrast to the other theological controversies among Lutherans resolved in the Formula of Concord, the one concerning the doctrine of Christ's descent into hell was comparatively minor. Complete agreement on the issues involved in this matter was attained with relative ease. This was because there had always been a large measure of consensus among the Lutherans as to the confessional importance, the Biblical basis, and the theological significance of the statement, "He descended into hell."

The Lutherans agreed as to the confessional importance of the doctrine of Christ's descent into hell. They knew that this teaching was found in both the Apostles' and the Athanasian Creeds. The *descensus* was a doctrine of the ancient and undivided church, part of the theological legacy of the Catholic and Orthodox Church through the Greek and Latin fathers. As

253

part of the Christian, Apostles', or Baptismal Creed, faith in the *descensus* was part of the very affirmation required for incorporation into the church, the body of Christ. As part of the Athanasian or Bishops' Creed, denial of the *descensus* was regarded as a sufficient deviation from orthodox Christianity to warrant excommunication. Unlike some of the Reformed Christians and Free Churchmen who deleted this sentence from the Apostles' Creed, the Lutherans felt that it must absolutely be retained as an article of Christian belief. To them it dealt with a central, not a peripheral, aspect of the Christian faith. The Lutherans were persuaded that Evangelical Christians did not have the liberty to deny this part of their Catholic legacy.

The Lutherans were agreed *that* this doctrine had a Biblical basis, and there was a large measure of consensus as to *what* that textual foundation was. The Scriptural source of the doctrine of the *descensus* was 1 Peter 3:18-19 RSV:

> Christ also died for sins once for all, the righteous for the unrighteous, that He might bring us to God, being put to death in the flesh but made alive in the spirit; in which He went and preached to the spirits in prison.

The Lutherans realized that certain other passages had been cited in connection with the doctrine of the *descensus*. But they were convinced that these texts had often been either misapplied or misinterpreted. They referred specifically to two proof texts often quoted by Reformed Christians. One was:

> Thou dost not give me up to Sheol,
> of let Thy godly one see the Pit.
> (Ps. 16:10 RSV)

The Lutherans taught that neither this verse nor its quotation Acts 2:27 had been correctly comprehended by the Calvinists. Lutheran theologians were in substantial accord that the Davidic description had been distorted in the doctrines of Zwingli and Calvin. They also concurred that the Petrine confession, "God raised him up, having loosed the pangs of death, because it was not possible for him to be held by it" (Acts

254

2:24 RSV), referred primarily to the resurrection and not the *descensus*. So there was a large measure of concord among the Lutherans concerning the exegetical foundation of the doctrine.

There was also an amazing amount of agreement among the Lutherans as to the theological significance of 1 Peter 3:18-19 and of the confessional statement derived from it, "He descened into hell." This doctrinal consensus consisted in a series of common negations and some common affirmations.

On the one hand, the Lutherans were pretty much of one mind when it came to what this text did *not* mean:

1. None of the Lutherans, as had Origen and some of the ancients, interpreted this passage in a mythological sense. To the Lutherans the sentence, "He descended into hell," referred to a real event in the life of Jesus. It was an historical occurrence in the career of Christ, not a story made up by the apostles to illustrate some philosophical idea.

2. None of the Lutherans, as had the Docetists of old, regarded the passage in a symbolical fashion, as being a metaphor, or an analogy, a sign, pointing beyond itself to some higher, nobler, or "more spiritual" truth. While there was a tendency among the Zwinglians to regard this text as being a poetic way of reporting the death of Jesus, the Lutherans maintained their Biblical realism at this point and refused to allow either the canonical text or the credal statement to be allegorized.

3. None of the Lutherans, as had Augustine, Aquinas, and Beza, viewed the text as applying to a preincarnational experience of Christ. Some theologians, both Roman and Reformed, had taught such an interpretation. It had been a minority viewpoint in every period of church history—ancient, medieval, and modern. Both Thomas Aquinas, the schoolman of Paris, and Theodore Beza, the schoolmaster of Geneva, had held such a position. Along with Augustine of Hippo they held that the passage in 1 Peter referred to to a sermon Jesus had preached before his incarnation at His conception. Such a teaching would even commend a rewording of the Apostles' Creed, or, at least, the relocation of the sentence about the *descensus* to an earlier portion of the creed. All the Lutherans

rejected this teaching, insisting that 1 Peter described an action that occurred after the incarnation.

4. None of the Lutherans, as had some of the Reformed and Free Church writers, felt that this passage was simply a sentence describing Christ's death. For many, if not most of the Reformed theologians, the statement, "He descended into hell," simply meant that Jesus "descended into Hades," or went to the "realm of the dead." It was, for them, a poetic way of teaching the death of Jesus.

The Lutherans rejected this interpretation because of its obvious conflict with the clear meaning of 1 Peter 3:18-19 and because of its deviation from the logical sequence of events recited in the Apostles' Creed. The creed taught that He "was *crucified, dead,* and *buried; He descended* into hell." After having made it obvious that Jesus had died, and by what instrument, and with what consequences, the creed continued to a separate event, the *descensus.* For the Lutherans the *descensus* had a much richer meaning than being merely a metaphorical way to describe the termination of a life.

5. None of the Lutherans, as had some of the scholastic writers of the Middle Ages, held that the *descensus* meant that Christ had gone and preached salvation either to the Old Testament saints, or that he had gone to the Elysian Fields to share the Gospel with the noble heathen who had lived and died before his earthly advent. The Lutheran Reformers rejected the medieval Roman Catholic teaching of the *limbus patrum,* the land of the devout Jewish believers, and, they consequently rejected also the notion that Christ had visited that supernatural location in order to release these ancient worthies so that they might now enter Paradise. The Lutheran Reformers were equally insistant in their denial of the Zwinglian notion that Jesus had visited with the venerable dead of the pagan world in order to make it possible for Socrates, Hercules, and other Greek and Roman philosophers to enter heaven. While such conceptions might be suitable for the poetry of a Dante, they were unacceptable in the serious theology of a Luther and his heirs.

6. None of the Lutherans, as had the framers of the

Heidelberg Catechism, held that the Petrine passage and the creedal affirmation designated the crucifixion of Jesus. The Lutherans were agreed that the *descensus* was more than merely another way of describing the agony of Christ on the cross.

On the other hand, the Lutherans were in substantial agreement as to how the doctrine ought to be regarded:

1. The Lutherans believed the doctrine ought to be viewed on the basis of the material principle of the Reformation, the Protestant teaching of *sola gratia,* or salvation by grace alone. Since justification by grace alone through faith was the central affirmation of both the Reformation and of the Scriptures, the teaching of Christ's descent into hell must have a soteriological significance. It was part of salvation history.

2. The Lutheran theologians believed the doctrine ought to be viewed on the basis of the formal principle of the Reformation, the Protestant teaching of *sola scriptura,* or the Word alone as the ultimate source and standard of Christian dogmatics. The passage would have to be understood on the basis of divine revelation, not ecclesiastical tradition or human speculation.

Precisely because there was so much consensus on the doctrine, it was to prove doubly frustrating when disagreement developed. The Epitome briefly and succinctly recorded the questions that caused contention:

> When and how, according to our simple Christian Creed, did Christ go to hell? Did it happen before or after His death? Did it occur only according to the soul, or only according to the deity, or according to body and soul, spiritually or corporeally? Does this article belong to Christ's suffering or to His glorious victory and triumph? (Ep IX 1, Tappert ed.).

In part this "dispute among some theologians of the Augsburg Confession" (Ep IX 1) was an inheritance from the earlier discord over the doctrine that had prevailed among "the ancient teachers of the Christian church" (SD IX 1). In part it was due to the ministry of John Aepinus.

Superintendent John Aepinus of Hamburg, who died in

1553, was a contemporary of Philipp Melanchthon and of John Calvin. He was a second-generation Protestant. Known as a staunch Lutheran, widely respected for his pastoral competence and scholarly ability, John Aepinus triggered the controversy over the *descensus* in 1544. In a series of sermon-lectures Aepinus taught that the descent into hell was a continuation of Christ's humiliation. In fact, it was the ultimate degradation experienced by the Son of God. On no conditions ought it to be regarded as part of the Lord's exaltation. Other Lutherans quickly replied to Aepinus. They pointed him to the very words of Jesus from the cross, "It is finished" (John 19:30). This meant that the atonement had been completed. If one accepted Aepinus' interpretation of the matter, the words of Jesus would have to read, "I am finished," for the Lord still would have had to face the terrors of hell. Aepinus did not change his position. Still other Lutheran theologians referred to the prediction of Christ that immediately after his death He would be in Paradise (Luke 24:43). That was as far from hell as one could be. Paradise implied peace, not passion. Furthermore, at his parting moment Jesus had said, "Father, into Thy hands I commit My Spirit!" (Luke 23:46). The way Aepinus interpreted the passage in 1 Peter seemed to contradict these texts and the obvious meaning of the historical sequence in the Apostles' Creed. But the Hamburg superintendent persisted in his opinion. Since Luther had died in 1546, the city council of Hamburg appealed to Philipp Melanchthon, the Wittenberg Professor, for a *Gutachten* (opinion) on this matter. He was the author of the Augustana and was now the theological leader of Lutheranism. Melanchthon's reply was not persuasive and Aepinus died three years later without having altered his views. While his teachings had not seriously disrupted the general life of the German Lutheran churches, they had, nevertheless, served as a source of friction. The authors of the Formula therefore felt it salutary to include this brief but sufficient Article on the descent of Christ into hell.

The article is in complete accord with what Luther had said on this subject, particularly in his Small and Large Catechisms, his sermon at Torgau in 1533, and the Smalcald Articles. It is also in harmony with what Melanchthon had stated in the Augsburg Confession and its Apology.

Article IX of the Formula of Concord includes five positive affirmations that complete the already sizable Lutheran consensus on the doctrine of the *descensus:*

1. Lutherans believe that the *descensus* involved Christ in both of His natures, the God-Man, both truly divine and truly human. It was an act of the whole Christ.

2. Lutherans believe that the *descensus* occurred after the burial of Jesus Christ on Good Friday and before His resurrection on Easter. The Biblical sequence of events was the Lord's death, the appearance of His spirit in the presence of His Father in heaven, the vivication, and the descent of Christ, body and soul, into hell.

3. Lutherans believe that the *descensus* was part of Christ's exaltation, not His humiliation. Jesus made a triumphal entry into the very citadel of the devil, harrowed hell, and crushed the ancient adversary under his heel.

4. Lutherans believe that the *descensus* is an article of the Christian faith because it is based solidly on Biblical revelation, not because it stimulates the human imagination. Believers are cautioned not to go beyond the Sacred Scriptures nor to use unreliable traditions in order to obtain more information than what has been provided by the divinely inspired apostolic author. Speculation is not appropriate.

5. Lutherans believe that the *descensus* is a doctrine full of comfort and good cheer for Christians. The assurance of Christ's conquest of hell is a source of courage through this life and in the hour of death. There is, indeed, nothing that can separate the believer from his Lord, either in this life or the next. Jesus Christ is the Lord, Redeemer of the faithful, the Harrower of hell.

CONFESSION AND CEREMONIES

Kurt Marquart

$\mathcal{A}$rticle X deals with "ecclesiastical ceremonies" (Latin) or "church customs, called *adiaphora* or things indifferent" (German). It is of the nature of the Formula of Concord to examine under a magnifying lense, as it were, highly particular controversial points, rather than broad areas of Christian doctrine. But the "points" all belong to an "area," of course—in the case of Article X to the doctrine of the nature of the church and of church fellowship and confession. The article has important dogmatic implications not only for the specific issue of "ceremonies" but for the *ecclesiology* of the Book of Concord.

The "adiaphoristic" controversy, to which Article X addresses itself, arose directly out of the Augsburg and Leipzig Interims of 1548. Although the Interim was a dead letter by 1552, when the Emperor was forced by the Lutherans into a stalemate, the issue itself remained the subject of furious debate among the deeply divided Lutherans. The precise point at issue is defined in SD X 1—3: In matters neither commanded nor forbidden in God's Word, may one at the demand of the enemies of the Gospel yield to a forced restoration of ceremonies that have fallen into disuse? Some said yes, since the points at issue were only *adiaphora*. Others said no, since at a time of persecution, when the opponents seek to destroy the pure Gospel by force or trickery, one must make a clear confession and dare not yield even in such externals. The Formula's decision naturally was in favor of the latter view.

What were the specific ceremonies or *adiaphora* in question? Andreä in his six sermons which prepared the way for the Formula made the interesting remark that "this matter arose not just over the surplice and that sort of thing." Evidently there was enough dispute about surplices "and that sort of thing" to warrant the defensive assurance that this in itself was not really the problem. The fact is that in the matter of vestments the Lutheran Reformation was from the outset characterized by much variety. In many places the full eucharistic vestments were kept, and they survived into the days of rationalism; in others even the white surplice was abhorred as an obnoxious reminder of popery. During the controversy about the Interim there were popular cartoons depicting the surplice as the thin edge of a wedge which at the other end burgeoned into the full-blown papacy. The Augsburg Confession's well-known ceremonial conservatism was inevitably tempered by Luther's own studied indifference, born of a healthy contempt for a superstitious fussiness in such matters.[1]

Before turning to the question of real *adiaphora,* Article X disposes of a number of things that had been falsely disguised as *adiaphora.* Thus the Leipzig Interim tried to make palatable as "*adiaphora*" matters that really were not that at all, e.g., "extreme unction" and the reintroduction of the Corpus Christi observance. Also, the required abstinence from meat on Fridays and Saturdays was presented as mere civil obedience to Imperial authority and therefore acceptable. This is the sort of thing meant in Article X's reference to matters given out under the "title and guise" or "pretext" of external *adiaphora,* which however—despite being "coated with another paint"—ran counter to God's Word and were therefore not *adiaphora* (SD X 5). Probably the most serious and far-reaching concession in this regard was the Leipzig Interim's restoration of the jurisdiction of the papal bishops over the Evangelical clergy as regards ordination and discipline. The Formula of Concord (SD X 19—23) shows that the Smalcald Articles contemplated and offered such restoration of episcopal jurisdiction not unconditionally, but only on understanding that the bishops would first become real bishops and begin to govern the church with the Gospel. Even then, however, jurisdiction was to be granted them not of necessity but for the sake of love and unity, and without unnecessary pomp and nonsense. None of these preconditions had been met by the bishops of the Leipzig Interim, who were unreconstructed Romanists. In no way therefore could submission to them be validly treated as an *adiaphoron*.

Nor does Article X accept as genuine *adiaphora* such ceremonies as create the impression or—in order to avoid persecution[2]—are meant to give the impression "as if our religion did not differ greatly from the papistic, or as if the latter were not highly abhorrent to us" (SD X 5). The same applies to ceremonies intended to reconcile and merge both incompatible religions into one, and to such others as are meant to cause or encourage a return to the papacy, hence apostasy from the pure doctrine of the Gospel and the true religion (SD X 5). All this is forbidden in 2 Cor. 6:14, 17 (SD X 6).

One final class of ceremonies that are not genuine *adiaphora* are those described as "useless, foolish spectacles, which serve neither good order, nor Christian discipline, nor evangelical propriety in the church" (SD X 7). Since no examples are given in the Formula itself, judgments will presumably differ, according to times and circumstances, as to what constitutes "useless, foolish spectacles." Flacius lists such things as "dragging about the palm-donkey, with the image [of Christ] seated thereon."

But what of genuine *adiaphora?* This after all is the real problem Article X sets out to solve in principle. There follow, in the Solid Declaration, three basic points of very unequal length,

262

each introduced with the solemn formula, "we believe, teach, and confess." The first such point defines the important principle that genuine *adiaphora,* that is ceremonies neither commanded nor forbidden in God's Word, *are not as such, or in and of themselves, divine worship or any part of it* (SD X 8). The proof text is Matt. 15:9: "In vain do they worship Me, teaching for doctrines the commandments of men." This position, at first sight, appears to involve a paradox:[3] On the one hand *adiaphora* are neither worship nor any part of it, yet on the other hand, actual worship is not possible without concrete particulars of time, place, and manner, in other words, *adiaphora!* But the point of course is that *adiaphora* are not *in and of themselves* worship, or service to God. This evangelical principle is integral to the Reformation's very cornerstone (see AC and Ap XV also Ap XXIV 51-52), cutting off at the source all false pretensions of self-chosen human piety (cf. Ap XXIV 92), all notions of meritorious observances, and all false claims of human tradition and authority in the church, in short, the superstitious religiosity of which the "natural man" is so incorrigibly fond. The principle, however, is a finely honed dogmatic instrument and requires skill and precision in application; it is not to be wielded like a bludgeon or a meat-ax! It would be wrong to infer from it, for instance, that ceremonies and liturgical forms simply don't matter, and may be left to proliferate—or stagnate!—like weeds or Topsy! The technical term "indifferent things" for *adiaphora* was never meant to suggest "indifference" in the popular sense of boredom, contempt, or carelessness. The Formula of Concrd nowhere retracts the Augsburg Confession's considered judgment that "nothing contributes so much to the maintenance of dignity in public worship and the cultivation of reverence and devotion among the people as the proper observance of ceremonies in the churches" (Of Abuses, introduction, 6; Tappert, p. 49).

The a-liturgical orientation of our modern Reformed-pietistic environment moreover jumps only too easily to the conclusion that Article X simply consigns everything liturgical to the realm of *adiaphora,* so that as long as Word and Sacraments still come to expression somehow, all outward arrangements are free and "indifferent." That too would be a grave misunderstanding. The term *adiaphora* applies only to that strictly circumscribed area of external details neither commanded nor forbidden in God's Word. In no way does FC X abrogate Article XXIV of both the AC and the Apology, in which the Lutheran Church officially confesses its doctrinal stand on the nature of Christian worship—including such concrete particulars as the divinely given relation between preaching and the Sacrament (Ap XXIV, 33—40, 71—72, 80, 89), and the "right use" of the historic Christian "mass" (AC XXIV 35 German; Ap XXIV 99) or the "liturgy" (Ap XXIV 79—81) or the "Eucharist" (Ap XXIV 74—77, 87). It would be a reductionist fallacy to confuse all such deeply theological issues with mere *adiaphora.*

The second major point about genuine *adiaphora* is that "the church of God of every place and time" (SD X 9) has the perfect right and authority to alter them so long as this is done without offence, in an orderly manner, so as to redound to the church's edification. Here too one may yield to the weak, as St. Paul teaches and shows by his own example. The Biblical texts appealed to are Rom. 14; Acts 16 and 21, and 1 Cor. 9. The reference to "good order" and "Christian discipline" in this connection means no doubt also to safeguard the proper, evangelical functioning of the public ministry, about which a significant assertion is made in the very next paragraph (cf. also AC XXVIII, esp. 49—60).

The third "we believe, teach, and confess" (SD X 10—17) finally, gets to the heart of the whole matter: at a time of confession, when the enemies of God's Word seek to suppress the pure teaching of the holy Gospel, one must confess fully and uncompromisingly, in word and deed, nor yield even in *adiaphora.* This is required of the whole church of God, of every individual Christian, "but especially [of] the servants of the Word as the leaders (*Vorsteher*) of the church of God," that is, "those whom the Lord has placed over (*praefecit*) his church to govern it" (SD X 10 Latin). Here it is not a question of accommodating oneself to the weak, but of resisting idolatry, false doctrine, and spiritual tyranny. The classical texts cited are

264

Paul's assertions of Christian liberty, Col. 2 and Gal. 2 and 5. It is pointed out that although circumcision was at that time an *adiaphoron*, which Paul also used in Christian freedom (Acts 16:3; 1 Cor. 7:18-19), he absolutely resisted any compulsion in this matter, "that the truth of the Gospel might be preserved" (Gal. 2:5 RSV). At stake here, then, is not some minor point or pedantry, but "the chief article of our Christian religion" (SD X 14).

Concessions in externals, without prior agreement in doctrine, simply confirm the idolaters in their idolatry, but sadden and offend the orthodox, and weaken them in their faith (SD X 16). This every Christian must avoid by his soul's salvation, Matt. 18:6-7. Above all, one must consider Christ's words: "Whoever shall confess Me before men, him will I also confess before My heavenly Father," Matt. 10:32 (SD X 17).

There follow quotations from Smalcald Articles and from the Treatise on the Power and Primacy of the Pope, as well as references to Luther's private writings, to show that all this "has always been the belief and confession regarding such *adiaphora*, on the part of the most eminent teachers of the Augsburg Confession" (SD X 18). The paragraphs cited repeat major ecclesiological themes of the Reformation, e.g., the classic formulation of the Smalcald Articles on the papalist hierarchy: "We do not concede to them that they are the church, nor are they. Nor are we going to pay attention to what they command or forbid under the name of the church. For, thank God, a child of seven knows what the church is, namely the saints, the believers and lambs, who hear their Shepherd's voice" (SA-III XII 1—2)! Or: "Therefore as little as we may adore the devil himself as Lord or God, so little may we tolerate his apostle, the pope or antichrist in his reign as head or lord. . ." (SA-II IV 14).

From the Treatise the principle is cited: "No one shall burden the church of God with his own traditions of whatever kind. For in this matter it must be held as firmly settled that no man's power or authority may take precedence over God's Word" (11). There follows immediately, also quoted from the Treatise, the admonition "to turn away from and execrate" the reign of the very antichrist (41). The Biblical basis given in the

Treatise and repeatedly by FC X is the Lord's command to beware of false prophets, in Matt. 7:15, an allusion to Paul's statements in Gal. 1:8-9 and Tit. 3:10, and Paul's explicit admonition in 2 Cor. 6:14—18. There follows again the classic formulation on illicit churchfellowship, from the treatise: "Difficult indeed it is to separate oneself from so many countries and people and to profess a distinct doctrine; but here stands God's command, that everyone is to beware of, and not make common cause with such as profess false doctrine or intend to maintain it by means of cruelty" (Treatise 42; FC SD X 23).

After these quotations from the earlier Confessions, FC X refers also to some of Luther's private writings, without however citing actual excerpts. The reference to Luther is in keeping with the principle stated already in Article VII, namely: "Since therefore Dr. Luther must rightly be regarded as the most eminent teacher of the churches which hold to the Augsburg Confession . . . so the oft-mentioned Augsburg Confession's proper sense and meaning can and ought to be taken more properly and better from no one else's than from Dr. Luther's doctrinal and polemical writings" (SD X 41). The specific writings intended in Article X are "A Report to a Good Friend Regarding Both Kinds of the Sacrament, Against the Bishop of Meissen's Decree" (1528), and Luther's letters to Augsburg (1530), especially to Melanchthon, as well as the important "Exhortation of Martin Luther to All The Clergy Assembled at Augsburg for the Diet of 1530" (*LW* 34, 9—61). Here Luther's consistent principles regarding *adiaphora* are set forth in detail and unmistakably. Melanchthon's anxious inquiries, for instance, characterised by timid subleties, are answered by Luther, under dates of July 21, Aug. 3, and Aug. 4, 1530, with firm, assured principles, such as the distinction between spiritual and civil powers, the spiritual freedom and dignity of the church and of individual Christians, and the sole prerogative of God in His Word to define what shall constitute worship.

True to its design as an honest, responsible instrument of theological and ecclesiastical pacification, the Formula also in this Article contents itself with calm considerations of principle. Inflammatory details and personalia are left out altogether—so much so that there is not even an explicit reference to the term "Interim," although it was of course quite clear that this was at the heart of the whole controversy about *adiaphora*. But the underlying principles are so clearly stated, "that everyone can understand what a Christian church and every individual Christian, especially the preachers, must do or refrain from doing with a good conscience in *adiaphora,* especially at a time of confession, that God be not angered, love not injured, the enemies of God's Word not strengthened, nor the weak in faith offended" (SD X 25). There follow five brief rejections of the corresponding errors.

By far the most important ecclesiological pronouncement in Article X, however, and perhaps in the whole Formula of Concord, is the concluding paragraph (SD X 31):[4]

> Accordingly the churchs will not condemn one another on account of differences in ceremonies, if in Christian liberty one has fewer or more of them, so long as they are otherwise at one [einig] with each other in the doctrine and all its articles, also in the right use of the holy sacraments, in accordance with the well-known maxim: "*Dissonantia ieiunii non dissolvit consonantiam fidei:* Disagreement about fasting shall not break up unity [Einigkeit] in the faith."

The significance of this formulation lies in the fact that it is obviously a parallel to and hence a commentary on that much-debated heart and core of evangelical, Lutheran ecclesiology, AC VII, which is herewith cited, in part, for purposes of comparison:

> For this is enough for the true unity of the Christian church, that the Gospel be preached there unanimously according to its correct sense pure understanding and that the Sacraments be given out in accordance with the divine Word. And it is not necessary to the true unity of the Christian church that uniform ceremonies, instituted by men, be everywhere observed, as Paul says to the Ephesians, chapter 4: "One body, one Spirit, even as you are called to the one

hope of your calling, one Lord, one Faith, one baptism" (AC VII 2—4).

Both paragraphs are about church unity. Both base unity on agreement in Christ's pure Gospel and sacraments. Both declare that differences about man-made ceremonies do not affect unity. It is a serious misunderstanding therefore to argue[5] that "unity" (Einigkeit) means one thing in the Augsburg Confession and something quite different in the Formula, namely internal, spiritual unity in the former case, and outward, "organizational" harmony and union in the latter. For one thing, the Augsburg Confession clearly speaks not simply of an intangible unity, but of one that can be expressed and apprehended in actual, i.e., external and palpable, preaching and sacraments; and for another, the Formula regards outward agreement in doctrine and sacraments not as some man-made "organizational" trifle, but as a precious expression of the divinely given unity of faith. In other words, the Formula here simply restates and applies the great, truly evangelical and truly ecumenical, ecclesiology of AC VII. The unity of that one holy church which is and remains in this life an article of faith, not of sight, is founded on the "pure marks," that is, on the church-creating pure Gospel and sacraments of Christ. And precisely these same "pure marks" are the sole determinants governing and limiting proper churchly relations, e.g., mutual recognition among concrete churches. Orthodox church fellowship therefore intends to represent publicly and officially not some other, narrower entity, but precisely the one church confessed in the Creed. Both the Augsburg Confession and the Formula solemnly protest against all sectarianism in the premises. The one church of Christ counts for everything. Separation is permissible only for the sake of the one, ecumenical Gospel of Christ. Where that is violated, separation is mandatory.

As a gloss or commentary on AC VII, FC SD X 31 safeguards the AC against any minimalistic misunderstanding of what is meant by the "Gospel." The AC's pure preaching of the Gospel is clearly equivalent to the Formula's agreement "in the doctrine and all its articles." To be sure, the Augsburg

Confession requires no mere paper doctrine, much less subscription formalities only, but actual right proclamation. This very proclamation, however, is necessarily dogmatic or doctrinal. No mere "minigospel" constitutes orthodoxy or justifies church fellowship. None of the Gospel's full-orbed splendor and integrity dare be sacrificed. The whole organism of Christian doctrine is to be maintained "in all its articles." The contrast is not between Gospel and other doctrines but between God-given Gospel-doctrine, all of it, and human traditions or ceremonies.

The understanding of Gospel-doctrine as consisting of individual "articles" is not an innovation in FC SD X 31. Already the Augsburg Confession clearly understood the "right teaching of the Gospel" as embracing the basic "articles" it set forth (Preface, 24; Title, "Articles of Faith and Doctrine," etc.). Nor is the organic, holistic understanding of Gospel-doctrine lost in the Formula: There is a "chief article" (SD X 14), and Law and Gospel are the chief "kinds" or "heads" of doctrine (SD V 1, 23, 24), the single judge, rule, and norm for *all* doctrines ("*dogmata*") being Holy Scripture alone, *sola sacra scriptura* (Ep, Rule and Norm, 7). What then is an "article" or "part" of doctrine? It is simply a larger or smaller area or aspect of the one Christian truth. So for instance the Lord's burial and descent into hell are, when the occasion demands it, differentiated "as distinct articles" (SD IX 1). Luther's usage in the Large Catechism is instructive: the Creed, which had heretofore been divided into "twelve articles" ("though there are many more articles if all items written in Scripture and belonging to the Creed were to be taken separately"), Luther briefly comprises in "three main articles" (LC II 5—6). But for the learned and more advanced, "one can greatly expand all three articles and divide them into as many parts as there are words" (LC II 12). Again, "expounding all these individual parts does not belong in the short children's sermons, but into the great sermons throughout the year, especially at the times set aside for the purpose of treating each article at length: of the birth, suffering, resurrection, ascension of Christ, etc." (LC II 32).

In sum, the whole point of Article X is that the church's

distinctive treasure, the full, many-faceted Gospel, including the sacraments in their God-given integrity, must be maintained and confessed, without additions or subtractions, uncompromisingly—and not only in theory, much less as a legal fiction, but in fact and reality. Christian truth by its very nature demands practical implementation in actual church life, in other words, honest, consistent, and decisive ecclesiastical and individual confession by word and deed. The absolute primacy of the Christic-Apostolic foundation (Eph. 2:20) determines this dynamic ecclesiology and sets it forever apart from all caricatures, be they of the subjectivist-disintegrative variety or of the institutionally fossilizing one.

PREDESTINATION AND ELECTION

Robert Preus

No discussion of predestination or an election of grace is offered in any of the Luther Confessions prior to the Formula of Concord. Only the slightest adumbration of the doctrine is found as the earlier Confessions speak of the elect (AC XVCII 3). This may appear strange, inasmuch as the doctrine received prominence in Luther's *Bondage of the Will* and in Melanchthon's first edition of his *Loci communes*.[1] It must be recognized, however, that neither Luther nor Melanchthon is treating predestination in his respective discussion as a necessary and fundamental element of the Gospel, but rather as a part of a polemic against freedom of the will and in the context of divine providence. This may explain why the matter was not in the Confessions prior to the Formula of Concord.

But why then was it discussed even in the Formula at all? There had been no formative treatment of the doctrine which added anything to what Luther and Melanchthon had said so emphatically in their earlier writings. Calvinism, however, had not been silent on the matter. Beza had articulated a supralapsarian doctrine, thus going beyond Calvin. Peter Martyr, Jerome Zanchi, and others had engaged in bitter controversies with Lutherans. The Reformed *Belgic Confession* and *Gallic Confession* had also clearly expressed the Calvinistic position. Furthermore, Luther's good friend, Nikolaus von Amsdorf, had in his earlier years set forth a kind of double predestination,[2] and the synergistic Lutheran, John Pfeffinger, had taught that God elected us to eternal salvation because we believed in Christ.[3]

It was wise therefore for the writers of the Formula of Concord to offer a discussion on predestination. Its relation to the Gospel and its evangelical application and use among Christians had never been sufficiently considered by Lutherans before. Moreover, the bitter debates of Flacius and the Gnesio-Lutherans with Strigel, Pfeffinger and others on the bondage of the will and on original sin that led to Articles I and II of the Formula of Concord necessitated a special article on predestination; for the three subjects cannot be considered in isolation from each other (SD XI 44). Luther recognizes this as he writes his *Bondage of the Will;* if one errs on one of the three topics he will likely err also regarding the other two, and he will end up erring on the central article of justification by faith.

Terminology and Orientation for Teaching the Article of Predestination

A common and most useful penchant in the Formula of Concord is to define terms and offer an orientation for presenting each article of faith. Article XI, accordingly, begins with a definition of foreknowledge (*Vorsehung*) and predestination (*die ewige Wahl Gottes; Verordnung Gottes*). Foreknowledge is usually spoken of in an unbiblical and ecclesiastical sense, meaning that God knows in advance all that occurs but is not necessarily the cause of such events and occurences. Although such foreknowledge, used in the sense of divine providence, does set limits on evil and controls all things

272

for God's glory, nevertheless it is in no sense the cause of evil. The cause of evil is the perverse will of the devil and men (SD XI 7; cf. AC XIX). Occasionally the term "foreknowledge" is used synonymously with predestination or election (SD XI 10, 12).

God's eternal election, or predestination, however, not only foresees all things, who will be saved and who will be lost, but effects, foreordains, and causes everything that pertains to the salvation of individual sinners. Unlike foreknowledge, it pertains only to the children of God. But in this case it is "a cause which creates, effects, helps, and furthers our salvation and whatever pertains to it" (SD XI 8; cf. Ep XI 5; Tappert ed.).

The definition and understanding of predestination must be seen in a context or setting. It must not be viewed as a kind of deterministic foreknowledge that would discourage repentance, faith, prayer, or a godly life. It is not the object of philosophical or rational speculation. We are not to search out "the absolute, secret, hidden, and inscrutable foreknowledge of God" (SD XI 13). Predestination must be viewed in the context of the Gospel, in the light of Christ's universal redemption, the effectiveness of the means of grace, justification by faith, the sanctification of the Spirit, and certainty of eternal life for all who are elected, called, and justified (SD XI 15—22). The "eight points" mentioned in the Solid Declarations are not a *part* of the entire election of God in the wide sense (as conjectured by 17th-century Lutheran Orthodoxy and by 19th-century Lutheran synergists in this country), but are the entire Gospel *context* for the doctrine of election. These great themes are to be considered along with election (*zusammengefasst werde; simul mente complectamur*), if it is not to be subsumed under other Gospel themes and then ultimately denied or overlooked.[4]

The Nature of Election

Viewing predestination organically as a part of the Gospel, we can finally gain a whole picture of what election really is. Election is an ordination (*Verordnung*) of the children of God to eternal life (SD XI 13).[5] But this election contains also an eternal predestination to faith (*zur Kindschaft; ad adoptionem in filios,* SD XI 24) and to everything that in time pertains to the elect's salvation. God in eternity determined not merely to send Christ to be the Savior of sinners and decreed not merely to save men by the means of grace—these eternal decrees are not election at all, but the setting for the doctrine as we have pointed out—but God in eternity has also "graciously considered and elected to salvation each and every individual among the elect who are to be saved through Christ, and also ordained [*verordnet; decrevit*] that in the manner just recounted [in the eight points] He wills by His grace, gifts, and effective working to bring them to salvation and to help, further, strengthen, and preserve them to this end" (SD XI 23, Tappert). This is what election is. It always includes a choosing of individuals (SD XI 25, 45). Election teaches that God is concerned about every individual's justification and conversion (SD XI 45). But more than that: God has determined for each person the time and hour of his call and conversion (SD XI 56). Everything God has done in time to save a sinner He determined to do in eternity.

Since election is a part of the Gospel there is no predestination to damnation. The eight points which offer the context for teaching the doctrine of election make this abundantly clear. The false doctrine that God does not desire all men to repent and believe the Gospel or that He is not serious as He extends the Gospel call to all men is explicitly rejected (Ep XI 17—19). Only the elect are the object of predestination (Ep XI 5). The paradox drawn from this position is simply accepted throughout the Formula of Concord and those who would curiously probe the mystery are simply warned not to do so (Ep XI 6). It is indeed God who gives His Word in one place and not another; and He removes it from one place and not another; He hardens those who will not repent (SD XI 56—57). But "we should not explore the abyss of God's hidden knowledge" (*Abgrund der verborgenen Versehung; abyssum arcanae et occultae praedestinationis divinae;* SD XI 33; cf. Ep XI 13).[6] We remain with the revelation of God's foreknowledge which we find in His Word (SD XI 43), and this Word speaks only of an election and predestination of the children of God.

God's predestination to salvation and "everything that pertains to it" (Ep XI 5) includes faith. It is an eternal election to adoption of sons (SD XI 24; Eph. 1:5). This position, not only excludes all work-righteousness and synergism (Pfeffinger and later Cardinal Robert Bellarmine's doctrine of predestination *ex praevisa fide*), but also the subtile view of later Lutheran orthodoxy, first introduced by Aegidius Hunnius, that God elected individuals to eternal life *intuitu fidei,* in view of faith, which God in eternity foresaw.[7] For instance, the Epitome rejects the following proposition: "That it is not only the mercy of God and the most holy merit of Christ, but that there is also within us a cause of God's election, on account of which he has elected us to eternal life" (Ep XI 20; cf. SD XI 88).

The Evangelical Nature of the Doctrine of Election

Although God punishes sins with obduracy and blindness (SD XI 83), nevertheless, the cause of sin and damnation lies totally in man's rejection of God's grace (Ep XI 12), and there is no predestination to damnation, as we have seen. This means that predestination and election must be viewed and presented from the perspective of the Gospel of grace and preached and applied as Gospel. The Formula often affirms the universal grace of God and His earnest will to bring all to faith and to save them, and this within the discussions on predestination (SD XI 14, 24, 28; Ep XI 17—19).[8] Our election is based solely on the work of Jesus Christ (SD XI 75). It does not depend on us, nor is it due to some muster-like, arbitrary action of God (SD XI 5, 9). Its cause is only the mercy of God and the most holy merit of Christ (SD XI 88). That is why it is such a comforting doctrine. We seek our election "in Christ" (SD XI 89), in the gospel of reconciliation (SD XI 25—27), and in the fact that the promise of the Gospel extends to all men (SD XI 28—33). This is extremely important. The Solid Declaration teaches that we make sure of our personal election by simply applying to ourselves the many verses of Scripture telling of God's universal love (e.g., John 3:16), Christ's universal atonement (e.g., John 1:29; 1 John 1:7; 2:2), and the universality of the Gospel call (e.g., Matt. 11:28; Rom. 3:22). As I learn to know that God in history has loved me and saved me in Christ, that He in time has now called me effectually through the Gospel, I know also that

He has loved me and saved me and called me from all eternity. In that my certainty of election consists. My certainty of election comes about as I appropriate to myself and particularize God's universal grace in Christ.

And God's election is certain and secure. God's decree of election is irrevocable. True, the children of God fall away. This fact, attested in Scripture, must be maintained against Calvinism (SD XI 10, 42). But the elect who fall will be restored again (SD XI 75). In fact, the doctrine of election is to be taught in such a way that every believer may be certain that by God's almighty grace he will not fall (SD XI 12, 43, 46). This is indeed the great force and comfort of the doctrine of election: that God who in eternity has loved us in Christ and predestinated us to sonship and everlasting life will be faithful to His promises, and He will allow no one to pluck us out of His hand (Ep XI 13; SD XI 29—32). One of the great concerns of Luther and the Reformers was to have the assurance of salvation. How do we acquire such certainty? Not by looking to ourselves—as Romanists and synergists taught—but by looking to all the promises of God and firmly relying on them. And among these Gospel promises is this, that He has loved us in Christ and chosen us from eternity to be His own, and nothing can hinder His eternal purpose. Any presentation of the Gospel, any interpretation of Scripture that would thwart this comfort which the doctrine of the election of grace affords can only be false and must be rejected (Ep XI 13; SD XI 92).

The antitheses attacked by the Formula of Concord in the article on predestination are (1) Calvinism with its denial of universal grace and a universal atonement, (2) synergism with its preoccupation with man's actions in conversion and its denial of *sola gratia,* and (3) enthusiasm with its denial that God brings us to faith in Christ and certainty of our salvation solely through the means of grace. In every case these heresies rob the believer of His comfort, comfort which only the effective Gospel of universal grace and *sola gratia* can bring us and instill in us. Thus, it is out of an evangelical and practical concern that even the polemics of Article XI emanate (Ep XI 1, 11, 13; SD XI 12, 43—45). Rather than undermining the article of justification by faith alone, the correct doctrine of predestination upholds it and confirms it; for it enhances the glory of God, refutes all false opinions about the powers of the human will, and comforts the believer abundantly (SD XI 43—49). In this it serves the same evangelical function as does the article of justification by faith (cf. Ap IV 2).

In refusing to answer the *cur alii, alii non* question (SD XI 53—59) and maintaining the paradox that salvation is entirely God's doing and is utterly undeserved, whereas the cause of damnation is entirely man's doing (SD XI 60, 78, 82), the Formula of Concord teaches the Biblical and only possible evangelical doctrine of predestination. And this is the only way the evangelical doctrine can be maintained against Calvinism, Synergism and Enthusiasm (a form of synergism at this point). This theological hermeneutic, or approach, of our Confession places a higher priority on scripturalness than on apparent consistency and is the genius of the Formula of Concord.[9] The teaching side by side in Article XI on Election (particular election) of *universalis gratia* and *sola gratia*—which are both Gospel and both Biblical—is unique to Lutheranism and indicates the faithful and profound Biblical and evangelical commitment of our Lutheran Confessions.

OTHER FACTIONS AND SECTS

C. George Fry

*D*uring the 16th century there were four Reformations. Three of these are immediately obvious:

1. There was a national or royal Reformation in England, led by Henry VIII and his children. This produced a unique territorial expression of Christianity. Limited to England, Ireland, and Wales, the Anglican Church claimed to be simultaneously Catholic, Evangelical, and Reformed. Its identifying traits were an episcopal polity, a formal and fixed liturgy, much theological variety, and control by the English monarchy. The attitude of the Lutherans toward this faction had been made clear in the correspondence of Martin Luther and Henry VIII. Henry had regarded Luther as "a bat straight out of hell," the "very limb of Satan" himself. While Luther felt that some of the Anglican divines veered toward Luthern con- fessionalism, he was persuaded that the prevailing attitude

within the church was antievangelical. Because of this previous identification of the theological issues, because of the limited amount of geographical space occupied by Anglicanism, and because the Anglicans were no specific threat to Lutheran unity or doctrinal purity, no specific mention of them had to be made in the Formula.

2. There was a traditional or papal Reformation within the Roman Church. This encompassed various men and movements and expressed itself in the rebirth of medieval forms of piety, the resurgence of scholasticism, the revival of monasticism, the decisions of the Council of Trent (1545—63), and in the revitalization of the papacy. The unifying force in this Reformation was common loyalty to the pope of Rome. Previous confessions, starting with the Augsburg Confession, had spoken to the points of convergence and divergence between the Lutherans and the Roman Catholics. No further mention of them remained to be made in this article.

3. There was the confessional, doctrinal, or evangelical Reformation centered in central Europe but intended for the church universal. This Reformation had two foundations: the formal principle, that the ultimate source and standard of faith and life was Sacred Scripture (not tradition, reason, or extracanonical revelation) and the material principle, that the central teaching of the Christian religion was salvation by grace alone received through faith. This Evangelical Movement (holding to the authority of Scripture and the centrality of grace) began with Luther but had divided into two main streams—the Lutheran Reformation, under the leadership of the city of Wittenberg and the Saxon Reformers, and the Zwinglian and Calvinist Reformation, under the leadership of the cities of Zurich and Geneva and the Swiss Reformers. Efforts in a colloquy at Marburg in October 1529 and subsequently had failed to achieve a unification of the Evangelicals. The differences were simply too great. Since these had been discussed in the other portions of the Formula, it was not felt helpful to treat them in Article XII. As regards disagreements among the Lutherans themselves, it had just been noted in the Formula that these confessional disputes had already received "a basic

settlement." That was the subject of the 11 previous articles.

Article XII concerned itself with none of these Reformations—neither Lutheran, nor Reformed, nor Roman, nor Anglican. It moved to an entirely distinct group: the sects.

4. There was a radical or underground Reformation. This was the opinion of the framers of the Formula and they sought to respond to its peculiar problems.

The verdict of the Confessional Fathers has been shared by subsequent generations of historians. Scholars have been persuaded that the sects formed a fourth kind of Reformation, a sort of "theological counterculture" across the entire expanse of Western Christendom. Often the sectarians have been lumped together under a common label, such as "the Left-Wing Evangelicals," or "the Radical Reformers," or "the Free Church Protestants," or "the Enthusiasts, Spiritualists, and Rationalists." None of these names really fits. Many of the sectarians were not evangelical, nor were they genuinely Protestant or truly free. The sectarians, however, are difficult to classify. This Reformation gave expression to a wild variety of theological opinions, a kind of runaway doctrinal proliferation, such as had not been seen in the Christian world since antiquity. Furthermore, no confessional unity was ever manifested among the sectarians. Because there were many different leaders (many of them relatively obscure), appearing almost spontaneously among the people, simultaneously in many different places, teaching a multiplicity of views on sundry subjects, and lasting for lesser or shorter periods of time, it is virtually impossible to detect common patterns to this movement. No biographical, historical, geographical, psychological, or political typologies seem immediately applicable. Furthermore, since the Radical Reformation was often an illicit movement, frequently engaged in open revolution, it almost universally provoked political repression. For these reasons, it is not easy to generalize about the sectarians.

The late German sociologist Ernst Troeltsch provided historians with a helpful instrument. He believed that all denominations coming out of the Reformation could be classified as either the "church type" or the "sect type." As much as the Anglicans, the Romans, the Reformed, and the Lutherans might differ from one another on certain basic doctrines, they all at least shared certain common beliefs concerning the church, the state, and secular society. These were the very assumptions, however, that were questioned by the sectarians. The Left-Wing Reformers, as much as they disagreed with one another, generally held the following views concerning the church, the state, and secular society:

1. Most of the sectarians taught that the established churches were in a condition of moral and doctrinal degeneration. The Radicals (those who wanted to get at the source of the problem; "radical" is from the Latin, *radix,* "root") felt that Martin Luther, John Calvin, Thomas Cranmer, and Ignatius Loyola had been very superficial in their estimate of what was wrong with the church. They had worked for a "re-formation" of the existing theology and institutions. The Radicals thought that this was not enough. They were persuaded that there had been a great apostasy of the Catholic Church somewhere after the close of the apostolic period. With the closing of the New Testament age, the true church of Jesus Christ had either disappeared (not to be reborn until the 16th century) or gone underground (the so-called "tunnel theory" of church history). What ought to occur in the "true Reformation" was a total repudiation of past tradition (the work of the Antichrist), the complete reconstruction of Christian faith and life, and a thoroughgoing return to the first century, a restoration of the church of Peter and Paul (complete with miracles, apostles, visions, and revelations). This would mean the separation of church and state (as opposed to the Lutheran, Anglican, and Reformed notion of the territorial or national church) and the expulsion of so-called "unregenerate members" of the church. They rejected the idea of an inclusive Christian community composed of both saints and sinners (as taught in the Evangelical and Catholic churches). For the sectarians the "true church" of Christ on earth was composed only of the saints. Only "spiritual people" were to be admitted to church membership. Radical congregationalists, the sectarians usually held that only the local assembly of believers constituted a "church" in the New Testament sense. This "assembly" or

"congregation" was made up only of the perfect and the godly, for no sinners were to be tolerated in it. The ecclesiology of the sectarians is known as that of "the gathered church" or "the believers' church" in contradistinction to the "inclusive church" (be it territorial, national, regional, or ecumenical) composed of both saints and sinners (often found in the same person!) advocated by the mainline Reformers. The sectarians admitted only adults to membership in their societies, admission depended on some unusual, unique qualifying experience (it might be christological, as "accepting Christ"; or pneumatological, as "receiving the Spirit"; or psychological, as "obtaining illumination," or "the quickening of the conscience," or "hearing the voice of reason"). The church was composed of individuals (not families), adults (not children), who had an experience (emotional not intellectual), and who were holy (perfect, not imperfect). The Christian churches were small, separated from the world, and a mark of discipleship was persecution. Often the sectarians stressed some kind of theological aberration, a unique doctrine, an obsession with one belief, an unusual theological emphasis (as a peculiar mode of baptism), or a restoration of an ancient heresy (as Arianism).

2. Most of the sectarians taught Christians to avoid any kind of participation in the state. This avoidance could take either an active or a passive form. It could mean violent opposition to the government (in the form of revolution) or nonviolent noncooperation with the normal activities of the state (as a refusal to pay taxes, serve in the military, swear oaths, or hold public office).

3. Most of the sectarians taught their followers to practice strict separation from secular society. Regarding European Christendom as itself an abomination, the sectarians wanted no part of "ordinary daily life." Preaching strict segregation from Evangelical and Catholic Christians, whom they regarded as "apostates" at best, "Gentiles" or "unbelievers" at worst, the Radicals lived in a kind of 16th-century ghetto mentality. The Confessional Fathers saw much of this "as basically nothing else than a new kind of monkery." Among the sectarians there were all manner of aberrations in connection with nearly all the

natural orders—the home, work, play, the school, and culture. Deviance seemed to be the norm among them.

The framers of the Formula realized that the sectarian movement was a multifaceted and complex phenomenon, exhibiting many contradictory traits. Like many modern historians, the Confessional Fathers realized that the sectarians as a whole were of a different breed from the church-type Christians (as Lutherans, Anglicans, Romans, and Reformed). For that reason it was possible to discuss them in a single article of the Formula. But like most contemporary scholars, the Lutheran theologians were able to see the diversity as well as the unity among the groups on the Left. For that reason, like several 20th-century sociologists, the fathers classified the sectarians as falling into three main types: the Anabaptists, the Spiritualists (as Schwenkfelders), and Rationalists (the New Arians and the New Anti-Trinitarians).

The Anabaptists

The Fathers began by admitting that "the Anabaptists have split into many factions, some of which teach many errors, others teach fewer" (Ep XII, 2; quotations in this chapter are from the Tappert ed.). It was difficult to generalize about the Anabaptists for four reasons:

1. There was the apparent multiplicity of leadership. The Anabaptist movement had many different advocates—Andreas Carlstadt, the Zwickau Prophets, Thomas Münzer, Conrad Grebel, Felix Manz, Balthasar Hubmaier, Hans Denck, Hans Hut, Jacob Wiedemann, Melchior Hoffmann, Menno Simons, etc. Unlike Lutheranism, Zwinglianism, or Calvinism, all of which were guided by one strong individualism, Anabaptism was championed by literally hundreds of local leaders, few of whom had even a regional significance, none of whom attained the international reputation of a Martin Luther, an Ulrich Zwingli, or a John Calvin.

2. There was the apparent anonymity of much of the membership. While Lutheranism, Zwinglianism, and Calvinism won adherents from all elements of society, from princes to peasants, professors to peddlers, and kings to cobblers, the

Anabaptist Movement (with some noteworthy exceptions) seemed to be popular particularly among the poor, the oppressed, the unlettered, the silent and sullen masses of Europe. This fact, coupled with the lack of a clearly defined leadership, made the Anabaptist cause either somewhat inarticulate, or, worse still, at times sounding forth in a cacophony of sounds like a modern-day tower of Babel.

3. There was the appalling notoriety evident in much of the Anabaptist movement. Some of the Anabaptist societies were so radical in their conduct and convictions as to seriously shock conventional sensibilities.

One of the most extraordinary Anabaptist experiments had been conducted in the West German highlands in the ancient and venerable city of Münster. This Westphalian metropolis, located near the modern-day Dutch border, had been moving from Roman Catholicism toward Evangelicalism. In 1533, however, two proletarian adventurers from the Lowlands initiated a very bizarre chapter in the history of Münster. John of Leyden (John Beuckelsz), a tailor, and John of Harlaam (John Matthys) seized control of the town (after a series of alleged supernatural visions), repressed and expelled all residents who refused to conform to their agenda for reform, restored a kind of patriarchal kingdom (complete with 12 tribes, polygamy, and a kind of communism of goods), and declared this to be the New Jerusalem on earth. On June 25, 1535, a joint Lutheran-Roman Catholic army, under leadership of Philip of Hesse, had suppressed the "Münster Saints" and put an end to this aspect of the Radical Reformation.

More widespread had been the troubles inaugurated by a Thuringian priest, Thomas Münzer. Pastor of the church in Zwickau, Münzer had progressive passed from Roman Catholicism to Lutheranism to his own variety of Anabaptism. Regarding himself as the recipient of direct revelations from God, Münzer proclaimed himself the "true leader" of the Reformation. Despising the means of grace, the established clergy, the inherited traditions, and formal theology, Münzer introduced an iconoclastic regime in the church. This was coupled with a radical social program that called for drastic changes in the economic and political structure of the German states. An open rebellion, the Peasants' Revolt of 1525, was, in large measure, the result of his agitation. On May 15 of that year Münzer died in battle leading a peasant army against the Lutheran princes.

Meanwhile the Anabaptist virus had appeared almost spontaneously on the home territory of both the Saxon and Swiss Reformations. In Wittenberg itself Andreas Karlstadt, one of Martin Luther's closest colleagues on the college faculty, had become infected with the Radical disease. During Luther's absence at the Wartburg during 1521—22, Karlstadt had tried to take charge of the Lutheran Reformation. Advised by the Zwickau Prophets, a band of three self-styled 16th-century Isaiahs (two were weavers, one was a university dropout), who claimed to receive immediate revelations from God, Karlstadt had introduced dangerous and drastic aberrations into the Saxon Reformation. Only Luther's timely return to Wittenberg in the spring of 1522 had saved the situation from further deterioration. At the same time Conrad Grebel and Felix Manz had started to teach Anabaptist doctrines in Zurich, right under the nose of Ulrich Zwingli. For a while it seemed as if they would either convert the Swiss Reformer to their beliefs or else subvert the Swiss Reformation.

Not only in Westphalia and Thuringia, Saxony, and Switzerland, but across the whole Holy Roman Empire Anabaptist preachers appeared in the 1520s and later. Melchior Hoffmann, a Swabian furrier, taught that Strasbourg was to be the site of the imminent second advent. Hans Denck, the rector of St. Sebald's School (Lutheran) in Nuremberg, embraced the Anabaptist heresy. Hundreds more followed in their footsteps— such as Balthasar Hubmaier, student of the famed Roman Catholic theologian, John Eck, or Hans Hut, who advocated anarchy, or Jacob Wiedemann, who urged a kind of Biblical Communism, or the saintly Menno Simons, founder of the Mennonites, who tried to bring some of the central affirmations of Evangelical Christianity into a place of prominence in Anabaptist thinking, or Jacob Amman, who tried to summon the simple people of Germany and Switzerland into a return to the imagined simplicity of a New Testament life-style. All across the Lutheran lands in the half century preceding the Formula of Concord there had been a small but persistent threat from the Anabaptist counterculture.

4. There was the appalling variety and inconsistency of the Anabaptist doctrines. Some Anabaptists were pacifists, others were rabid militarists. Some held to Biblical authority, others were ardent visionaries, relying on supplementary communications from the Deity. Some strove to live in apostolic humility and simplicity, while others urged a radical discontinuity with the traditional Christian life-style. It was very difficult to speak of an Anabaptist theology.

The framers of the Formula, however, recognized the validity of the name "Anabaptist" for this particular collection of sectarians. As Anabaptists they believed in adult baptism, after conversion by immersion in free-flowing water. The word "Anabaptist" is from the Latin and means "rebaptizer," or "one who baptizes a second time." This was not the name they gave themselves, but it was an accurate description of them by the Lutherans and the Roman Catholics. They denied the efficacy of infant baptism by sprinkling and pouring, and insisted on rebaptizing adherents they attracted from the established churches. Their rite of initiation and their peculiar ecclesiology furnished a name that served as an umbrella under which to group a variety of sectarians.

The Lutheran Fathers then discussed 17 false doctrines that could be discovered among the Anabaptists. As Professor Willard Dow Allbeck has suggested, these errors can be grouped in three categories (the classification of the Fathers themselves):

1. The Anabaptists held errors "which cannot be tolerated in the church." Among these are such teachings as these: that Christ was only a gifted man (not God's Son), that the Lord's flesh and blood did not come from Mary, that justification is based on piety and sanctity, that baptism should be reserved for adults because children under the age of reason are not yet sinners, that children raised by Christian parents are not really sinners, that it is possible to have a church on earth made up only of saints, that Roman Catholics and Lutherans ought to be

286

avoided (out of fear of contamination by association), that one ought not preach, teach, pray, or otherwise worship in any building ever used by the Roman Catholic Church. To the Confessional Fathers, these notions were not to be tolerated in the Lutheran Church.

2. The Anabaptists held errors "which cannot be tolerated in the government." Just as the Anabaptists sinned against the church, so they also transgressed against the divine order in the state. Among these heresies were the following ideas: that government is not a God-pleasing estate, that Christians ought not serve in civil office, that a Christian may not use the agencies of the government for defense or justice, that a Christian cannot swear an oath in court, and that capital punishment is contrary to the New Testament ethic. To the Confessional Fathers it was evident that these teachings would undermine the legislative, executive, and judicial power of the government, destroy the instrument God had intended for social order, and plunge Germany into anarchy.

3. The Anabaptists held errors "which cannot be tolerated in domestic life" (cf. FC Ep XII 2). The Anabaptists revolted against God's purpose in society, as well as in the state and the church. In the realm of the natural orders (home, work, play, culture, school) they had devised such strange doctrines as these: a Christian cannot own private property but must practice a kind of New Testament communalism of goods: a Christian cannot in good conscience engage in certain occupations, particularly those of being an innkeeper, a merchant, or a cutler; and that divorce between married persons is acceptable if they are of different religious faiths, and that the separated spouses are then free to remarry. It was obvious to the Confessional Fathers that the Anabaptist beliefs and practices would undermine the very fabric of the common life.

The Spiritualists

During the 16th century there had been a random sampling of individuals who believed that it was no longer necessary to rely on the means of grace in order to come to a saving knowledge of God. Mediate truth and grace were superseded by

287

*im*mediate wisdom and favor. It was felt that the Spirit of God was active in a unique and wonderful way in the current generation.

One of these Spiritualists was Kaspar von Schwenkfeld (or Schwenckfeld, or Schwenkfeldt) von Ossig. Born at Ossig (or Ossigk, or Ossing) near Liegnitz in 1489 (some say 1490), Schwenkfeld had been educated at Cologne and at Frankfurt-on-the-Oder. Originally a Roman Catholic, he embraced Lutheranism and introduced the Reformation into Silesia. Rather early, however, he departed from Evangelical Lutheran theology and devised his own philosophy, which was accepted by a small group of followers called "Confessors of the Glory of Christ," or simply the Schwenkfelders. The significance of this sect was not in its size but in its assertions and the Lutheran Fathers identified seven heretical teachings of the Schwenkfelders (or Schwenkfeldians) (by dividing the first point the Epitome comes up with eight points). For the purposes of discussion, these can be grouped in three categories:

1. The Schwenkfelders held to christological errors. They affirmed that the humanity of Christ was absorbed by His divinity after the resurrection so that "now both natures in Christ possess only one divine essence, property, will, and glory and that the flesh of Christ belongs to the essence of the holy Trinity" (Ep XII, 21). This serious christological misconception caused the Schwenkfelders to assert "that all who say that Christ according to the flesh is a creature do not have a right understanding of Christ as the reigning king of heaven" (Ep XII, 20).

2. The Schwenkfelders held to errors concerning the means of grace. They denied, for instance, that the preaching and teaching of God's Word is "a means through which God the Holy Spirit teaches people and creates in them the saving knowledge of Christ, conversion, repentance, faith, and new obedience" (Ep XII, 22). The Spirit could work apart from the Word. The two dominical sacraments, Baptism and the Lord's Supper, were also deprived of power. As far as Baptism was concerned, it was "not a means through which the Lord God seals the adoption of children and effects rebirth" (Ep XII, 23).

288

In connection with the Eucharist, "bread and wine in the Holy Supper are not means through and by which Christ distributes His body and blood" (Ep XII 24). For all practical purposes, the Schwenkfelders felt it was possible to dispense with the necessity of Word and Sacraments.

3. The Schwenkfelders held ecclesiological errors. They believed it was possible for a Christian to attain perfection in this life, that the congregation of believers ought to introduce sufficient discipline to make this possible, and that it was not only desirable and feasible, but indeed, necessary to have a sinless clergy. Since the Schwenkfelders taught that "a minister of the church cannot teach profitably or administer true and genuine sacraments unless he is himself truly reborn, righteous, and pious" (Ep XII, 27), it was obvious they were reintroducing the ancient Donatist heresy—a view that had destroyed the objective validity of the means of grace, undermined Christian certainty, introduced a radical subjectivity regarding Word and Sacrament, threatened the efficiency of the ministry, as well as its authority, confused sanctity with salvation, and if carried to its logical extreme, would utterly dissolve the unity of the Christian community.

The Rationalists

The Anabaptists had a peculiar understanding of the church. The Schwenkfelders had a distorted comprehension of the means of grace. The Rationalists had a perverted and sub-Christian notion of God. Relying on human logic to fathom the mysteries of the divine nature, these teachers came to all manner of strange conclusions. Rationalism, or the rule of reason in religion, led to two sects: the New Arians (a revival of the heresy of the fourth century) and the anti-Trinitarians.

The ancient Arian error had been revived by a variety of men in the 16th century: the Spanish physician, Michael Servetus, who had labored not only in Iberia but in France before meeting his death in Calvin's Geneva; and the Italian Unitarians—uncle and nephew—Lelio and Fausto Sozzini (Laelius and Faustus Socinus), who failed to win much support in either Saxony or Switzerland, but who eventually found both princely and popular favor in Poland and Rumania (Transylvania). Though the danger was not immediately evident in the German lands, the Fathers were genuinely prophetic in condemning this mentality, for, in a significant way, it paved the road for the resurgence of humanism and rationalism in the subsequent epoch, the Era of Illumination, the so-called Age of Reason. The deism that came to dominate much of sophisticated German, French, British, and American society between 1648 and 1815 was in many respects glorified Arianism, transformed Unitarianism. It was strangely appropriate that the Formula should conclude with this condemnation of a heresy both ancient and modern, both transitory and resurgent, both small in adherents but eventually enormous in influence. The Fathers identified these dangerous errors of the Rationalists:

1. Their deviation from the ancient Catholic and confessional norms of the Nicene and Athanasian Creeds;

2. Their confession of subordinationist views of Jesus Christ;

3. Their denunciation of the Trinity, and their subsequent relapse into some kind of paganism (a tritheism, a kind of polytheism), or

4. Their exaltation of the Father at the expense of the Son and the Spirit, and, therefore, the substitution of a Muslim notion of divinity for the Christian affirmation of the Trinity.

It is significant that the Fathers conclude this article with this prophetic anticipation of the struggles to be fought against modern rationalism and neopaganism in the subsequent centuries and with the historical recollection of the very starting point of the Reformation, the effort by Dr. Martin Luther to reform and renew the Western Church through the proclamation of the evangelical Word and thus return it to its genuine catholic and apostolic foundations.

NOTES

Historical Background

1. On Melanchthon's influence on Luther see Lowell C. Green, "Faith, Righteousness, and Justification: New Light on Their Development Under Luther and Melanchthon," *The Sixteenth Century Journal* IV, 1 (1973), 65—86, and Martin Greschat, *Melanchthon Neben Luther: Studien zur Gestalt der Rechtfertigungslehre zwischen 1528 und 1537* (Witten: Luther Verlag, 1965).

2. Joachim Rogge, *Johann Agricolas Lutherverständnis, unter besonderer Berücksichtigung des Antinomismus* (Berlin: Evangelische Verlagsanstalt, 1960), esp. pp. 140—148; see also Gustav Kawerau, *Johann Agricola von Eisleben, Ein Beitrag zur Reformationsgeschichte* (Berlin: Hertz, 1881), esp. pp. 129—222.

3. On the Cordatus controversy on good works, see Greschat, pp. 217—230. On Amsdorf's criticism of Melanchthon during this period, see Robert Kolb, "Nikolaus von Amsdorf, Knight of God and Exile of Christ, Piety and Polemic in the Wake of Luther," (Ph.D. dissertation, University of Wisconsin-Madison, 1973), pp. 99—111, and 118—120; see also Robert Kolb, *Nikolaus von Amsdorf (1483—1565), Popular Polemics in the Preservation of Luther's Legacy* (Nieuwkoop: DeGraaf, 1978), pp. 49—61; Robert Kolb, "Nikolaus von Amsdorf on Vessels of Wrath and Vessels of Mercy: a Lutheran's Doctrine of Double Predestination," *Harvard Theological Review,* LXIX (1976), 3—4 (July—Oct.), 325—343.

4. The geography of the Saxon Reformation, particularly at the time of Luther's death, makes understanding political factors in its unfolding story somewhat difficult. First, Upper Saxony or the southern part of the entire region, now called simply Saxony, must be distinguished from Lower Saxony, roughly the area comprised by the current West German state of Lower Saxony. Lower Saxony was only a geographical designation in the 16th century; the most important political units in Lower Saxony were the several duchies of Braunschweig and the cities of Hamburg,

Lübeck, Lüneburg, and Bremen. Upper Saxony was both a geographical and a political designation (though the adjective "upper" was seldom used). Its duke had become an elector of the Holy Roman Empire. Elector Frederick II left his lands at his death in 1464 to his two sons, Ernst and Albert, who ruled them in common until 1485 when they divided their lands between them. The "Ernstine" branch of the family received the electoral title along with the special electoral territories in the middle of Frederick's domains and the western part of the dukedom, Thuringia. The "Albertine" branch of the family received the eastern lands, called Meissen, and the university of Leipzig. This division existed from 1485 to 1547; the settlement of the Smalcaldic War made a significant change in the arrangement. Until 1547 Ernstine Saxony had been electoral Saxony, and Albertine Saxony had been ducal Saxony. After 1547 the electorate was in the hands of the Albertine branch, and ducal Saxony became the designation of the Thuringian, Ernstine part of Upper Saxony. The Ernstine electors to 1547, succeeding Ernst himself (1485—86), were Frederick the Wise (1486—1525), John the Steadfast (1525—32), and John Frederick (1532—47). The Albertine dukes were Albert (1485—1500), George (1500—39), Heinrich (1539—41), and Moritz (1541—47). Moritz assumed the electorate for the Albertine branch in 1547 and was succeeded at his death by his brother August (1553—86). Elector John Frederick's sons, John Frederick the Middler and John William, ruled Ernstine ducal Saxony from 1547 until John William's death in 1573.

5. On the Smalcaldic War, see Franz Lau and Ernst Bizer, *A History of the Reformation in Germany to 1555,* trans. Brian A. Hardy (London: Black, 1969), pp. 157—207; Georg Mentz, *Johann Friedrich der Grossmütige 1503—1554,* III (Jena: Fischer, 1908), 1—112; Hildegard Jung, *Kurfürst Moritz von Sachsen, Aufgabe und Hingabe* (Hagen: Eigenverlag der Verfässerin, 1966), pp. 104—167.

6. The text of the Augsburg Interim is found in *Das Augsburger Interim von 1548, Deutsch und lateinisch,* ed. Joachim Mehlahausen (Neukirchen: Neukirchner Verlag, 1970). For discussions of the Interim, see Lau-Bizer, pp. 208—219; Walther von Loewenich, "Das Interim von 1548," *Von Augustin zu Luther, Beiträge zur Kirchengeschichte* (Witten: Luther Verlag, 1959), pp. 391—406; Gustav Wolf, "Das Augsburger Interim," *Deutsche Zeitschrift für Geschichtwissenschaft* NF II (1897/1898), 45—64; Georg Beutel, *Über den Ursprung des Augsburger Interims* (Dresden: Paessler, 1888), esp. pp. 61—103, in which he traces the origin of the "Interim" to the work of the theologian of Cologne, Johann Gropper.

7. Gustav Bossert, *Das Interim in Württemberg* (Halle: Verein für Reformationsgeschichte, 1895), pp. 15—16. On the enforcement of the Interim, see Lau-Bizer, 213—215; and Christian August Salig, *Vollständige Historie der Augspurgischen Confession und derselben Apologie . . .,* I (Halle: Renger, 1730), 583-605.

8. Nikolaus von Amsdorf, Caspar Aquila, and Erasmus Alber were among the earliest and sharpest critics of the Augsburg Interim; see Kolb, *Amsdorf,* pp. 72—82.

9. Published in *Corpus Reformatorum,* eds. C. G. Bretschneider and H. E. Bindseil (Halle and Braunschweig: Schwetschke, 1834—60), VI, 924—942; henceforth abbreviated *CR.* The tract was titled *Bedenken aufs Interim des Ehrwirdigen und Hochgelarten Herrn Philip Melanthonis* (Magdeburg, 1548).

10. The text of the Leipzig Interim is printed in *CR* VII, 258—264; see also cols. 48—62, 215—221. On the Leipzig Interim, see Emil Sehling, *Die Kirchengesetzgebung unter Moritz von Sachsen 1544—1549 und von Georg von Anhalt* (Leipzig: Deichert,

292

1899), Johann Herrmann, "Augsburg—Leipzig—Passau, (Das Leipziger Interim nach Akten des Landeshauptarchivs Dresden 1547—1552)," (Dissertation, University of Leipzig, 1962), and Luther D. Peterson, "The Philippist Theologians and the Interims of 1548: Soteriological, Ecclesiastical, and Liturgical Compromises and Controversies within German Lutheranism," (Ph.D. dissertation, University of Wisconsin-Madison, 1974). On specific aspects of the Leipzig Interim, see Albert Chalybaeus, *Die Durchführung des Leipziger Interims* (Chemnitz: Oehme, 1905); Robert Stupperich, "Melanchthons Gedanken zur Kirchenpolitik des Herzogs Moritz von Sachsen (nach bisher unveröffentlichen Papieren aus den Jahren 1547/63)," *Reformatio und Confessio, Festschrift für D. Wilhelm Maurer zum 65. Geburtstag am 7. Mai 1965*, ed. F. W. Kantzenbach and Gerhard Mueller (Berlin, Hamburg: Lutherisches Verlagshaus, 1965), pp. 84—92; Jung, pp. 185—220.

11. See Sehling's study and Franz Lau, "Georg III. von Anhalt (1507—1553), erster evangelischer 'Bischof' von Merseburg, Seine Theologie und seine Bedeutung für die Geschichte der Reformation in Deutschland," *Wissenschaftliche Zeitschrift der Karl-Marx-Universität Leipzig, Gesellschaftsund sprachwissenschaftliche Reihe* 3 (1953/54), 139—152.

12. On Pfeffinger's life, see Friedrich Seifert, "Johann Pfeffinger, der erste lutherische Pastor zu St. Nicolai und Superintendent in Leipzig," *Beiträge zur Sächsischen Kirchengeschichte* IV (1888), 33—162.

13. A bibliography of secondary literature of Flacius is provided by Arthur Carl Piepkorn, "Matthias Flacius Illyricus: A Biobibliographical Sketch Related to the FRR's Extensive Holdings," *Bulletin of the Library of the Foundation for Reformation Research* IV (1969), 37—38, 46—47. Mijo Mirkovic, *Matija Vlacic Ilirik* (Zagreb, 1960), has not really replaced Wilhelm Preger, *Matthias Flacius Illyricus und seine Zeit* (2 vols., Erlangen: Blaesing, 1859—61), since the former work is written in Croatian, though it does provide a German summary. In English, see Henry Reimann, "Matthias Flacius Illyricus," *Concordia Theological Monthly* XXXV (1964), 69—93. On Flacius' involvement in the Interims controversies, see Hans Christoph von Hase, *Die Gestalt der Kirche Luthers, Der Casus Confessionis im Kampf des Matthias Flacius gegen das Interim von 1548* (Göttingen: Vandenhoeck & Ruprecht, 1940).

14. For lists of these titles, see F. Hülsse, "Beiträge zur Geschichte der Buchdruckerkunst in Magdeburg," *Bibliographiae Reconditae* I (Amsterdam: Schippers, n.d.), pp. 618—738 (reprinted from *Geschichtsblätter für Stadt und Land Magdeburg* XV, XVI, XVII [1880—82]). On the party strife within Late Reformation Saxon Lutheranism see Robert Kolb, "Dynamics of Party Conflict in the Saxon Late Reformation, Gnesio-Lutherans vs. Philippists," *The Journal of Modern History*, XLIX, 3 (Sept. 1977), D1289—1305; and "Parties, Princes, Pastors, and Peace: The Formulation of Concord, 1577," *Academy, Lutherans in Profession*, XXXIV (1977), 2—13.

15. Deren zu Magdeburgk so widder die Adiaphora geschrieben haben vorigne schreibens beschlus auff der Adiaphoristen beschüldigung vnnd lesterung die zeit jhrer belagerung vnd itzt zum teil neulich vnter diesen friedshandlungen wider sie ausgangen (1551), 1f. (Aiv)r.

16. *CR* VIII, 841.

17. *Auff des Ehrenwirdigen Herren Niclas von Ambsdorff schrifft so jtzundt neulich*

293

Mense Nouembri Anno 1551 wider Georgen Maior öffentlich im Druck ausgegangen. Antwort Georg: Maior (Wittenberg, 1552), lvs. Cv-Cijv.

18. e.g., in *Ein Sermon von S. Pauli vnd aller Gottfürchtigen menschen bekerung zu Gott* (1553).

19. On the unfolding of the Majoristic controversy, see Preger, I, 354—380; Peterson, [see note 10]; and Robert Kolb, "Georg Major as Controversialist: Polemics in the Late Reformation," *Church History,* XLV, 4 (Dec. 1976), 455—468.

   On Menius, see Preger, I, 380—417; Peterson; Kolb, "Amsdorf, Knight of God," pp. 278—311; and Alvin H. Horst, "The Theology of Justus Menius," (Th.D. dissertation, Concordia Seminary, St. Louis, 1973).

   On Melanchthon's disavowal of Major's proposition, see *CR* VIII, 411—412; IX, 405—408, 474—475.

   On Major's withdrawal (but not repudiation) of his proposition, see his *Bekentnis . . von dem Artickel der Iustification . . .* (Wittenberg, 1558), lf. Biijr.

20. Amsdorf advanced his proposition first in the preface of his edition of Luther's *Das achzehend vnd neunzehend Capitel vnd ein Stuck aus dem zwentzigsten S. Johannis von dem Leiden Sterben vnd Aufferstehung vnsers Herrn Jhesu Christi* (Jena, 1557). He defended his proposition in *Das die Propositio (Gute werck sind zur Seligkeit schedlich) ein rechte ware Christliche Propositio sey durch die heligen Paulum vnd Lutherum gelert vnd geprediget* (1559).

21. On Melanchthon's view of the role of the human will in conversion, see the second edition of his *Loci communes, CR* XXI, 375—376; cf. the third edition, cols. 656—658; see also Hartmut O. Günther, "Die Entwicklung der Willenslehre Melanchthons in der Auseinandersetzung mit Luther und Erasmus," (Dissertation, University of Erlangen, 1963).

22. The text of Pfeffinger's 1555 disputation on the freedom of the will is reprinted in his *Demonstratio Manifesti Mendacii, Sychophanticus germanice editus titulo ad Amsdorff, Necessaria propter Veritatis assertionem & auersionem Scandali . . .* (Wittenberg, 1558), see esp. lvs. Br-Dr. Pfeffinger was careful to avoid stating precisely the role of man's natural powers in conversion, but the implication, picked up readily by his opponents, was present that these natural powers to enable man to assent, etc.

23. Amsdorf's *Offentliche Bekentnis der reinen lere des Euangelij Vnd Confutatio der jtzigen Schwermer* (Jena, 1558), lvs. (Div)r-Ev; Flacius' and Stolz's *Refutatio propositionum Pfeffingeri de Libero arbitrio* (1558). Pfeffinger replied with his *Nochmals gründlicher, klarer warhafftiger Bericht vnd Bekentnis der bittern lautern Warheit reiner Lere . . . Vnd vnuermeidliche notwendige Verantwortunge Johannis Pfeffingers Doctoris Wider den Lügengeist vnd Lesterschrifften newlich in Druck vnter dem Namen Matthiae Flacij Illyricii ausgegangen* (1559). On the dispute between Pfeffinger and Amsdorm, see Kolb, *Amsdorf,* pp. 188-201.

24. On the composition of *Illvstrissimi Principis Ac Domini, Domini Iohannis Friderici Secvndi . . . Solida & ex Verbo Dei sumpta Confutatio & condemnatio praecipuarum Corruptelarum, Sectarum, & errorum . . .* (Jena, 1559), see the biography of one of the members of the Jena theological faculty, Julius Hartmann, *Erhard Schnepf, der Reformator in Schwaben, Nassau, Hessen und Thüringen* (Tübingen: Osiander, 1870), pp. 117—122, and August Beck, *Johann Friedrich der Mittlere, Herzog zu Sachsen* (Weimar: Böhlau, 1855), I, 309.

25. Flacius' anthropology is presented in his report of the Weimar Disputation,

294

Disputatio de originali peccato et libero arbitrio (1563), e.g. his views on the concept of the image of Satan in fallen man, pp. 1, 43—63, 109—115, 286—287. His position is analyzed by Hans Kropatscheck, "Das Problem theologischer Anthropologie auf dem Weimarer Gespräch von 1560 zwischen Matthias Flacius Illyricus und Viktorin Strigel," (University of Göttingen, 1943). Lauri Haikola treats Flacius' position in *Gesetz und Evangelium bei Matthias Flacius Illyricus* (Lund: Gleerup, 1952), esp. pp. 48—192. On Strigel's anthropology, see Albert Pommerien, *Viktorin Strigels Lehre von dem Peccatum Originis* (Hannover: Stephanusstift, 1917).

26. See Flacius' "De peccato originali, aut veteris Adami appellationibus & essentia," in *Altera Pars, Clavis Scripturae, seu de Sermone Sacrarum literarum, plurimas generales Regulas continens* (Basel: Quecum, 1567), pp. 479—498. On his dispute with other Gnesio-Lutherans and with Andreä, see Preger, II, 228—412. Andreä had also played a role in the attempt to establish Strigel's "Declaration" of his understanding of the free will and its role in conversion as a binding statement on the clergy of ducal Saxony, see Conrad Schüsselburg, *Haereticorum Catalogus* (Frankfurt am Main: Saurius, 1597—99), V, 88—91; see also pp. 452—459, 462—465, and Salig, III, 882—886, Beck, I, 381—382.

27. On the Eisenach synod and particularly the debate between Amsdorf and Flacius which followed it, see Kolb, *Amsdorf*, pp. 145—155. Schlüsselburg supplies most of the extant documents from the dispute between Mörlin and Poach, IV, 65—86, 213—345. Flacius and Wigand presented their position in theses published in *de voce & re Fidei, quod que sola iustificemur, contra Pharasaicum hypocritarum fermentum, Liber* (1563 edition), pp. 208—218. Johann Seehawer deals with this controversy in *Zur Lehre vom Brauch des Gesetzes und zur Geschichte des späteren Antinomismus* (Rostock: Boldt, 1887), pp. 18—58.

28. On this controversy see Christian Wilhelm Spiecker, *Lebensgeschichte des Andreas Musculus, General-Superintendent der Mark Brandenburg . . .* (1858; Nieuwkoop: De Graff, 1964), esp. pp. 45—114.

29. Seehawer deals with this controversy, pp. 59—91. Flacius and Strigel touched on the definition of the gospel in the Weimar Disputation, and Johann Wigand took issue with earlier expressions of the Philippist position in his *De Antinomia veteri et nova, Collatio et Commonefactio* (Jena, 1571). This provoked Christoph Pezel to reply in *Apologia verae doctrinae de definitone evangelii . . .* (Wittenberg, 1571).

30. On the influences on Osiander's theology, see Gottfried Seebass, *Das reformatorische Werk des Andreas Osiander* (Nuremberg: Verein für Bayerische Kirchengeschichte, 1967), pp. 71—72, 80—82, and Emanuel Hirsch, *Die Theologie des Andreas Osiander und ihre geschichtlichen Voraussetzungen* (Göttingen: Vandenhoeck & Ruprecht, 1919), pp. 5—9, 27—40, 165—170 (though Hirsch must now be read in the light of recent studies listed in subsequent notes).

31. *An Filius Dei Fuerit Incarnandus, si peccatum non introiuisset in mundum. Item. De Imagine Dei Quid Sit* (Königsberg: Lufft, 1550).

32. Among the most important statements of Osiander's position on justification are his *Disputatio de Justificatione, praesidente D. Andrea Osiandro Theologiae primario Professore* (Königsberg: Lufft, 1550; 2. and 3. editions, 1550 and 1551), *Von dem Einigen Mitler Jhesu Christo vnd Rechtfertigung des Glaubens, Bekantnus* (Königsberg: Lufft, 1551; other editions and a Latin translation followed); and *Widerlegung: der vngegrundten vndienstlichen Antwort Philippi Melanthonis . . . Wider mein Bekantnus . . .* (Königsberg: Weinreich, 1552). See Martin Stupperich,

Osiander in Preussen, 1549—1552 (Berlin: de Gruyter, 1973), and Theodor Mahlmann, *Das neue Dogma der lutherischen Christologie* (Gütersloh: Mohn, 1969), pp. 93—124, for details on Osiander's position.

33. Stupperich, pp. 166—171.

34. Reactions to the theology of Osiander are discussed in Stupperich, pp. 137—302, and in Jörg Rainer Fligge, "Herzog Albrecht von Preussen und der Osiandrismus, 1522—1568," (Dissertation, University of Bonn, 1972), pp. 117—153.

35. The course of Osiandrism after Osiander's death is discussed by Fligge, pp. 183—586.

36. *Farrago confusanearum et inter se dissidentium Opinionum de Coena Domini ex Sacramentariorum libris congesta* (1552); *Recta Fides de Coena Domini* (1553). On the debate between Calvin and Westphal, see Ernst Bizer, *Studien zur Geschichte des Abendmahlsstreits im 16. Jahrhundert* (Gütersloh: Bertelsmann, 1940), pp. 275—278, and Francois Wendel, *Calvin,* trans. Philip Mairet (New York: Harper & Row, 1963), pp. 102—104, 342—351; Joseph N. Tylenda, "The Calvin-Westphal Exchange: The Genesis of Calvin's Treatise Against Westphal," *Calvin Theological Journal,* IX (1974), 182—209.

37. Timann's work, *Farrago sententiarum consentientium in Catholica doctrina de Coena Domini* (Frankfurt am Main: Braubach, 1555), was also translated into German. On Hardenburg, see Wilhelm H. Neuser, "Hardenberg und Melanchthon. Der Hardenbergische Streit (1534—1560)," *Jahrbuch der Gesellschaft für niedersächsische Kirchengeschichte* 65 (1967), 142—186; Hanns Engelhardt, "Das Irrlehreverfahren des niedersächsischen Reichskreises gegen Albert Hardenberg 1560/61, *ibid.* 61 (1963), 32—62; and Jürgen Moltmann, *Christoph Pezel (1539—1604) und der Calvinismus in Bremen* (Bremen: Einkehr, 1958), pp. 16—22. On the Lutheran theologians of Bremen, particularly Johann Bötker, see Mahlmann, pp. 44—61.

38. *Repetitio sanae doctrinae de vera praesentia corporis et sanguinis in coena, additus est tractatus complectens doctrinam de communicatione idiomatum* (1561); see Mahlmann, pp. 205—238.

39. Melanchthon's memorandum is dated Nov. 1, 1559; *CR* IX, 960-966. On Hesshus' role in the Heidelberg dispute, see Peter F. Barton, *Um Luthers Erbe, Studien und Texte zur Spätreformation* (Witten: Luther Verlag, 1972), pp. 158—225, and Mahlmann, pp. 78—82.

40. On Brenz's Christology, see Mahlmann, pp. 125—204, and Otto Fricke, *Die Christologie des Johannes Brenz im Zusammenhang mit der Lehre vom Abendmahl und der Rechtfertigung* (Munich: Kaiser, 1927). On the Stuttgart synod and Andreä's role in it, see Rosemarie Müller-Streisand, "Theologie und Kirchenpolitik bei Jakob Andreä bis zum Jahr 1568," *Blätter fur württembergische Kirchengeschichte* 60/61 (1960/61), 325—333; Melanchthon's comment on Colossians, to which Hagen appealed; is discussed in Erdmann K. Sturm, *Der junge Zacharias Ursin* (Neukirchen: Neukirchener Verlag, 1972), pp. 73—82.

41. Each side issued its own reports on the Colloquy at Maulbronn. From the Württembergers came *Wahrhafftiger und gründtlicher Bericht von dem Gespräch zwischen des Churfürsten Pfaltzgrafen und des Hertzogen zu Würthemberg Theologen von des Herrn Nachtmahl zu Maulbronn gehalten* (Frankfurt am Main, 1564; also in Latin). The Palatine account appeared the next year with a critique of

296

the Württemberg account, *Protocoll, Das ist, Acta oder Handlungen des Gesprechs, . . . von der Ubiquitet oder Allenthalbenheit des Leibs Christi und von dem buchstäbischen verstand der wort Christi, Das ist mein Leib* . . . (Heidelberg, 1565). See Bizer, pp. 335—352, and Müller-Streisand, pp. 371—378.

42. *De duabas naturis in Christo, de hypostatica earum unione, de communicatione idiomatum et de aliis quaestionibus inde dependentibus* . . . (Jena: Richzenhan, 1570). The second edition of this work, published in 1578, has been translated into English, *The Two Natures in Christ,* trans. J. A. O. Preus (St. Louis: Concordia, 1971).

43. See Moltmann, pp. 60—75, on the crpyto-Calvinist movement in electoral Saxony. The most thorough study of the movement, based on the state archives records in Dresden, is that of Robert Calinich, *Kampf und Untergang des Melanchthonismus in Kursachsen in den Jahren 1570 bis 1574 und die Schicksale seiner vornehmsten Häupter* (Leipzig: Brockhaus, 1866).

44. Selnecker's *Exegema collationis . . . cum theologis Wittenbergensibus 28. Julii Anno 1570 Wittebergae institutae* (Wolfenbüttel, 1570), and Andreä's *Gründlicher, warhafftiger und bestendiger Bericht: Von christlicher Einigkeit der Theologen und Predicanten* (Wolfenbüttel, 1570), esp. lvs. Liiijv—Oiijr, ascribe a position to the Wittenbergers which they did not want to claim; see Calinich, pp. 31—35. On the development of Selnecker's understanding of the Lord's Supper, see Mahlmann, pp. 239—244.

45. *Catechesis, continens explicationem simplicem et brevem Decalogi, Symboli Apostolici, Orationis Dominicae, Doctrinae de poenitentia et sacramentis, contexta ex Corpore Doctrinae Christianae . . . ecclesiae regionum Saxonicarum et Misnicarum* . . . (Wittenberg, 1571). The Jena critique is contained in *Warnung vor dem unreinen und sakramentirischen Katechismus etlicher zu Wittenberg* (Jena, 1571).

46. *Von der Person und Menschwerdung unseres Herrn Jesu Christi der wahren christlichen Kirchen Grundfest wider die newen Marcioniten . . . Eutychianer und Monotheleten unter dem Flacianischen Haufen* (Wittenberg, 1572).

47. The document was popularly called the "Consensus Dresdensis," and it was published under the title *Kurze christliche und einfältige Wiederholung des Bekenntnis der Kirchen Gottes in des Churfürsten zu Sachsen Landen* . . . (Dresden, 1571). The consensus was criticized in the *Einhellige Bekenntnis vieler hochgelahrten Theologen und fürnehmer Kirchen von dem 1. Neuen Catechismo der neuen Wittenberger und von ihrer 2. Neuen Grundfeste, auch von ihrem darauf beschlossenen 3. Neuen Bekenntnis* (Jena, 1572).

48. See Calinich, pp. 87—93, and Moltmann, p. .64.

49. *Exegesis perspicua et ferme intergra de Sacra Coena, Scripta ut privatim conscientias piorum erudiat* . . . (Leipzig, 1574). On events surrounding the discovery of its origin, see Calinich, pp. 100—124.

50. On the incident involving the letter, see August Kluckhohn, "Der Sturz der Kryptocalvinisten in Sachsen 1574," *Historische Zeitschrift* 18 (1867), esp. pp. 102—107, and Calinich, pp. 115—124. On the fate and future of the leaders of this party, see Calinich, pp. 125—172, and Moltmann (on Pezel), pp. 76—166.

51. On the course of the dispute, see Walther Sohm, *Die Schule Johann Sturms und die Kirche Strassburgs in ihrem gegenseitigen Verhältnis 1530—1581, Ein Beitrag zur*

Geschichte deutscher Renaissance (Munich/Berlin: Oldenbourg, 1912), pp. 195—236; on Marbach's earlier career in the city, see pp. 161—194. On the theological aspects of the controversy, see Jürgen Moltmann, *Prädestination und Perseveranz, Geschichte und Bedeutung der reformierten Lehre "de perseverantia sanctorum"* (Neukirchen: Neurkirchener Verlag, 1961), esp. pp. 72—109; James M. Kittelson, "Marbach vs. Zanchi, The Resolution of Controversy in Late Reformation Strasbourg," *The Sixteenth Century* Journal, VIII, 3 (Oct. 1977), 31—44.

52 David G. Truemper, "The Descensus ad Inferos from Luther to the Formula of Concord," (S.T.D. dissertation, Lutheran School of Theology at Chicago, 1974), outlines the views of a number of Evangelical theologians, pp. 152—217, discusses the controversies in Pomerania, centering on Jacob Thiele, in 1554, pp. 273—276, in southern Germany between Johann Matsperger and Johann Parsimonius in 1565, pp. 277—291, and the Hamburg controversy, pp. 218—271, and presents the positions of Melanchthon, pp. 202—211, and Flacius, pp. 188—194, in some detail. He also discusses Luther's "Torgau" sermon, pp. 292—312. Truemper's study supplements and corrects the study by Erich Vogelsang, "Weltbild und Kreuzestheologie in den Höllenfahrtsstreitigkeiten der Reformationszeit," *Archiv für Reformationsgeschichte* 38 (1941), 90—132.

53. On Melanchthon's emphasis on the concept of pure doctrine, see Greschat, pp. 89—109.

54. See Lewis W. Spitz, "Particularism and Peace, Augsburg—1555," *Church History* 25 (1956), 110—126.

55. *Provocation oder erbieten der Adiaphorischen sachen halben, auff erkentnis vnd vrteil der Kirchen* (Magdeburg: Lotter, 1553).

56. "Linde Fürschläge, dadurch man gottselige und nothwendige friedliche Vergleichung machen könnte zwischen den Wittenbergischen und Leipzigischen Theologen in causa Adiaphoristica und den andern, so wider sie geschrieben haben," reprinted from manuscript in Preger, II, 9—10. For a fuller discussion of the events surrounding this and other Flacian attempts at unity, see Preger, II, 1—103.

57. The texts of the documents related to the Coswig colloquy are found in *CR* IX, 23—72.

58. The texts of Evangelical documents related to the colloquy at Worms are found in *CR* IX, 221—395.

59. The text of the "Recess" is found in *CR* IX, 489—507.

60. See note 24 above.

61. *Supplicatorii libelli quorundam Christi ministrorum de synodo propter controversias gravissimas congreganda, partim antea editi, partim nunc recens ad conventum Naumbergensem missi et exhibiti* (Oberursel, 1561); see Preger, II, 86—91.

62. The first of the documents that describe the colloquy and its results were published by the Jena faculty: *Bekentnis Von der Rechtfertigung fur Gott vnd Von guten Wercken* (Jena, 1569), and *Bekentnis Vom Freien Willen. So im Colloquio zu Alterburg hat sollen vorbracht werden von Fürstlichen Sechsischen Theologen* (Jena, 1570). The electoral Saxons replied by issuing their massive transcripts of the position papers read at the colloquy, *Gantze vnd vnuerfelschete Acta vnd Handlung des Colloquij . . . zu Altenburgk* (Wittenberg, 1570; also issued in Latin, Leipzig, 1570). The ducal Saxons replied with their *Bericht vom Colloquio zu Altenburgk, Auf den endlichen Bericht, etc.* (Jena, 1570), and the electoral Saxons offered their

objections to that reply in their *Warhafftiger bericht vnd kurtze Warnung der Theologen beider Vniuersitet Leipzig vnd Wittemberg, Von Den newlich zu Jhena im Druck ausgangenen Acten des Colloquij so zu Aldenburg in Meissen gehalten* (Wittenberg, 1570).

63. On Andreä's two efforts to establish Lutheran unity between 1568 and 1573, see Theodore R. Jungkuntz, *Formulators of the Formula of Concord, Four Architects of Lutheran Unity* (St. Louis: Concordia, 1977), pp. 19—45; Robert Kolb, *Andreae and the Formula of Concord, Six Sermons on the Way to Lutheran Unity* (St. Louis: Concordia, 1977). On the general development of the Formula of Concord and related historiography, see Lowell C. Green, *The Formula of Concord, Sixteenth Century Bibliography #12* (St. Louis: Center for Reformation Research, 1977).

64. *Sechs Christlicher Predig Von den Spaltungen so sich zwischen den Theologen Augspurgischer Confession von Anno 1548. biss auff diss 1573. Jar nach vnnd nach erhaben, Wie sich ein einfältiger Pfarrer vnd gemeiner Christlicher leye, so dardurch möcht vererget sein worden auss seinem Catechismo darein schicken soll* (Tübingen, 1573). The most extensive presentation of the details surrounding Andreä's efforts and those of others to create the Formula of Concord is found in Heinrich Heppe, *Geschichte des deutschen Protestantismus in den Jahren 1555 bis 1581* (Marburg: Elwert, 1852—59), esp. volumes 2—4, and his *Geschichte der lutherischen Concordienformel und Concordie* (Marburg: Elwert, 1857—59). Heppe, a Reformed theologian, indicates his disapproval of the Formula of Concord in his treatments of it.

65. The letters are printed in Johann Georg Bertram, *Das Evangelische Lüneburg* (Braunschweig: Schröder, 1719), pp. 172—177. They are dated March 22 and March 23, 1574, respectively.

66. *Drey und dreissig Predigen von den fürnembsten Spaltungen in der christlichen Religion, so sich zwischen den Bäpstischen, Lutherischen, Zwinglischen, Schwenckfeldern, und Widerteuffern halten, Gepredigt zu Esslingen* (Tübingen: Morhart, 1568).

67. *Kirchenordnung . . . Wie es mit lehr und ceremonien unsers fürstenthumbs Braunschweig . . . gehalten werden sol* (Wolfenbüttel: Horn, 1569), reprinted in Emil Sehling, ed., *Die evangelischen Kirchenordnungen des XVI. Jahrhunderts* VI, 1 (Tübingen: Mohr/Siebeck, 1955), 83—280; see esp. pp. 98—102 on this point.

68. See Andreä's letter to Chemnitz, May 1, 1574, in Bertram, p. 178.

69. His *Loci theologici quibus et loci communes P. Melanchthonis explicantur,* edited by Polycarp Leyser, appeared first in 1591. His *Examen concilii Tridentini* was published in four parts 1565—73. The first sections of this work are available in English translation, *Examination of the Council of Trent, Part I,* trans. Fred Kramer (St. Louis: Concordia, 1971).

70. See notes 38 and 42 above. A modern biographical study of Chemnitz is sorely needed; Theodor Pressel's *Martin Chemnitz* (Elberfeld: Friderichs, 1862), C. G. H. Lentz's *Dr. Martin Kemnitz* (Gotha: Perthes, 1866), and *Hermann Hachfeld's Martin Chemnitz nach seinem Leben und Wirken* (Leipzig: Breitkopf & Härtel, 1967) are insufficient. See Jungkuntz [cf. note 63], pp. 46—68.

71. A modern biography of Chytraeus is also needed to replace Theodor Pressel's *David*

Chytraeus (Elberfeld: Friderichs, 1862), and Otto Krabbe, *David Chytraeus* (Rostock: Stiller, 1870). See Jungkuntz [cf. note 63], pp. 69—88.

72. No adequate biography of Selnecker exists; on his views on the Lord's Supper, see Mahlmann, pp. 239—244. See Jungkuntz [cf. note 63], pp. 89—114.

73. Documents relating to the Lichtenberg meeting are found in Leonhard Hutter, *Concordia Concors, De origine et progressu Formulae Concordiae Ecclesiarum Confessionis Augustanae* (Wittenberg: Berger, 1614), lvs. 75—80r.

74. See pp. 72—74 above. Spiecker remains the best biographical study of Musculus.

75. Documents relating to the Torgau meeting are found in Hutter, lvs. 84—91r. See Ernst Koch, "Striving for the Union of Lutheran Churches, The Church-Historical Background of the Work Done on the Formula of Concord at Magdeburg," *The Formula of Concord, Quadricentennial Essays, The Sixteenth Century Journal*, VIII, 4 (Dec. 1977), 105—121.

76. Critiques of the Torgau Book from Hesse, Zweibrücken, Holstein, and Braunschweig are found in Hutter, lvs. 98v—114r. The reaction to the Formula of Concord is discussed in several essays in *Discord, Dialogue, and Concord, Studies in the Lutheran Reformation's Formula of Concord*, eds. Lewis W. Spitz and Wenzel Lohff (Philadelphia: Fortress, 1977), pp. 119—207.

77. Hutter offers materials relating to the Bergen Book, lvs.

78. E.g., Christoph Irenaeus' *Mercklich Partickel: Der langst gesuchten Formel Concordien, eynigkeit vnd vergleichung D. Jacobs Andreae in Religions sachen* (1580) attacked Andreä and the Formula's doctrine of original sin.

79. See Hutter, lvs. 101—111r.

80. Zacharias Ursinus helped prepare the *De libro Concordiae . . . . Admonitio Christiana* (Neudstadt an der Haardt: Harnisch, 1582), the official reply from the government of Johann Kasimir of the Palatinate. Chemnitz, Selnecker, and Kirchner replied in their *Apologia, Oder Verantwortung dess Christlichen Concordienbuchs.* (Heidelberg: Spies 1583).

Rule and Norm of Doctrine

1. John Gerhard, *Loci Theologici*, I, 9, in *The Doctrinal Theology of the Evangelical Lutheran Church*, translated by C. A. Hay and H. E. Jacobs, 3d ed., rev. (© 1899, reprinted Minneapolis, Minn., 1961), p. 55.
2. *Examen theologicum acroamaticum*, translated in *The Doctrinal Theology of the Evangelical Lutheran Church* by Hay and Jacobs, p. 51.
3. Theodore G. Tappert, ed., *The Book of Concord* Philadelphia, Pa.: Muhlenberg Press [now Fortress Press], 1959), p. 12.
4. Tappert, p. 12.
5. This and the following references in this chapter are to the Tappert edition.
6. Tappert, p. 6: "divine truth."
7. Cf. Tappert, p. 14, lines 4—5.
8. Tappert, p. 7: "a pure declaration of the truth."
9. Tappert, p. 10.
10. Tappert, p. 8.
11. Cf. Tappert, p. 507, lines 19—20.

Article I

1. A useful source for the understanding of Melanchthon's thinking and action is H. Engelland, *Melanchthon, Glauben and Handeln* (München: C. Kaiser, 1931). Evaluations of Melanchthon's influence on Lutheran theology and practice are offered by Richard R. Caemmerer's essay, "The Melanchthonian Blight," *Concordia Theological Monthly*, 18 (1947), 321-338; Jaroslav Pelikan's chapter, "Melanchthon and the Confessional Generation" in his book *From Luther to Kierkegaard* (St. Louis: Concordia Publishing House, 1950), pp. 24—48; Clyde L. Manschreck, "The Role of Melanchthon in the Adiaphora controversy," *Archiv für Reformationsgeschichte*, 48 (1957): 165—181; H. C. von Hase, "Occasions for Confession, 1548—1948," *The Lutheran World Review* 1:2 (1948): 27—37. The evaluations of Melanchthon by Franz Hildebrandt, *Melanchthon: Alien or Ally* (Cambridge: Cambridge University Press, 1946) may be pertinent for the considerations of some contemporary issues. See also Julius Gross, "Seit der Reformation." *Geschichte des Erbsündendogmas*, vol. 4 (München/Basel: Ernst Reinhardt Verlag, 1972).

2. *Sancti Augustini Enchiridion de fide, spe et caritate*, VII 23 ff.; also *De correptione et gratia*, VI 9: Civitas   XIII, XIV.

3. Theodore G. Tappert, ed., *The Book of Concord* (Philadelphia, Pa.: Muhlenberg Press [now Fortress Press], 1959), pp. 302—303.

4. Luther repeated this theological perspective in his thesis written for a theological exercise: *Disputatio de homine*, 1536; WA 39 I, 175—177.

5. Am. ed., I, 141—236.

6. *Ibid.*, I, 155, par. 1—3.

7. See G. Jacob, *Der Gewissensbegriff in der Theologie Luthers* (Tübingen: Mohr, 1939).

8. J. W. Preger, *Matthias Flacius Illyricus und seine Zeit*, I (Erlangen: Bläsing, 1859—61).

Article II

1. *The Bondage of the Will*. Trans. by J. I. Packer and O. R. Johnston (Westwood, N.J.: Revell, 1957), p. 78. Cited hereafter as *BOW*.

2. *BOW*, p. 261; WA 18, p. 749.

3. cf. *ibid.*, p. 107.

4. *BOW*, p. 80—81.

5. *Ibid.*, p. 105.

6. *Luther's Works*, Am. ed., 31, ed. H. J. Grimm (Philadelphia, Pa.: Fortress Press, 1957), p. 49.

7. *Ibid.*, p. 48.

8. *BOW*, p. 137.

9. *BOW*, p. 217.

10. *Ibid.*, p. 83—84, 215.

11. *BOW*, p. 206.

12. *BOW*, p. 171.

13. *BOW,* p. 208.

14. cf. *BOW,* p. 213.

15. C.F.W. Walther, *The Proper Distinction Between Law and Gospel.* (St. Louis, Mo.: Concordia, 1929), p. 8.

16. Harry J. McSorley, *Luther: Right or Wrong?* (Minneapolis, Minn.: Augsburg, and New York, N.Y.: Paulist/Newman Press), p. 21.

17. *BOW,* p. 105.

18. *BOW,* p. 157.

19. *Ibid.,* p. 298.

20. *Op. cit.,* p. 262.

21. *Luther's Works,* Am. ed., 26, ed. J. Pelikan (St. Louis, Mo.: Concordia, 1963), p. 9.

Article III

1. *Rebuttal,* 0 3 r.

2. *Concerning the One Mediator, A 4 v.*

3. *Disputation,* Theses 73 and 74.

4. *Ibid.,* Thesis 3.

5. *Rebuttal,* L 2 r; cf. *Concerning the One Mediator,* B 1 v.

6. *Rebuttal,* M 1 r and J 3 v.

7. *Concerning the One Mediator,* J 1 v.

8. *Ibid.,* J 2 v.

9. *Ibid.,* X 4 v.

10. *Concerning the One Mediator,* H 2.

11. *Rebuttal,* G 3.

12. The material of this paragraph is taken from Reinhold Seeberg, *Lehrbuch der Dogmengeschichte,* IV, 2, 499—500.

13. *Exegesis of John 16,* B 3 a.

14. The material here was in large part suggested by F. H. R. v. Frank, *Die Theologie der Concordienformel,* II 31—43.

15. Frank, *op. cit.,* pp. 65—66.

16. *Ibid.,* p. 55.

Article V

1. Summarized from G. Thomasius, *Dogmengeschichte,* 427—428. Thomasius uses both the Theses of 1537 and the *Kurze Summarien der Evangelien* of the same year.

2. See F. H. R. v. Frank, *Theologie der Concordienformel* II, 267. The source is a sermon of Agricola's on Luke 7:37-39.

3. Frank, 277 and 327.

4. This material comes from Frank, 289—290 and 331—332.

5. But one wonders, first, whether the writers have not unnecessarily complicated the conversion process, and, secondly, whether it is really the case that the Law cannot be understood properly without a knowledge of the Gospel. One could grant quite readily that the preaching of the Law is sharpened considerably by a consideration of the action of God in Christ which alone could undo the curse of sin and satisfy the demands of the Law (see the quotation from Luther above, section 12). But, it is another thing again to say that this sharpening is necessary before true penitence is possible. The Scripture passages the Formula quotes in support of its position are really no help. Christ in the Sermon on the Mount (Matt. 5:21 ff.) is not engaged in an evangelical preaching of the Law; He is simply expounding the deepest meaning of the Law itself. The reference to 2 Cor. 3:13-15 and the veil of Moses as well as the veil that lies over the minds of those who hear Moses read in the synagogue does not really concern the specific concern of our article, Law and Gospel, but the proper understanding of the Old Testament. The Old Testament, indeed, cannot be understood from its own presuppositions without the light thrown on it from the fulfillment in Jesus Christ. The reference to Rom. 7:6, 14 is even less valid than the passages already mentioned.

Article VI

1. *Luther's Works,* American ed., eds. J. Pelikan (Companion Vol. and 1—30) and H. T. Lehman (31—55) (St. Louis, Mo.: Concordia, and Philadelphia, Pa.: Fortress Press, 1955—), 31, 45—46. Cited hereafter as *LW.*
2. *LW* 31, 47.
3. *LW* 26, 4 and 6.
4. *LW* 26, 132.
5. *LW* 26, 4.
6. *LW* 26, 11—12.
7. *LW* 27, 71-72.
8. *LW* 27, 82.
9. *Concordia Triglotta,* p. 669—670.
10. *LW* 35, 370—371.
11. *LW* 41, 114.
12. *LW* 41, 114.
13. *LW* 41, 113—115.
14. *LW* 47, 116.
15. *LW* 47, 108, 109, 107.
16. *LW* 47, 113.
17. *Ibid.*
18. *LW* 47, 110.
19. *LW* 47, 111.
20. *LW* 47, 114, 110.
21. *LW* 53, 278—281.
22. *LW* 47, 109.

23. *Ibid.*

24. W. Elert, *Law and Gospel* (Philadelphia, Pa.: Fortress Press, 1967), p. 38—39.

25. Elert, *op cit.,* p. 32.

26. *LW* 47, 110.

27. P. Althaus, *The Divine Command* (Philadelphia, Pa.: Fortress Press, 1966), p. 29.

28. Althaus, *op. cit.,* p. 38ff.

29. Althaus, *op. cit.,* p. 45.

30. Althaus, *op. cit.,* p. 46f.

31. See also Wilfried Joest, *Gesetz und Freiheit: Das Problem des Tertius usus legis bei Luther und die neutestamentliche Parainese* (Goettingen, 1961).

32. *Bondage of the Will.* Trans. by J. I. Packer and O. R. Johnston (Westwood, N.J.: Revell, 1957), p. 261.

33. *Ibid.,* p. 192.

34. *LW* 47, 118.

35. *Ibid.,* p. 119.

36. *Ibid.*

Article VII

1. In the liturgical forms for Holy Communion used by Lutheran churches in America it is generally stated that the pastor shall distribute *bread* and *wine.* This Reformed practice is also retained in the rubrics of the various orders proposed by the ILCW (Inter-Lutheran Commision on Worship). But if we consult the liturgies of the 16th-century church orders, we find that the consecrated host and chalice are always called the *body* and *blood* in the distribution or manducation. Braunschweig, 1528: "vnde nemen den licham des Heren. . ." in *Die evangelischen Kirchenordnungen des sechszehnten Jahrhunderts,* ed. Aemilius Ludwig Richter (Weimar, 1846 and Nieuwkoop, 1967) hereafter abbreviated "Richter"—Vol. I, p. 115. Margravate of Brandenburg and Nürnberg, 1533: ". . . soll [der Pfarherr] den leyb Christi raychen yedermann . . ." *Ibid.,* p. 207. Pomerania, 1535: "vnd Communicatio des lyues vnde blodes Christi ynn beyder gestalt . . ." *Ibid.,* p. 258. Electoral Brandenburg, 1540: "Nunc Communicantes accedunt et cum eis corpus porrigitur . . ." *Ibid.,* p. 327. Württemberg, 1559: "Als bald darauff geht das Volck herzu ordenlich/vnnd entpfahet an einem ort des Altars den Leib Christi/am andern ort das Blut Christi. . . . der Kirchendiener [mage] in Darreichung des Leibs vnd Bluts Christi/zu einem jetlichen vngefahrlich volgende Wort sprechen. In der Darreichung des Leibs Christi. Nimm hin vnd iss/das ist der Leib Christi/der für dich gegeben ist." *Summarischer vnd einfältiger Begriff/wie es mit der Lehre vnd Ceremonien in den Kirchen vnsers Fürstenthumbs . . . gehalten vnd volzogen werden solle,* "Württembergische Grosse Kirchenordnung 1559" (Tübingen, 1559 and 1968, Fol. lxxv and lxxvv.

2. Over against a certain carelessness today regarding distribution of the body and blood of the Lord, the disposal of the consecrated elements that remain after the communion, and the occurrence of accidents, one must contrast the diligence of

Luther, who saw the dropping of the host or spilling of the chalice as a sacrilege. See Edward F. Peters, *The Origin and Meaning of the Axiom: "Nothing Has the Character of a Sacrament Outside of the Use,"* in *Sixteenth-Century and Seventeenth-Century Lutheran Theology* (dissertation, Concordia Seminary, St. Louis, Mo., 1968), pp. 188—196. On the other hand, Melanchthon felt that a wafer that fell to the floor was only bread [*ibid.,* p. 77 f.], a judgment that many Lutherans today would prefer. Luther would certainly be horrified by a "contemporary" communion services where a loaf of bread is broken and crumbs fall to the floor, or at the careless practices involved in distributing and collecting individual glasses and cleansing them afterwards.—Luther's position is rejected, and Melanchthon's espoused, in the influential handbook by Georg Rietschel, *Lehrbuch der Liturgik,* 2 vols. (Berlin: Reuther & Reichard, 1900 and later) (§ 48). Rietschel calls Luther's position (that the Real Presence is consummated during the recitation of the *Verba*) "a decidedly Catholic interpretation," p. 434. Luther D. Reed calls the sacramental body and blood of Christ the "bread and wine" in *The Lutheran Liturgy* (Philadelphia: Muhlenberg Press, 1947 and later), pp. 351—353; he seems to combine what Luther might call a Zwinglian doctrine with a High Church Anglicanism ritual. The whole question of Luther's abolition of the canon of the mass needs to be restudied more sympathetically then in Reed (pp. 322—337), or in the grossly incompetent analysis by Gregory Dix, *The Shape of the Liturgy* (London: Dacre Press, 1945), pp. 625—639.

3. Luther's understanding of the means of grace emphasized his theology of the incarnation, in which God conveys spiritual gifts through earthy means. See Hans Grass, *Die Abendmahlslehre bei Luther und Calvin,* 2d ed. (Gütersloh: C. Bertelsmann, 1954), pp. 176 ff. Grass contrasts Calvin in an unfavorable light, seeing his understanding of the means of grace as seriously hindered by a false Neoplatonic dichotomy of the spiritual and the earthy, pp. 224 ff.

4. Some occurrences of "Eucharist" in Luther include WA 6, 231 (1520), WA 8, 441 (1521), WA 26, 41 and WA 30 I, 122 (1528), WA 39 I, 149, 169, 170, 171 (1536), and Luther's acceptance of the Wittenberg Concord of 1536, CR 3, 75; but the term is rare, especially in Luther's later years. It is found in Melanchthon in CR 1, 901 (1527), SA VI, 299 (1558), and in CR 23, 63 and 65 (1559). Its usage is justified by Brenz in the *Württembergische Große Kirchenordnung* 1559, Fol. xviii. The preachers at Bremen who opposed the Calvinist, Albert Hardenberg, used the term—see Philipp Julius Rehtmeyer, *Antiquitates Ecclesiasticae Inclytae Urbis Brunsvigae . . .* , Part III, Beylagen (Braunschweig, 1710), Document No. 4, p. 84. Even the Tetrapolitan Confession (1530) of the Reformed used this word—see *Reformed Confessions of the 16th Century,* ed. Arthur C. Cochrane (Philadelphia: Westminster, 1966), p. 75. Paul Rorem comments: "It is incorrect therefore to call the sacrament by that name which denotes only the remembrance, 'eucharist,'" in "Luther's Objection to a Eucharistic Prayer," *The Cresset,* Vol. XXXVIII, No. 5 (March 1975), p. 16.

5. The demand for frequent communion today is often accompanied by loose pastoral practices and even open communion. The attempt to legitimize this demand by insisting that communion was offered weekly by the reformers is not supported by the evidence. Perhaps there was weekly communion at places such as Wittenberg, but this does not seem to have been general practice. Proponents of weekly communion sometimes appeal to AC XXV and Apol XXV; however, there it is said

that if communion is available on Sundays and feast days, it is accompanied by strict pastoral practices, with no one admitted who has not been privately absolved or at least previously announced. The *Württembergische Große Kirchenordnung* prescribed monthly communion in the larger places, Fol. lxxij v. Since in the Middle Ages communion had been received as a rule once a year, this represented a dramatic increase. At any rate, documents and liturgical practices from the past are not to be incanted legalistically. The Confessions speak in the indicative, not the imperative, mood. See my article, "Toward an Evangelical Understanding of the Lutheran Confessions," *The Lutheran Quarterly,* Vol. IX (August 1957), especially pp. 240—246.

6. Not only did Melanchthon write three of the seven Lutheran Confessions, but he strongly influenced the writers of the rest, and even the teaching of many who later turned against him. For example, that important manifesto of the Gnesio-Lutherans, the Weimar Confutation of 1559 (of which Flacius is said to have been a principal writer), moved within a Melanchthonian framework in Part V, "Confutatio Erroris Zwinglij." Like him (CR 21, 843—853), they accepted the pitfalls of developing the Supper out of a general doctrine of the sacrament, fol. 30—31, condemned the adoration and called it *artolatreia,* fol. 19, quoted Augs. Conf. X with the *exhibere* of the *Variata* of 1540, fol. 31v, and used that Latin verb continuously (cf. fol. 20, 22, 23, 25v, 26v, and 27). Likewise they abstained from deriving the real presence out of the ubiquity of Christ, except for rejecting the antithesis of the "Zwinglians," fol. 26v—27, notwithstanding the contrary impression of Melanchthon (CR 9, 765—766). (On this point see the work of Theodor Mahlmann, referred to in footnote 11.) The Confutation also employed the rhetoric of Melanchthon in his distinction between the word and its meaning, *rheton* and *dianoia* (CR 13, 442-443), fol. 22.

7. See Gerhard Friedrich Bente, "Historical Introductions to the Lutheran Symbols," in *Concordia, or Book of Concord. The Symbols of the Ev. Lutheran Church* (St. Louis: Concordia, 1922), pp. 1—266. Bente was dependent on Franz Hermann Reinhold Frank, who was also excessively biased against Melanchthon in his great work, *Die Theologie der Concordienformel,* 4 vols. (Erlangen: Theodor Blaesing, 1858—65); the Lord's Supper is treated in Vol. III, pp. 1—164. Bente paid the price of his overhasty condemnations of Melanchthon, pp. 175—185. Supposing that reformer's doctrine of the Lord's Supper to consist in covert Calvinism, he regarded the hallmark of Luther's doctrine to be the phrase, "nothing has the character of a sacrament outside of the use," a phrase that was actually from Bucer and Melanchthon. This prompted Bente to misinterpret Beatus Saliger, who was probably a true representative of Luther, calling him an "extremist . . . who taught that in virtue of the consecration before the use (*ante usum*) bread and wine are the body and blood of Christ." The term *ante usum* here evidently meant the time between the consecration and the manducation: Bente is espousing the Melanchthonian notion that the body is in, with, and under the bread only in the distribution and consumption (if, indeed, Melanchthon limited it to that extent), and calling the position of Luther and Saliger "extreme." Bente's historical introduction has been very influential.

8. The *Consensus Tigurinus* is given in *Documents Illustrative of the Continental Reformation,* ed. B. J. Kidd (Oxford: Clarendon Press, 1911; reprint 1967), No. 319, pp. 652—656.

9. Friedrich Brunstäd insists that Melanchthon, rightly understood, did not diverge

essentially from Luther's doctrine, in *Theologie der lutherischen Bekenntnisschriften* (Gütersloh: C. Bertelsmann, 1951), p. 154. Michael Rogness takes a similar position in his monograph, *Melanchthon, Reformer Without Honor* (Minneapolis: Augsburg, 1969), pp. 129—135. Rogness notes that Melanchthon did not precisely echo "Luther's strong feeling toward the 'physical' presence" of Christ, p. 134; however, neither Luther nor his followers accepted the term "physical" as denoting the sacramental presence of Christ, a concept also rejected in SD VII 127. Nevertheless, Reformed writers to this day continue to ascribe that term to the Lutheran position. See also note 19.

10. See *The Book of Concord*, tr. and ed. T. G. Tappert (Philadelphia, Pa.: Fortress Press, 1959), p. 568, fn 9. A fuller treatment in Bente, *op. cit.*, pp. 185—190. A balanced explanation is given in George J. Fritschel, *The Formula of Concord: Its Origin and Contents* (Philadelphia: Lutheran Publication Society, 1916), pp. 175—193.

11. Theodor Mahlmann, *Das neue Dogma der lutherischen Christologie* (Gütersloh: Gerd Mohn, 1969), pp. 19—43; this book is indispensable for studying the Lutheran doctrine of the Sacrament.—Actually, this error by the editors of the Jena edition of Luther in 1558, which was to have such enormous results in the history of doctrine, had been spotted long before Mahlmann. Unfortunately, the influential Martin Chemnitz had incorporated this error in his *Examen Decretorum Concilii Tridentini*, ed. Eduard Preuss (Berlin: Gustav Schlawitz, 1861), p. 300, in his *Fundamenta sanae doctrinae, de vera et substantiali praesenti, exhibitione, et sumptione corporis & sanguinis Domini in coenae* (Frankfurt and Wittenberg: Tobias Maevius, 1653), p. 68, and in his *De duabus naturis in Christo* (*ibid.*), p. 193. However, so early as 1614, Hutter had revealed the mistake. See Leonhard Hutter, *Concordia concors . . .* (Wittenberg: Clement Berger, 1614), fol. 8 v—9. But Hutter's discovery was overlooked until Karl Gottlieb Bretschneider, in editing the *Corpus Reformatorum*, rightly identified it as stemming from Melanchthon and printed it as such, CR 9, 1086—88. In 1927, Otto Albrecht also exposed this long-standing error in literary criticism, WA 48, pp. 236—237, with a corrected reprint of the Latin original and also the German translation of the Jena edition.

12. On Melanchthon's position, see Mahlmann, pp. 75—77. The editors of the critical Göttingen edition claim Melanchthon as the source of the statement condemned in SD VII 4, but the citations of CR 9, 460, CR 21, 363 f., and the secondary literature do not establish that Melanchthon was the "forerunner" of this viewpoint. In his defense, we refer to his words of 1559: "Christ is present not merely in efficacy but also in substance" (CR 21, 863).

13. In the Sixth Sermon of Andreä, we come upon this startling denunciation of the doctrine of the communication of the idioms: "At this point it is impossible but that anyone who rightly understands the matter will at once say: 'Phooey to you, Devil!' (*pfui dich Teuffel*)" (Heppe III/B, p. 68). He charges that the Crypto-Calvinists have substituted this concept for Zwingli's "alloeosis," that is, that one thing is said, but another meant; "for them it means nothing else than an exchange of the names, according to which one nature [the divine] is taken for the other [the human]." (Heppe III/B, p. 67).

14. Ironically, in countering the rumor that Luther changed his position, the scholar who prepared the Latin version (likely Lucas Osiander of Tübingen) tampered with the original words of Luther (WA 26, 499 f.), adding a spurious statement that all

doctrines must be tested by the Sacred Scriptures, which were like the Lydian Stone as a norm (30).

15. The Lutherans reported back to their church-bodies: "As a result of our studies and discussions we see no insuperable obstacles to pulpit and altar fellowship and, therefore, we recommend to our parent bodies that they encourage their constitutent churches to enter into discussions looking forward to intercommunion and the fuller recognition of one another's ministries" (*Marburg Revisited: A Reexamination of Lutheran and Reformed Traditions,* ed. Paul C. Empie and James I. McCord [Minneapolis: Augsburg, 1966], p. 191). When one examines the essays on which this conclusion was based, however, one can only say that they did not adequately present Lutheranism. The principal Lutheran contribution, Theodore G. Tappert's essay, pp. 55—69, contains a number of inaccurate statements and oblique judgments; however this is not the place for a detailed criticism. Such statements as the Leuenberg Agreement and the 1976 ALC-LCA "Statement on Communion Practices" are weak in conviction and rife in ambiguity. See also the exposure of the shallow statement of the Oberlin Conference, which stated: "Rejecting any one-sided preoccupation with the elements in isolation, we agree that in the entire eucharistic action the whole Christ is personally present . . . ," in Hermann Sasse, *This Is My Body: Luther's Contention for the Real Presence in the Sacrament of the Altar* (Minneapolis: Augsburg, 1959), pp. viii—ix.

16. Joseph McLelland criticizes the reformers for discussing the question of "how" Christ is present (*Marburg Revisited,* p.42, 49), and then proceeds to belittle the Lutherans for holding the *manducatio impiorum* (pp. 51, 53). Torrance's proposal does not solve the problems raised (p. 53), and McLelland's whole essay suffers from his lack of clarity in theology and accuracy in details of history. Compare his citing the false report that Luther praised Calvin's doctrine (p. 44).

17. This element of comfort is brought out by Friedrich Brunstäd, *Theologie der lutherischen Bekenntnisschriften* (Gütersloh: Bertelsmann, 1951), pp. 165—170. Brunstäd, who was also a philosopher, gave a biting criticism of the Neoplatonism of Zwingli and Calvin, and noted of Calvin's position: "With this one has returned to Zwingli; the elevation of faith into heaven is, like by Zwingli, a movement of man toward God, and not the coming of Christ to us. This is the decisive difference" from the Lutheran position (p. 166). See also the comments on the dangers of making faith constitutive of the Sacrament in Ernst Bizer, *Studien zur Geschichte des Abendmahlsstreits im 16. Jahrhundert* (Gütersloh: Bertelsmann, 1940), pp. 328—331.

18. Sasse, *op. cit.,* p. 126; p. 178.

19. See Williston Walker, *John Calvin: The Organiser of Reformed Protestantism, 1509-1564* (New York: Schocken Books, 1969 reprint of 1906 edition), pp. 184, 396, 423. Walker, of course, is missing the mark, since the word "physical presence" stems from Calvin, not Luther. The statement is made that "Luther understood the words 'This is my body' to mean that Christ is physically present in the sacrament," in Roland H. Bainton, *Women of the Reformation in Germany and Italy* (Minneapolis: Augsburg, 1971), p. 64. Also Clyde L. Manschreck, in his book, *Melanchthon: The Quiet Reformer* (Nashville: Abingdon, 1958), pp. 228—248, treats the difference between Melanchthon and Luther as of that between a spiritual and a physical view.

20. Dix (work cited in note 2), pp. 48 ff. For a reply to these notions among Lutherans,

308

see especially Oliver K. Olson, "Luther's 'Catholic' Minimum" *Reponse*, XI (1970), 17—31; "Contemporary Trends in Liturgy Viewed from the Perspective of Classical Lutheran Theology," *The Lutheran Quarterly*, Vol. XXVI (1974), 110—157.

21. Peters (work cited in note 2).

22. *Ibid.*, pp. 335—357. Compare Sasse, *op. cit.*, pp. 174—176.

23. Grass asserted (work cited in note 3), pp. 112 ff., that the axiom "Nothing has the character of a sacrament" was characteristic of Luther, whereas Peters, *op. cit.*, p. 119, writes that the axiom played only a peripheral role in Luther's thinking. Peters is more correct. He finds the axiom only in WA Br 10, 348 and WA Br 11, 259. In addition, Grass has cited a statement in a disputation, given in WA 39 II, 147; however, that thesis was written by Melanchthon rather than Luther; nevertheless, Luther did speak approvingly of Melanchthon's thesis in his comment (WA 39 II, 160).

24. Hans-Werner Gensichen, *Damnamus!*, translated by Herbert J. A. Bouman as *We Condemn: How Luther and 16th-Century Lutheranism Condemned False Doctrine* (St. Louis: Concordia, 1967), especially chapters 1—3 and 11—13.

25. On this and related problems, see, besides the cited works by Peters and Sasse, Tom G. A. Hardt, *Venerabilis & Adorabilis Eucharistia. En Studie i den Lutherska Nattvardsläran under 1500-Talet* (Uppsala: Ljungberg, 1971).

Article VIII

1. For a more detailed analysis of this point, see Hardt, *Venerabilis & Adorabilis Eucharistia*, 161 f.

2. Roensch has shown that there is an "Apostolic Tradition" in the Lutheran Confessions, not, of course, in the sense of Episcopal succession, but a tradition of genuine Apostolic doctrine; hence also the many references to the "Fathers" in Article VIII. See *Grundzüge der Theologie der Lutherischen Bekenntnisschriften*, p. 37f.

3. See Walter Albrecht's detailed exposition of this aspect of the Personal Union of the two natures of Christ in his "The Enhypostasia of Christ's Human Nature," CTM VI, 8 (August 1935), pp. 561—588.

4. Nestorius and his doctrine have in recent years fared much better than Cyril of Alexandria and his position. Pelikan suggests that the fact that modern research has been more kind to the Antiochians than to the Alexandrians is due largely to Harnack's anti-Trinitarian bias ("Chalcedon After 15 Centuries," CTM, XXII, 12, p. 928). Early in this century the discovery of a work of Nestorius, *The Book of Heracleides,* led to a renewed study of his doctrine. J. B. Bethune-Baker (*Nestorius and His Teaching,* 1908) and Friedrich Loofs (*Nestorius and His Place in the History of Doctrine,* 1914) have exerted great efforts to rehabilitate him. Bethune-Baker maintains that the "Two Persons" was not the teaching of Nestorius (p. 82f) and Loofs believes that one can "avoid theological and rational impossibilities" only by returning to the lines of the Antiochian Christology of Nestorius as developed by the modern kenotic theories of I. A. Dorner, M. Kaehler and R. Seeberg (p. 130). These theologians reduce the divine nature of the Son of God in His incarnation and hold that the man Christ had His own personality distinct from

that of the Son of God. J. N. D. Kelly (*Early Christian Doctrines*, pp. 310—317) examines the doctrine of Nestorius, and while granting that "he was not a Nestorian in the classic sense of the word" (p. 316), believes that when all this is granted, his theory regarding the Personal Union was not adequate because all that it amounted to was the "truism that Jesus Christ, the historical Figure, was a single object of presentation, a concrete psychological unity" (p. 317). Ernst Kinder has recently made the judgment that in the teaching of Nestorius "there is no essential union between the two [i.e., the *Logos* and the Man Jesus] . . . . (the *Logos* dwells in the Man Jesus as the Holy Spirit dwells in the believer). . . . In principle it remains an ethical union—and the person of Jesus Christ is cleft into two egos" (*The Encyclopedia of the Lutheran Church*, p. 476).

5. J. N. D. Kelly's translation, which brings out the "emphatic *omnino non*" (*The Athanasian Creed*, p. 97).

6. The formula follows the arrangement of Chemnitz, *genus idiomaticum, genus apotelesmaticum, genus majestaticum*. Today we follow the arrangement of Gerhard, placing the *genus majestaticum* before the *genus apotelesmaticum*.

7. Chemnitz, the chief author of this Article, presents this first genus in considerable detail, *The Two Natures*, Ch. XIII, pp. 171—179.

8. See Zwingli's answer to Luther's "That These Words of Christ, etc.," June 20, 1527, St. Louis ed. of Luther's works, XX, 1194f.

9. See Chemnitz, *The Two Natures*, Chap. XI, "On the Use of This Doctrine," pp. 147—156.

10. A precise but shorter definition is found in Chemnitz, *The Two Natures*, pp. 242—243: "On the basis of Scripture . . . we must attribute to Christ's human nature not only its essential attributes and natural conditions, but also, especially because of the hypostatic union with the deity, innumerable supernatural qualities . . . and characteristics which are contrary to nature."

11. Pieper (11, 154, 219) asserts that the Roman Catholic theologians also deny this participation of the human nature in the divine attributes.

12. On the antithetical statements in SD VIII 63, Brunstäd suggests that they are not directed solely against the *Alloeosis* theory, but also against the "Swabian speculation" (Brenz and Andreä), which goes directly to the union of the natures and speculates over the communion of natures in itself, while Chemnitz, on the other hand, limits himself very specifically to only what the Scriptures definitely say about the two natures of Christ. (Brunstäd, *Theologie der Lutherischen Bekenntnisschriften*, p. 44f).

13. J. N. D. Kelly, *Early Christian Doctrines*, p. 319.

14. Chemnitz expounds this distinction in great depth, *The Two Natures*, pp. 242—246.

15. See Thesis VI of "The Catalog of Testimonies," Trig., pp. 1139—1141.

16. See Kelly, *Early Christian Doctrines*, pp. 313 and 321.

17. For the history of the use of the soul-flesh analogy, see Kelly, *The Athanasian Creed*, pp. 98—104.

18. Schaff gives us a rather typically worded objection, "It (i.e., Chalcedonian Christology) does not do justice to the genuine humanity of Christ in the Gospels, and to all those passages which assert its real growth. It overshadows the human by the divine," *The New Schaff-Herzog Encyclopedia of Religious Knowledge*, III, p.

310

55. LCUSA's "Who Can This Be?" suggests that in actuality Lutheran "teaching often yielded to the docetic tendency" (p. 15).

19. See Luther's Palm Sunday sermon on Phil. 2:5-11, St. Louis, ed., XII, 466—477. Chemnitz devotes an entire chapter to the Humiliation, *The Two Natures,* pp. 487—495. Pieper (II, 286—292) makes a careful exegetical analysis of Phil. 2:5-9.

20. The modern "Kenosis Theory" which identifies humiliation with the incarnation and postulates that the Son of God could become man only by relinquishing His divine operative attributes is intensively examined by Pieper (II, 292—296). He also (296—301) reviews the Crypto-Kenotic Controversy within the Lutheran church, carried on by the Tübingen and Giessen theologians (1619—27). See also Elert, *The Structure of Lutheranism,* I, 236—253.

21. The reference is to the decrees of the Council of Chalcedon. Chemnitz analyzes the words of Scripture that describe the Personal Union, *The Two Natures,* p. 117 f.

22. The term "ubiquity" has been used to name this doctrine. But the term is neither Luther's nor that of the Lutheran Confessions. It was rather a "snarl" word coined by the Sacramentarians to ridicule the Lutheran doctrine. As such the term carried the connotation of something the Lutherans never taught—that Christ's body was somehow locally extended through the universe, not independent of time and space (SD VII, 100, 119).

23. Schaff has said that Chemnitz, in distinction to Brenz, taught only a relative ubiquity, depending on Christ's will (*The New Schaff-Herzog Encyclopedia of Religious Knowledge,* III, 57). Schlink seems to take the same position when he writes that "it is not correct to say, 'The whole Christology of the Formula of Concord essentially reproduces the teaching of Chemnitz' (Seeberg, *Textbook of the History of Doctrines,* Vol. III, Book III, Part II, p. 387 f.)." Schlink, in disagreement with Seeberg's judgment, comments, "We are here faced with a compromise in which neither Chemnitz nor Brenz had his way" (*Theology of the Lutheran Confessions,* Note 25, p. 189). But a close examination of Chemnitz's *The Two Natures* will not sustain this viewpoint. First, Chemnitz in his "Dedicatory Epistle to Prince Christian, Duke of Saxony" is emphatic that he has in this work published a clear statement that shows the "teaching of Luther on the person of Christ" (p. 22; see also references to Luther on pp. 20 and 21). He could hardly have been unaware that Luther taught the genearl omnipresence of Christ's human nature. It is inconceivable to think that Chemnitz was not honest and independent scholar enough to state that he here disagreed with Luther's position—if he did. Further, those who believe that Chemnitz did not teach a general omnipresence besides the multipresence, point to his words in *The Two Natures,* p. 463: "Some Questions are asked which are foul to hear and abominable to imagine . . . such as whether the divine nature, which is everywhere, is found in excreta and sewage." These words are reminiscent of Luther taking up the argument that "if Christ's body is everywhere, ah, then I shall eat and drink Him in all the taverns, from all kinds of bowls, glasses, and tankards!" (*LW* 37, 67). Chemnitz had, in the paragraph preceding, declared that "the humanity in and with the Logos rules all things, *not in the sense of being absent, far away, or removed by an immense interval of space*" (emphasis added), thereby indicating that Christ rules in an omnipresent way. In addition, Chemnitz often asserts that many clear Scripture passages make it plain that Christ's power communicated to the assumed human nature is infinite, universal, and supreme (pp. 319, 321, etc.). Hence, when Chemnitz feels that he must take note of this common way in which the

fanatics ridicule the Lutheran doctrine of the real presence in the Lord's Supper, he calmly answers: "Since we do not have express and definite promise that He wills to be sought and found in such places . . . it is safest and simplest to drop all such questions from our discussions and to limit ourselves to the boundaries of divine revelation so that we may seek Christ and lay hold on Him in the places where He has clearly promised that He himself wishes to be" (p. 463). Here Chemnitz aligns himself with Luther's teaching that "the right hand of God is everywhere, but at the same time nowhere and uncircumscribed, above and apart from all creatures." And Chemnitz is in total agreement with Luther's further contention, "It is one thing if God is present, and another if He is present for you. He is there for you when He adds His Word and binds himself, saying 'Here you are to find me'" (*LW* 37, 68). It is an important point to remember, because Luther and Chemnitz do not rest the real presence in the Lord's Supper on Christ's general omnipresence but on the command and promise found in the words of institution. They would not say with regard to the Lord's Supper as Vajta has said that "Christ is in the elements long before they are placed on the altar" (*Luther on Worship—An Interpretation*, p. 95). For a full discussion of Chemnitz's position, see Pieper, II, 198—205, and Hardt, *Venerabilis & Adorabilis Eucharistia*, Chap. III, "Possible—Necessarium," pp. 75—115.

24. Chemnitz's *The Two Natures*, p. 449; cf. his entire chapter XXX, "Christ Present in the Church According to Both Natures," for a careful presentation of Scripture in what modes Christ is present, especially pp. 448 and 499. The chief author of Article VIII wanted to "follow the Scripture with simplicity and firmness" (p. 425). His goal was to say no more and no less than the Scriptures say about this mystery.

25. Luther's words in his "The Disputation Concerning the Passage: 'The Word Was Made Flesh'" (*LW* 38, 239).

26. Forty years ago Sasse observed that not only idealistic philosophy of all kinds, but also Reformed theology, must take offense at such a statement, *Here We Stand*, p. 144.

Article X

1. Luther's "Admonition to the Entire Clergy Assembled at the Diet of Augsburg, 1530" urged a proper concern for the essentials of Christian faith and worship, i.e., the nature of Law, Gospel, sin, grace, repentance, faith, Christian liberty, free will, love, hope, Baptism, the Mass or the Sacrament of the Altar, church, bishop, ministry, catechism, duties, and the like. By way of contrast there followed a scathing denunciation of the customary preoccupation of the official church with a long list of superstitions and trifles, including indulgences, purgatory, vestments, organs, altars, vessels, paraments, bells, Ash Wednesday, veiling images, little palm-crosses, burying and raising crosses, half-mass on Good Friday, Easter candles, candlemas and wax-market, St. Martin's Day goose, and many similar things. Luther himself willingly retained some of these very things; what infuriated him was the false importance attached to them.

2. This problem, on a much vaster and more intensive contemporary scale, is reflected in the title of Trevor Beeson's recent book, *Discretion and Valour: Religious Conditions in Russia and Eastern Europe* (Glasgow: Collins, Fontana, 1974).

3. Cf. Friedrich Kalb (H. P. A. Hamann, tr.), *Theology of Worship in 17th Century Lutheranism* (St. Louis: Concordia, 1965), p. 106.

4. The Tappert edition of the Book of Concord numbers this paragraph "6." as if it continued the preceding list of 5 *negativa*. It is significant that the Epitome considers this paragraph so important that it makes it into a separate "we believe, teach, and confess" entry under "*affirmative*," *before* giving the "*negativa*."

5. So A. C. Piepkorn, "What The Symbols Have To Say About The Church," *Concordia Theological Monthly*, XXVI, 10 (Oct. 1955), 721—763. Note especially the statements on pp. 750—751 and 759: "The unity of the church (*unitas ecclesiae*) is carefully differentiated from the organizational integrity of the church (*communis integritas in ecclesia*) and harmony in the church (*concordia, caritas, tranquillitas in ecclesia*). The use of *Einigkeit* in the German Book of Concord for both *unitas* and *concordia* has obscured this differentiation . . . . The objective of human institutions, ordinances, and ceremonies is organizational integrity and external union (or at least intercommunion) at the individual and corporate levels in the bonds of fraternal charity. Whereas *unitas* is God-given, Christians have a role in this lesser, external unification. . . . The *Einigkeit* that the Formula contemplates is not the *unitas ecclesiae* of the Augsburg Confession, Article VII." This strong dichotomy is all the more strange in view of the article's general trend *against* any separation of the empirical from the "inner" church. Moreover, church fellowship on the basis of the God-given Gospel and Sacraments is precisely not on the level of "human," "organizational," etc. aspects. Finally, appeal to the usage of "Einigkeit" in political contexts (Preface, *Bekenntnisschriften*, p. 15, 6) is surely irrelevant.

Article XI

1. WA 18, 600 ff. CR, 21, 86 ff.

2. See Robert Kolb, "Nikolaus von Amsdorf on Vessels of Wrath and Vessels of Mercy: A Lutheran Doctrine of Double Predestination," *Harvard Theological Review*, LXIX (1976), 3—4 (July—Oct.), 325—343.

3. Franz Hermann Reinhold Frank, *Die Theologie der Concordienformel* (Erlangen: T. Blaesing, 1858—65), 4, 135, 267.

4. The later dogmaticians included the eight points as a part of election and thus considered election only in this wide sense—out of fear of Calvinism (See John Gerhard, *Loci theologici*. Tübingen: Cotta, 1764 IV, 200 ff; David Hollaz, *Examen theologicum acroamaticum*. Rostock and Leipzig, 1725. P. III, S. I, Cap. II, q. 5 (II, 26—27). This insecure interpretation is effectively refuted by Georg Stoeckhardt in *Lehre und Wehre* (1880, p. 137 ff.), "Lehrt die Concordienformel eine 'Gnadenwahl im weitern Sinn'?"

5. At times this ordaining to eternal life is called a decree in the Latin text. The Formula of Concord shows no hesitancy to use that term, which became so important in later Calvinist theology (cf. SD XI 14, 17, 21, 23; Ep XI 13). In the eight points mentioned above, the term is used for the many acts of God whereby He orders from eternity every detail of the individual's salvation, redemption, justification, preservation, etc. These eight points, which offer the setting for the doctrine of predestination, are taken from Chemnitz' *Examen Concilii Tridentini*, Berlin: Gustav Schlawitz, 1861, *de fide justificante*, III, 23, p. 197, where he says, "The doctrine of predestination places before us decrees formed by God and revealed in His Word, concerning the causes

and manner of salvation and condemnation." As he makes his points, every decision of God is called a decree. This indicates, as in the Formula of Concord, no fear of the word; and it indicates too that the eight points of the Formula of Concord do not all of them make up the doctrine of predestination, but that together as separate decrees of God, they offer the setting for the right doctrine of election.

6. Werner Elert (*The Structure of Lutheranism,* tr. Walter A. Hansen. St. Louis: Concordia Publishing House, 1962, p. 138) sees this emphasis in our Confessions going back to Luther's *Bondage of the Will* and his distinction between the *Deus absconditus* and the *Deus revelatus.* This "hidden predestination" is Law and must not be probed. Predestination in the strict sense as spoken of throughout the Formula of Concord is Gospel, and one is to find his own predestination or election from the promises of the Gospel. Elert sees no difference between Luther's doctrine of predestination and that of the Formula of Concord, nor need one ascribe to Luther a doctrine of double predestination (as does Otto Ritschl, *Dogmengeschichte des Protestantismus,* Göttingen: Vandenhoeck & Ruprecht, 1926, III, 15 ff.; IV, 106 ff.) that is denied in the Formula of Concord.

7. We cannot discuss this exceedingly complicated and prolix matter here. I refer the reader to two works which delineate and evaluate this false doctrine and its development: Francis Pieper. *Conversion and Election.* St. Louis: Concordia Publishing House, 1931; Robert Preus, "The Doctrine of Election as Taught by the Seventeenth Century Lutheran Dogmaticians," *Quartalschrift,* LV, 4 (Oct. 1958), 229—261; cf. also Gottfried Adam, *Der Streit um die Prädestination im ausgehenden 16. Jahrhundert.* Neukirchen-Vluyn: Neukirchener Verlag, 1970. In both cases the *intuitu fidei* form of the doctrine is shown to be unconfessional. As a matter of fact the Madison Agreement, which was the basis for church union (1917) among Norwegian Lutherans in this country who taught both views, admits as much. See Pieper, p. 12.

8. This was also Luther's position as he spoke of predestination (WA 18, 686, 6; cf. Elert, *op. cit.,* p. 138)

9. See Pieper, *op. cit.,* 32—51; Elert, *op. cit.,* 138—139. Edmund Schlink, on the other hand, (*Theology of the Lutheran Confessions,* tr. Paul F. Koehneke and Herbert J. A. Bouman. Philadelphia: Fortress Press, 1961, p. 292.) asks the incredible question whether the refusal of the Formula of Concord to teach double predestination does not logically and ultimately lead to the rationalistic *intuitu fidei* doctrine of later Lutheran orthodoxy.

GENERAL
BIBLIOGRAPHY

I. Sources

Andreä, Jakob. Tr. and ed. Robert Kolb, *Andreae and the Formula of Concord: Six Sermons on the Way to Lutheran Unity.* St. Louis: Concordia, 1977.

Balthasar, *Erste Sammlung Einiger zur Pommerischen Kirchen-Historie gehörigen Schriften.* . . . Greifswald: Andreas Bussen, 1723. *Andere Sammlung Einiger zur Pommerischen Kirchen-Historie gehörigen Schriften.* . . . Ibid., 1725.

Bertram, Johann Georg. *Das Evangelische Lüneburg: Oder Reformations- und Kirchen-Historieder Alt-berühmten Stadt Lüneburg,* "Beylagen zum II. Theile," after p. 760. Braunschweig: Ludolph Schröders Buchladen, 1719.

Chemnitz, Martin. *Examen Concilii Tridentini,* ed. Eduard Preuss. Berlin: Schlawitz, 1861. Reprint, Darmstadt: Wissenschaftliche Buchgesellschaft, 1972. Tr. Fred Kramer, *Examination of the Council of Trent,* Part 1. St. Louis: Concordia, 1971.

————. *Loci theologici . . . Quibus et Loci Communes D[omini] Philippi Melanchthonis Perspicve Explicantur, & quasi integrum Christianae doctrinae corpus, Ecclesiae Dei sincere proponitur,* ed. Polycarp Leyser. *Fvndamenta Sanae Doctrinae de Vera et svbstantiali Praesenti, Exhibitione, & sumptione corporis & sanguinis Domini in Caena* [*sic!*]. *Libellvm de Dvabvs Natvris in Christo, earundem hypostatica unione, &c. De Communicatione Idiomatum.* Partial tr. Jacob A. O. Preus, *Two Natures in Christ.* St. Louis: Concordia, 1970.

Church Orders. *Die evangelischen Kirchenordnungen des 16. Jahrhunderts,* ed. Emil Sehling, 7 vols., 1902—61; abbrev. Sehling, KO or KOO. *Die evangelischen Kirchenordnungen des sechszehnten Jahrhunderts.* Urkunden und Regesten zur Geschichte des Rechts und der Verfassung der evangelischen Kirche in Deutschland, ed. Aemilius Ludwig Richter, 2 vols., 1846. Reprint, Nieuwkoop: De

Graaf, 1967; abbrev. Richter. [Württembergische Grosse Kirchenordnung; 1559:] *Von Gottes gnaden vnser Christoffs Hertzogen zu Würtemberg vnd zu Teckh/ Grauen zu Mümpelgart/ etc. Summarischer vnd einfältiger Begriff/ wie es mit der Lehre vnd Ceremonien in den Kirchen vnsers Fürstenthumbs/ auch derselben Kirchen anhangenden Sachen vnd Verrichtungen/ bissher geübt vnnd gebraucht/ auch fürohin mit verleihung Göttlicher gnaden gehalten vnd volzogen werden solle.* Getruckt zu Tüwingen/ Im jar 1559.

Chytraeus, David. *On Sacrifice,* tr. John Warwick Montgomery. St. Louis: Concordia, 1962.

Concord, Book of. *Die Bekenntnisschriften der evangelisch-lutherischen Kirche.* Herausgegeben im Gedenkjahr der Augsburgischen Konfession 1930. Göttingen: Vandenhoeck & Ruprecht, 1963 (5th ed.). Tr.: *The Book of Concord: The Confessions of the Evangelical Lutheran Church,* ed. Theodore G. Tappert [Formula of Concord tr. Arthur Carl Piepkorn]. Philadelphia: Fortress, 1959. See also: *Concordia, or Book of Concord. The Symbols of the Ev. Lutheran Church.* With Indexes and Historical Introductions [This is the *Concordia Triglotta*]. St. Louis: Concordia, 1922.

Confutation, Weimar, of 1559. *Confutatio & Condemnatio praecipuarum Corruptelarum, Sectarum & errorum, hoc tempore ad instaurationem et propagationen Regni Antichristi Rom. Pontificii aliarumque fanaticarum opinionum, ingruentium & grassantium, contra ueram sacrae Scripturae, Confessionis Augustanae & Schmalkaldicorum Articulorum Religionem . . . Jena:* Thomas Rebart, 1559.

Heppe, Heinrich. *Geschichte des deutschen Protestantismus in den Jahren 1555—1581,* Vol. III, Part B: Beilagen. Marburg: N. G. Elwert, 1857. [Includes Six Sermons of Andreä, 1—75, the Swabian-Saxon Concord, 166—352, etc.].

Kidd, B. J. *Documents Illustrative of the Continental Reformation.* Oxford: Clarendon Press, 1911; reprint 1967.

Kirchner, Timotheus. Selnecker, Nikolaus, and Chemnitz, Martin. *Apologia, Oder Verantwortung dess Christlichen Concordien Buchs, In welcher die ware Christliche Lehre, so im Concordi Buch verfasset, mit gutem Grunde heiliger Göttlicher Schrifft vertheydiget . . .* Dresden: Matthes Stoeckel, 1584.

Luther, Martin. *D. Martin Luthers Werke.* Kritische Gesamtausgabe. Weimar [etc.]: Böhlau, 1883 ff. Abbrev. WA; Tischreden abbrev. WA TR; Briefe abbreviated WA Br. *Dr. Martin Luthers sämmtliche Schriften,* ed. Johann Georg Walch et al., 25 vols. St. Louis: Concordia, 1880—1910; abbrev. W^2. *Luther's Works,* ed. Jaroslav Pelikan, Helmut T. Lehmann, et al., 55 vols. St. Louis: Concordia, and Philadelphia: Fortress, 1955 ff., abbrev. AE or LW.

Maulbronn Formula. Ed. Theodor Pressel, "Zwei Aktenstücke zur Genesis der Concordienformel," *Jahrbuch für deutsche Theologie* XI/1 (1866): 640—711. Ed. George J. Fritschel, *Die Maulbronner Formel,* No. 2 in "Quellen aus der Zeit der C[oncordien-]F[ormel]." Dubuque: mimeograph, 1910; abbrev. Fritschel.

Melanchthon, Philipp. Ed. Karl Gottlieb Bretschneider and Heinrich Ernst Bindseil, *Philippi Melanthonis* [sic!] *Opera quae supersunt Omnia, in* "Corpus Reformatorum," Vols. 1—28. Halle: Schwetschke, 1834 ff.; abbrev. CR. Ed. Robert Stupperich, *Melanchthons Werke in Auswahl,* Studienausgabe, 8 vols. + supplements. Gütersloh:Bertelsmann and Gerd Mohn. 1951 ff; abbrev. SA or StA.

Pfaff, Christoph Matthaeus. *Acta et scripta publica ecclesiae Wirtembergicae.* Tübingen: Cotta, 1719.

316

Rehtmeyer, Philipp Julius. *Antiqvitates Ecclesiasticae Inclytae Urbis Brunsvigae, Oder: Der berühmten Stadt Braunschweig Kirchen-Historie*, Vol. III, Part B: Beilagen. Braunschweig: Christoph-Friedrich Zilligers Wittib und Erben, 1707. [Includes important documents, especially relating to Chemnitz].

Reu, Johann Michael. Quellen zur Geschichte des kirchlichen Unterrichts in der evangelischen Kirche Deutschlands zwischen 1530 und 1600, 11 vols. or parts. Gütersloh: Bertelsmann, 1906—35. Reprint pending.

Salig, Christian August. *Vollständige Historie Der Augspurgischen Confession und derselben zugethanen Kirchen.* Dritter Theil: Dokumenten. Halle: Renger, 1735.

Schlüsselburg, Conrad. *Haereticorum Catalogus,* 13 vols. Frankfurt am Main: Peter Kopf et al., 1597—99.

Schwäbische Concordie. Ed. Hermann Hachfeld, "Die schwäbische Confesion nach einer wolfenbütteler Handschrift," *Zeitschrift für historische Theologie,* NF XXX (1866): 234—301. Ed. George J. Fritschel, *Die Schwaebische Concordie, "Schwaebischer Kirchenbegriff zu einer heilsamen Union in Kirchensachen,"* No. 1 in "Quellen aus der Zeit der C[oncordien] F[ormel]." Dubuque: mimeograph, n.d.; abbrev. Fritschel.

II. Secondary Literature

Albrecht, Walter. "The Enhypostasia of Christ's Human Nature." *Concordia Theological Monthly,* VI, 8 (Aug. 1935), 561—588.

Anderson, Charles S. *Faith and Freedom: The Christian Faith According to the Lutheran Confessions.* Minneapolis: Augsburg, 1977. For laity.

Balthasar, Jacob Heinrich. *Historie des Torgischen Buchs.* . . . 6 vols. in 1. Greifswald & Leipzig: Johann Jacob Weitbrecht, 1741—56.

————. *Erste [Andere] Sammlung Einiger zur Pommerischen Kirchen-Historie gehörigen Schriften.* . . . [See *Balthasar* under Sources].

Bente, Gerhard Friedrich. "Historical Introductions to the Lutheran Symbols" in *Concordia Triglotta* [See *Concord, Book of* under Sources].

Benz, Ernst. *Studien zur Geschichte des Abendmahlsstreits im 16. Jahrhundert,* Vol. 46 in "Beiträge zur Förderung christlicher Theologie," Series 2. Gütersloh: C. Bertelsmann, 1940.

Bertram, Johann Georg. *Das Evangelische Lüneburg.* . . . [See *Bertram, Johann Georg* under Sources].

Bethune-Baker, J. B. *Nestorius and His Teaching: A Fresh Examination of the Evidence.* Cambridge: University Press. Reprint. New York: Kraus Reprint Co., 1969.

Brunstäd, Friedrich. *Theologie der lutherischen Bekenntnisschriften.* Gütersloh: C. Bertelsmann, 1951.

Carpzov, Johann Benedict. *Isagoge in libros ecclesiarum Lutheranarum symbolicos.* Leipzig: Johann Wittigau, 1665.

Elert, Werner. *Abendmahl und Kirchengemeinschaft in der alten Kirche hauptsächlich des Ostens.* Berlin: Lutherisches Verlagshaus, 1954. Tr. Norman E. Nagel, *Eucharist and Church Fellowship in the First Four Centuries.* St. Louis: Concordia, 1966.

Elert, Werner. *Der Ausgang der altkirchlichen Christologie.* Berlin: Lutherisches Verlagshaus, 1957.

————. *Das christliche Ethos. Grundlinien der lutherischen Ethik.* Tübigen: Furche, 1949. Tr. Carl C. Schindler, *The Christian Ethos.* Philadelphia: Muhlenberg, 1957.

————. *Der christliche Glaube. Grundlinien der lutherischen Dogmatik.* Hamburg: Furche, 1956.

————. "Gesetz und Evangelium," in *Zwischen Gnade und Ungnade.* Munich: Evangelischer Presseverband, 1948. Tr. Edward H. Schroeder, *Law and Gospel.* Philadelphia: Fortress, 1967.

————. *Morphologie des Luthertums,* 2 vols. Munich: C. H. Beck, 1931 and reprints. Vol. I tr. Walter A. Hansen, *The Structure of Lutheranism.* St. Louis: Concordia, 1962.

Frank, Franz Hermann Reinhold. *Die Theologie der Concordienformel historisch-dogmatisch entwickelt und beleuchtet,* 4 vols. Erlangen: Theodor Blaesing, 1858—65.

Fritschel, George J. *The Formula of Concord: Its Origin and Contents.* Philadelphia: Lutheran Publication Society, 1916.

Gensichen, Hans-Werner. *Damnamus: Die Verwerfung von Irrlehre bei Luther und im Luthertum des 16. Jahrhunderts.* Berlin: Lutherisches Verlagshaus, 1955. Tr. Herbert J. A. Bouman, *We Condemn: How Luther and 16th-century Lutheranism Condemned False Doctrine.* St. Louis: Concordia, 1967.

Gonzalez, Justo L. *A History of Christian Thought,* III. Nashville and New York: Abingdon, 1975.

Grass, Hans. *Die Abendmahlslehre bei Luther und Calvin: Eine kritische Untersuchung,* Vol. 47 in "Beiträge zur Förderung christlicher Theologie." Series 2. Gütersloh: C. Bertelsmann, 1954.

Green, Lowell C. *The Formula of Concord: An Historiographical and Bibliographical Guide,* No. 11 in "Sixteenth Century Bibliography." St. Louis: Center for Reformation Research, 1977.

Gritsch, Eric W. and Jenson, Robert W. *Lutheranism: The Theological Movement and Its Confessional Writings.* Philadelphia: Fortress, 1976.

Hardt, Tom G. A. *Venerabilis & Adorabilis Eucharistia: En Studie i den Lutherska Nattvardaläran under 1500-Talet,* Vol. 9 in "Acta Universitatis Upsaliensis: Studia Doctrinae Christianae Upsaliensis." Upsala: Ljungberg, 1971.

Hutter, Leonhard. *Concordia Concors. De Origine et Progressu Formulae Concordia Ecclesiarum Confessionis Augustanae.* Wittenberg: Clement Berger, 1614.

Jacobs, Henry E. *The Book of Concord,* Vol. II: Historical Introduction; Part III, Documents Pertaining to the History and Interpretation of the Formula of Concord. Philadelphia: G. W. Frederick, 1882-83.

Jungkuntz, Theodore R. *Formulators of the Formula of Concord: Four Architects of Lutheran Unity.* St. Louis: Concordia, 1977.

Kelly, J. N. D. *The Athanasian Creed: Quicunque vult.* London: Adam and Charles Black, 1964.

————. *Early Christian Doctrines,* 2d ed. New York: Harper & Row, 1960.

Klug, Eugene F. *Getting into The Formula of Concord.* St. Louis: Concordia, 1977. With new tr. of the Epitome by Otto F. Stahlke; for laity.

Kolb, Robert. *Nikolaus von Amsdorf: Popular Polemics in Preserving Luther's Legacy.* Nieuwkoop: De Graff, 1978.

318

Krauth, Charles P. *The Conservative Reformation and Its Theology.* Philadelphia: J. B. Lippincott, 1871.

Lau, Franz. "Georg III. von Anhalt (1507-1553), erster evangelischer 'Bischof' von Merseburg." *Wissenschaftliche Zeitschrift der Karl-Marx-Universität,* Leipzig, GVRS 3 (1953-54), 139—52.

Loofs, Friedrich. *Nestorius and His Place in the History of Christian Doctrine.* Reprint of the 1914 ed. published by the University Press, Cambridge, Eng. New York: Burt Franklin Reprints, 1975.

Mahlmann, Theodor. *Das neue Dogmas der lutherischen Christologie: Problem und Geschichte seiner Begründung.* Gütersloh: Gerd Mohn, 1969.

Maurer, Wilhelm. Art., "Formula of Concord." *The Encyclopedia of the Lutheran Church,* ed. Julius H. Bodensieck, II. Minneapolis: Augsburg, 1965. Pp. 868—75.

Neuser, Wilhelm H. *Die Abendmahlslehre Melanchthons in ihrer geschichtlichen Entwicklung (1519—1530),* Vol. 26, Part 2 in "Beiträge zur Geschichte der Reformierten Kirche." Neukirchen: Verlag des Erziehungsvereins, 1968.

Olsen, Arthur L. "Scripture and Tradition in the Theology of Martin Chemnitz." Ph. D. dissertation, Harvard University, 1966.

Olson, Oliver K. "Contemporary Trends in Liturgy Viewed from the Perspective of Classical Lutheran Theology," *The Lutheran Quarterly,* 26 (1974), 110—57.

Opsahl, Paul with William Rush and Robert Kolb, eds. *The Formula of Concord: Quadricentennial Essays,* published as special number of *Sixteenth Century Journal* VIII/4 (1977).

Pelikan, Jaroslav. "Chalcedon After 15 Centuries." *Concordia Theological Monthly,* XXII, 12 (Dec. 1951), 926—936.

Pieper, Franz. *Christliche Dogmatik.* St. Louis: Concordia, 1917—24. Tr. Theodore Engelder, Walter W. F. Albrecht, Fred E. Mayer, and Lorenz F. Blankenbuehler, *Christian Dogmatics.* St. Louis: Concordia, 1950—57 and reprints.

Piepkorn, Arthur Carl. "Martin Chemnitz' Views on Trent: The Genesis and Genius of the Examen Concilii Tridentini." *Concordia Theological Monthly,* 37 (1966), 5—37.

————. "What does 'Inerrancy' Mean?" Ibid. 36 (1965), 577—93.

————. *Profiles in Belief: The Religious Bodies of the United States and Canada,* 7 vols. New York: Harper, 1977 ff.

Peters, Edward Frederick. "The Origin and Meaning of the Axiom: 'Nothing Has the Character of a Sacrament Outside of the Use' in Sixteenth-Century Theology." Th.D. dissertation, Concordia Seminary, St. Louis, 1968.

Planck, Gottlieb Jakob. *Geschichte der protestantischen Theologie von Luthers Tode bis zu der Einführung der Konkordienformel,* III. Leipzig: Siegfried Lebrecht Crusius, 1800.

Preus, Robert. *Getting into the Theology of Concord: A Study of the Book of Concord.* St. Louis: Concordia, 1977.

————. *The Theology of Post-Reformation Lutheranism,* 2 vols. St. Louis: Concordia, 1970—72.

Quere, Ralph W. *Melanchthon's Christum Cognoscere: Christ's Efficacious Presence in the Eucharistic Theology of Melanchthon.* Nieuwkoop: De Graaf, 1977.

Reu, Johann Michael. *Two Treatises on the Means of Grace,* ed. Emil W. Matzner. Minneapolis: Augsburg, 1952.

Ritschl, Otto. *Dogmengeschichte des Protestantismus,* II: *Orthodoxie und Synkretismus in der altprotestantischen Theologie.* Leipzig: J. C. Hindrichs, 1912.

Roensch, Manfred. *Grundzüge der Theologie der Lutherischen Bekenntnisschriften.* Oberursel, West Germany. Oberursel Hefte #7, 1976.

Rogness, Michael. *Melanchthon, Reformer Without Honor.* Minneapolis: Augsburg, 1969.

Sasse, Hermann. *Here We Stand. Nature and Character of the Lutheran Faith,* tr. Theodore G. Tappert. New York: Harper & Brothers, 1938; reprint St. Louis: Concordia, [1977].

————. *This Is My Body. Luther's Contention for the Real Presence in the Sacrament of the Altar.* Minneapolis: Augsburg, 1959.

Schlink, *Theologie der lutherischen Bekenntnisschriften.* Munich: Chr. Kaiser, 1940; 3d ed., 1948. Tr. Paul F. Koehneke and Herbert J. A. Bouman, *Theology of the Lutheran Confessions.* Philadelphia: Muhlenberg, 1961.

Scaer, David P. *Getting into the Story of Concord: A History of the Book of Concord.* St. Louis: Concordia, 1977.

Secker, Philip J. "The Goodness of Creation and the Natural Knowledge of the Goodness of God in Nicholas Selnecker, David Chytraeus, and Martin Chemnitz." S.T.M. thesis, Concordia Seminary, St. Louis, 1967.

Seeberg, Reinhold. *Lehrbuch der Dogmengeschichte,* IV, 2. Darmstadt, Germany, 1954.

Sommerlath, Ernst. Art., "Lord's Supper." *The Encyclopedia of the Lutheran Church,* ed. Julius H. Bodensieck, II. Minneapolis: Augsburg, 1965. Pp. 1336—1342.

Spitz, Lewis W., ed. *Discord, Dialogue, and Concord. Studies in the Lutheran Reformation's Formula of Concord.* Philadelphia: Fortress, 1977.

Tappert, Theodore G. See *Concord, Book of* under Sources.

Thomasius, G. *Das Bekenntnis der evangelisch-lutherischen Kirche in der Konsequenz seines Prinzips.* Nürnberg: August Recknagel, 1848.

Weber, Hans Emil. *Reformation, Orthodoxie und Rationalismus,* 3 vols. or parts. Gütersloh: C. Bertelsmann, 1940 ff.